Tile
your
World

JOHN BRIDGE'S
NEW TILE SETTING BOOK

Mistflower Press

Houston

Also by John P. Bridge:
Ceramic Tile Setting, McGraw-Hill, 1992

First Edition
First Printing

Mistflower Press
P.O. Box 842243
Houston TX 77284-2243
USA

Publisher's Cataloging-in-Publication
Bridge, John P.
    Tile your world: John Bridge's new tile setting book
/ John P. Bridge. -- 1st ed.
    p. cm.
    LCCN 2003094951
    ISBN 0-9742754-3-3

    1. Tile laying--Amateurs' manuals. 2. Tiles --
Amateurs' manuals. I. Title.

TH8531.B75 2003   698
                                QBI33-1525

Printed in Canada

Design and layout:
Fine Line Design
204.755.2239

For Harold and Bob,
Teachers and mentors, they were also my brothers.

ACKNOWLEDGEMENTS

Even though it might seem so at times, nobody writes a book alone. My wife Patti proof read the manuscript more than once. Moreover, she put up with me during the course of the writing (which lasted well over a year), and for that I can't thank her enough. I'm not the world's easiest person to get along with when I am in the midst of a project.

I'm grateful to the people who contributed articles: Dave Gobis (foreword), Peter Nielsen, Jim Buckley, Todd Groettum, Bob Campbell, Andy Lundberg, William Carty, Paul Fisette, Jim Reicherts, Tim Thomas, John Kipper, Keith Bretzfield and Frank Woeste.

Carol Bedient proof read *Ceramic Tile Setting* in 1991, and I called on her again to edit *Tile Your World*. If you find any typos in the book, I assure you they were created after Carol did her thing. Nobody is more thorough than she.

Book designer, Rachelle Painchaud-Nash, has been immensely patient in sorting out my mess. Book designer I am not, but I'll be a better manuscript organizer in the future as a result of Rachelle's prodding.

Camille Arnold designed the logo for Mistflower Press. Thanks, Cami.

I owe a debt of gratitude to many others, not the least of whom are the moderators and other "regulars" at the John Bridge Forums on the Internet. I have gained vast quantities of knowledge from those folks. In addition to those who have already been mentioned, I thank Dave Misevich, Rob Zschoche, Sonnie Layne, Jim Cordes, Davy Stephens and Jason Butler.

Special thanks to Kelly "CX" Chaplin for reading the text and saving me the embarrassment of making several major errors.

And I thank Bud Cline.

There are dozens more. I thank you all.

CONTENTS

FOREWORD

Clemson, South Carolina
July 31, 2003

Welcome to *Tile Your World*. In purchasing John Bridge's new book you've set yourself on a course to discover some of the many facets of ceramic tile setting, methods that have served John well in his three decades in the trade. Is this book a do-all-tell-all analysis of preparing for and installing ceramic tile? No, no single person knows it all, and John is the first to admit it. John has, however, taken the time to continue his education throughout the years, and he has a great overall awareness of the latest products and techniques available.

Tile setters are opinionated, and all will not agree with the procedures set out herein, but that is to be expected. I myself don't agree with John one hundred percent of the time. When he talks of using "chicken war" (chicken wire – poultry netting) in place of metal lath or wire reinforcement, I cringe, and there are other issues upon which we will never agree. He has voiced opinions on various products and methods that have made me bristle on occasion, and to say that John Bridge is hardheaded would be an understatement. But in the end I know he's going to get the job done in a professional manner, and he will stand behind his work. That is what counts.

As with most things, tile setting offers many alternatives. Lacking a better analogy, I can liken it to washing a car. You shoot it with a garden hose. It knocks some of the dirt off, but it leaves something to be desired, so you take it to a car wash. Now it's clean, but there are small scratches in the paint job. A brush-free car wash, maybe? Yes, but there is still dirt in the nooks and crannies. It comes down to the old hands-on method. Time consuming and demanding of patience, but there's no matching it.

Tile setting is that way. Your floor, wall or other decorative application will reflect the method used to install it. By taking shortcuts, you might end up with an eye-pleasing result, but it's almost certain that down the road those shortcuts will render your project less than serviceable. Quality methods offer improved long-term performance.

There are standards in the tile industry which are issued by the American National Standards Institute (ANSI). These are published and distributed by the Tile Council of America (TCA), and you may wish to avail yourself of them for the more serious projects.

The tile industry is on the move. It has gained both in sales and in valuable new technology during the past decade. We are blessed with a plethora of new materials and methods. Most are aimed at making ceramic tile installation a more installer friendly task. There is still no substitute for good old-fashioned craftsmanship, however, and on that point John and I are in complete agreement.

Launch yourself into the world of tile, and let my friend, John Bridge, help you in his unique way to achieve satisfying and lasting results.

David M. Gobis
Executive Director, Ceramic Tile Education Foundation

TILE YOUR WORLD DISCLAIMER

Neither the author nor the publisher accepts responsibility for outcomes resulting from the employment of methods and applications defined in this book. Since skill levels vary and conditions constantly change, we cannot be held accountable for injuries suffered, damages incurred or losses sustained by anyone in the course of following the advice contained in these pages. You are encouraged to work safely at all times and to adhere to the instructions provided by tool and product manufacturers. It is your responsibility alone to purchase and use eye, ear and lung protective devices when doing the projects outlined herein.

A WORD TO THE PROS

I've written this book with the do-it-yourselfer in mind, but that does not mean the professional tile person will find it uninteresting or useless. Although I don't claim to be anybody special — just a well-rounded and informed tile setter — the information I've managed to compile here will aid novices and professionals alike. There is always another trick to learn, a new idea to digest. I'm always on the lookout for perspectives I haven't considered before, new knowledge to tuck into my bag of tricks. I know you are like me, and I hope you find some of what you're looking for here. I think you will.

While I'm addressing the novice one-on-one, I'll be looking over that person's shoulder from time to time to notice you watching and listening. Wish me luck, and wink once in a while to let me know I'm not too far off track.

INTRODUCTION

When I wrote *Ceramic Tile Setting* (TAB/McGraw-Hill, 1992) I was not of the opinion that do-it-yourselfers were capable of much more than tiling residential floors, bath tub surrounds and kitchen back splashes. I was convinced that the more complex tile and stone projects would continue to be done by professional tile and stone setters who possessed advanced technical knowledge in the field, men and women with years, even decades of experience doing the work – people like me. After all, what would keep the pros in business if everyone were capable of doing everything we were capable of doing? It just couldn't be.

But it is.

Ten years after the book was published I have a new respect for the "weekend warrior," the person who slogs away all week in order to pay the bills, while in the back of his mind is the work he'll be doing at the house come Saturday morning. I've gained this respect because despite everything I've done to discourage the average Joe from attempting advanced tile and stone work, he has done it anyway. And not only has he done it; he has excelled at it. Furthermore, the average Joe can just as easily be the average Jane. "He" can be, and often is, she.

From complete floor-to-ceiling ceramic tile showers to intricate inlaid floors, from Roman baths to complicated granite and marble tile countertops, there is nothing I can think of that some avid and persistent do-it-yourselfer hasn't accomplished. I have accepted this, and rather than fight a battle I can't win, I've taken the honorable way out. I've switched sides.

In 1999 I launched a web site, not really knowing what it might become or what I wanted it to be. By 2000 there was an online advice forum attached to the site, and people began asking questions about tile projects they either had in progress or in the planning stage. Before long, other professionals found the site and began answering questions and asking questions of their own. Both professionals and novices arrived from around the world — from the United States, Canada, Australia, New Zealand, South Africa, Ireland and the United Kingdom, and from other countries whose main language might or might not be English.

An online community developed, and this attracted even more people, all eager for information. The projects grew in size and complexity. The enthusiasts couldn't be discouraged or dissuaded. They listened to my admonitions and to those of the other pros on the site, and then they informed us they were going on with or without us. Not wanting to be left in the dust, my colleagues and I signed on for the ride. We would show these plucky novices in words and pictures how to do the things we do, and in the process we would attempt to debunk some of the poor advice they were getting elsewhere.

By 2001 the exchange of ideas was in full swing, and as I write in 2003, the men and women who operate the John Bridge Forums are not only leading "newbies" by the hand, but they are furthering the tile trade in the process. They are assisting people in tackling projects that challenge professionals, and by so doing they are causing professionals to become even more professional. As the masses become better informed about the intricacies of the tile trade, the pros are compelled to improve in order to stay ahead of the crowd.

We think this is a good thing. We don't think it threatens the people in the trade who want to make a living at it. We know that no matter how many people attempt doing their own work, there will always be others to hire the pros. The process does, however, expose and weed out the hacks, the would-be tile installers, the incompetents who would otherwise drag our trade down with them.

You can visit the John Bridge Forums at: http://johnbridge.com. I suggest you stop in often as you work your way through this book. You will soon realize that it is not just I putting sentences on these pages but a number of people throughout the country and throughout the world. What has been developed here could not possibly be conceived by one person. It is instead the cumulative thought of scores of professionals and non-professionals alike.

When I began writing, the working title of the book was *Extreme Tile Setting*, but I was talked out of that title in favor of the current one. The "extreme" thing may have by now been overdone in publishing as well as in other endeavors. Still, the theme remains present throughout the book. The American stage comedian Ghallager frequently uses the term "style" in his monologue, and I'm going to borrow it from him. Whatever we do here will indeed be done with style, and style will be taken to the extreme.

And what, then, is "extreme tile setting"? It is the practice of not only gluing tiles to a wall or floor but of doing everything else that goes into the complete project and doing it well. We will do whatever it takes to complete the job. We will frequently change trades without changing hats.

Extreme tile setting is not only completing projects with satisfactory results; it is tiling with a certain amount of flair. It is using one's imagination and casting one's eye toward the aesthetic qualities of one's work. Floors don't have to be mundane. They should be elegant and inviting. Showers might be small, but they don't have to be dark and confining. They can be bright, airy, interesting and exciting. I will sprinkle pictures of creative projects throughout the book. Projects completed by both professionals and amateurs alike will be displayed.

The project pictures typify the ideas I will attempt to instill within you as you traverse these pages. Along the way, we will come to understand that there are more ways than one to do a job. While we strive to observe long accepted practices and current standards within the tile industry, we won't back away from anything. We will shoot for the stars. We will...

Oh, enough of this. Grab up your gear, and let's get moving. We've got serious tile work to do!

HOW TO USE THE BOOK

It would be good if someone could write a book that covered all the projects or even most of the projects that people might want to attempt. It would be a huge and unique book, one that would take months, maybe years, to write and to digest. In the space we have I haven't attempted such a book, as if it were possible in the first place. Instead I've tried to give you many of the basics of our trade. There are certain procedures that have become more or less standard in this business of tile setting, a business which has resisted change at nearly every stage in its history and yet has somehow managed to modernize to meet the changing requirements of the construction industry. The book will acquaint you with the proven systems that have remained constant through the decades. At the same time, I will make every effort to apprise you of the new things that are taking place within our industry. Changes are occurring almost daily.

Tile setting for novices remains a relatively new trend. When I wrote *Ceramic Tile Setting,* those willing to attempt their own tile work were not numerous. There are many more now, but there remains a certain amount of reluctance. Tools and procedures seem a bit strange to most, and consequently, people tend to shy away. All of us are familiar with woodworking, a little plumbing maybe, and even electricity, but tile setting and masonry have not traditionally been do-it-yourself items. It's just a whole different ball game.

And so it will be best if you start reading this book from the front and continue without skipping sections, even though you might think those sections don't pertain to you or the project you have in mind. You may reach a point in the book where you can pick and choose what you want to read, but that will be well into the text. I trust you will know when you have arrived there.

I beg you keep in mind the writer is an American saddled with the usual linguistic peculiarities associated with that breed. Realizing the book will be read in countries with their own unique interpretations of the English language, I have made footnotes at the bottoms of pages which contain words and phrases that might not be readily understood. Additionally, I have frequently converted English Standard numerical statements to the metric system in deference to my cousins abroad who no longer subscribe to my system of measurement.

A complete index is provided at the back of the book.

SCHLUTER SYSTEMS AND THIS BOOK

A couple years ago you couldn't have given me a plastic matting product to use under my floor tile installations. No amount of talking would have convinced me it was a good idea. What was this "Ditra" stuff I'd been hearing about — another gimmick devised by some slick marketing person to suck money out of me and my customers?

And then my friend Dave Gobis (Ceramic Tile Education Foundation) invited me to South Carolina to attend a seminar that is given from time to time at the Tile Council of America and at the tile school where Dave is director. The seminar stretches over a three-day period and is presented by employees of Schluter Systems, LP, the American arm of a German company known as Schluter Systems, maker of Ditra® and a host of other tile-related products.

Figure 1: Schluter Systems L.P., Plattsburg, NY

After assuring Dave and everyone else within earshot that the seminar would probably be wasted on me, I accepted the invitation and attended. What I saw and heard changed me forever. An old broken down mud man was converted into a cutting-edge, high-tech tile installer. The Schluter folks made me, John Bridge, a true Renaissance man in the tile industry! I've been saying good things about them ever since.

I was completely sold on not only "Ditra" but on a number of other Schluter products, including Kerdi® matting, which can be used in tile shower construction. Not only was I impressed with the products; I soon came to respect the professionals I met while there. I have come to know first hand that Schluter is not only one of the most aggressive companies in the tile business when it comes to training and marketing, but it is also among the most straight-forward I have known in backing up its products. The company puts its money where its mouth is. All products and *installations* are completely warranted by the company when Schluter specifications and directions are followed. The company's technical support is nearly unmatched in the industry.

A question will undoubtedly arise as to whether Schluter has had anything to do with the publication of this book, and I will answer it now so there can be no misunderstanding down the road. The answer is yes. Schluter has not only influenced me and what I say, but the company has also subsidized the production of the book. The book would not be as good as it is without that support.

I would not want anyone to think that my friends at Schluter approached me and offered me money to write about their company's products. That is not the case, and in fact, the reverse is true. I went to Schluter with the idea and persuaded its management that the arrangement would be beneficial to both the company and to me.

People who know me also know I could never write favorably about products I am not completely confident in. Before you finish reading the book I am confident you will know me, too, and be similarly convinced that Schluter products are outstanding and well worth considering when you think about how your tile or stone project will come into being.

CHAPTER ONE

TILES, TOOLS AND BASIC METHODS

The History of Tile Setting According to John

As he emerged from the cave, Gherd scanned the horizon through the morning mist. It was not that he really expected the animals to be anywhere near, but he felt obliged to look — there was always a chance. Once more, though, he saw nothing, and this particular morning Gherd, the leader, knew the time had come. The clan would have to leave the only home it had ever known in order to pursue those precious beasts that ensured its survival. Food stocks were dangerously low, and soon children would be crying in hunger. Times had been better.

The leader, with the concurrence of the other men, decided the clan would set out to the north the following morning at first light. They gathered the possessions the women and children could carry – the men carried the weapons and crude tools – and they all began the journey northward. They trekked eleven days at something of a forced march before deciding they were well within the new grazing grounds where the men could once again bag the game that would both feed and clothe the members of the clan. Exhausted, they searched for shelter.

But not a single cave could be found. Hills were everywhere, and rocks and stones were abundant among them, but there appeared nothing that could be easily converted to living quarters. There weren't even any large trees which would offer partial shelter from the elements. The people could make fire, but a fire did little good in the open with no way to reflect or contain its heat. It was cold.

Gherd directed the women to begin erecting low walls of stone. There were plenty of rocks, but no way of cutting or shaping them. After much trial and error, the women determined to find stones with flat surfaces on at least one or two sides, for these were relatively easy to stack one upon the other. Since there was nothing to hold the rocks together save their own weight and friction, the walls thus built were barely high enough to provide meager shelter from the wind when one was sitting.

Spindly tree branches were thrown across the walls to complete crude structures that could at least partially protect the occupants from the cruel effects of the northern winter. The "huts," if they could be considered that, afforded no protection from snow and rain, and since there were many voids in the stone walls, much of the cold wind came through. But this was much better than simply lying out on the ground with no shelter at all, and the people resolved to do the best they could. They had no other choice, no other knowledge.

It would be years, ages in fact, before methods were developed for using mud and clay to both fill the voids in the stone walls and to hold the individual stones in place, and this new-found technology would afford the ability to make higher walls. It would be only then that the mason's trade would enter the evolution of things. Masonry is, after all, the art of placing one stone or clay unit upon another, cementing it there and expecting it to stay firm.

As procedures advanced from the feeble efforts of Gherd's people and their immediate offspring and moved on to the practice of using clay for the manufacture of crude bricks, larger, more intricate walls and structures were possible. Millennia passed, and there came a time when someone discovered that if one baked the clay bricks, they would become much stronger and less susceptible to water damage than their uncooked predecessors.

The invention of fired clay bricks – over 20,000 years ago – was one of two major turning points in the progression of the masonry trades. The other would not come until the age of the Roman Empire. It would be the Romans who would discover the means for making cement mortar, but I'm getting ahead of the story.

The first clay paving tiles were developed in the area of the world that is commonly referred to by Westerners as the Holy Land. This would have been about six thousand years ago, roughly four thousand years before the birth of Jesus of Nazareth. The tiles were unglazed and used primarily to pave the earthen floors of huts and other buildings.

As buildings became more elaborate, aesthetics began contemplating their looks. Why should all buildings be so drab and so unacceptably ugly? Why couldn't the structures, or at least portions of them, become things of beauty? Why couldn't pigments be added to the clay to form masonry units of a different color, and further, couldn't masonry units be covered with decorative cladding? If it was possible to make rather thick clay bricks, why wouldn't it be possible to make thinner, more ornate ones that could be installed over the mundane units used in basic construction? Would it be possible to apply colorings that could be baked on?

And so ceramic tiles were born, tiles that could in fact be covered with decorative "glazed" surfaces. The first of these appeared in Egypt and, being much too expensive for commoners, they were used to decorate the palaces and tombs of the nobility. Both interior and exterior tiles were developed. A select group of masons were trained to apply the new building products to the masonry walls their fellows built. In the future, craftsmen who did this work would be called tile fixers or tile setters.

As the art improved, tile-making saw rise in Persia. And from Persia the craft spread to Europe, first to the Low Countries and later to other areas, including England. This occurred while Egyptian tiles were making their way across North Africa. It was the Moors who introduced ceramic tiles into Southern Europe when they invaded Iberia, which is now Spain.

Spain and Portugal exported glazed tiles to the New World, where they were used to decorate mission churches and the homes of European governors. Eventually, tiles from the northern European countries were brought to the English and French colonies of North America. Still far too expensive for general distribution, the tiles were used almost exclusively by the wealthy.

Those were the old days, and these are the new. We have reached a point where nearly everyone can afford ceramic tiles. They have become standard in modern homes, and there is hardly a business that does not have, at the least, ceramic tile restrooms. Industry depends upon tile setters to effect walls and floors that are chemical resistant and durable in other ways.

With advanced methods, modern tiles are made to fill every need in construction and in decorating. In the past two decades, the consumption of ceramic tiles (fully-fired clay tiles) has nearly doubled in the United States and Canada. Tile has been, and would seem to remain, the people's choice when it comes to providing elegant and durable surfaces in homes and businesses. It is not likely this trend will change.

Types and Varieties of Clay Tiles

There are *ceramic* tiles, and then there are other "burnt clay" products. Nearly all of the materials we'll be dealing with, save quarry tiles and raw clay pavers, are classed as ceramic. It doesn't matter whether the tiles are glazed or unglazed, and size has nothing to do with the definition. Porcelain tiles are ceramic tiles. Softer wall tiles made from ceramic clay are ceramic tiles, and so are mosaic tiles, no matter what type of materials they are made from.

Burnt Clay Products

Burnt clay is what bricks are made from. The term derives from an ancient Sanskrit word meaning "burnt stuff." Pieces of burnt stuff dating back 24,000 years have been unearthed in Asia. Modern burnt clay products include bricks, brick pavers, brick paver tiles (thin bricks) and quarry tiles. Many of these masonry units are used primarily outdoors, but indoor use is certainly not unheard of. Extremely durable not only because they are baked hard but because the color pigment goes all the way through the piece, quarry tiles and thin bricks are

Figure 2: Examples of modern "burnt stuff." Quarry tiles and bricks resting on an installation of thin brick paver tiles.

often used in commercial construction. The range of available colors is almost unlimited. Clays come from the Earth in a myriad of shades and can be tinted to make even more shades. Different temperatures and methods of firing can also affect the final color of the products. (Figure 2)

Wall Tiles

Classic bathroom tiles that have been used for decades, four-and-one-quarter inches square and made from semi-fluid figurine clay, are considerably more durable than, say, glass tiles but still not a good choice for floors. Glazed in many different textures and colors, these "standard wall tiles" have been with us since the advent of inside plumbing and will be with us for many more years to come. We'll discuss "four-and-a-quarter" tiles further along.

There are many other types and sizes of "wall tiles," too numerous to cover in these brief

Figure 3: Standard 4- 1/4 in. wall tiles and typical trims.

passages. Wall tiles are essentially tiles that cannot hold up on floors. (Figure 3)

Floor Tiles

Most modern floor tiles are made by a process known as "dust pressing" or "dry pressing." Clay, containing very little moisture is packed into dies and is then placed into a pressing machine or "press," where extremely high pressure is exerted. This forms a "biscuit" that is then glazed or otherwise decorated and cooked in a kiln at high temperatures.

Figure 4: Glazed floor tiles.

Glazed "hard body" or "mono-cottura" tiles are produced in this manner. The tiles, however, do not have to be glazed, and many are not. Unglazed porcelain floor tiles, for example, are very popular for both residential and commercial applications. (Figure 4)

Terracotta Tiles and Saltillo Pavers

Terracotta is an Italian word that essentially means "cooked earth." Terracotta tiles are actually semi-cooked and do not achieve the hardness produced in other more modern tiles. Made from natural clay, terracottas range from grayish yellow to brownish orange. They are prized for their natural, "earthy," look.

Saltillo tiles are produced in the Saltillo area of Mexico. These are raw clay pavers, roughly cast by ancient methods. The making of the tiles has become a cottage industry to many of the people who live in and around Saltillo. The pavers are cooked with

Figure 5: Saltillo tiles with clear finish. Grout is masonry sand and portland cement.

banked open fires or in "beehive" ovens. They are soft, softer even than terracotta. Quality control is not a known quantity in Saltillo. The tiles are very irregular.

Similar tiles are made in other regions of Mexico and in some of the Mediterranean countries of Europe, including Spain. All of these "paver" type tiles vary dramatically in thickness and in overall size, ranging from small three or four inch pieces to tiles nearly two feet across.

Saltillo tiles, most terracotta tiles and other rough pavers are finished with sealer and a "top coat" when used indoors. The finish eventually wears off and must be replaced, so there is some maintenance involved. Outdoors it's a good idea to seal these products with a penetrating masonry sealer. (Figure 5)

Porcelain Floor Tiles

Porcelain tiles are in a class of their own. Practically waterproof, they are classed as vitreous, meaning they possess a moisture absorption rate of 0.5 percent or less with many tiles coming in at around 0.2 or 0.3 percent. Being dense makes them extremely hard and durable. Porcelain floor tiles can be glazed or unglazed. (Figure 6)

Figure 6: Glazed porcelain tiles with decorative insert.

Abrasive Resistance: Tiles with baked-on glazes, which are intended for floor installations, are rated for surface abrasion resistance. In the United States the testing is done under the auspices of the Porcelain Enamel Institute (PEI). Other countries have their own testing systems, and there are slight differences from country to country, but progress is being made to bring all testing systems into agreement.

There are five ratings or grades of resistance, I through V, with Grade V being the most durable. In my opinion, Grade I tiles should not be used on floors at all, and Grade II tiles should only be used in bathrooms and other areas where floors will see little foot traffic and practically *no* "shoe traffic." Grade III tiles are rated for all residential applications as well as for limited light commercial use. Grade IV can handle most commercial and some industrial applications, and Grade V covers everything else, including heavy industrial uses.

In choosing tiles for floor areas in your home, you won't go wrong if you stick to Grade III and above. You will find many floor tiles that work well for residential use in the Grade IV category. Most Grade V tiles look, well, "commercial."

Unglazed tiles are not rated, but persons selling tile will often attribute ratings to them. When someone says, "Now this is a Grade Five porcelain tile," you can assume that tile will wear out thousands of pairs of shoes before it shows any wear of its own.

Slip Resistance: Co-efficient of Friction (C.O.E., C. of F., or COF) is the term applied to slip resistance, and this is one area where there is no international agreement at all and little agreement within the country. To pursue the issue here would serve no purpose. It makes more sense to simply know that if a smooth surfaced tile gets wet, it's going to be slippery, and that heavily textured surfaces are more "slip resistant" than smooth ones. There are many unglazed tiles in clay and stone that are extremely slick when they get wet, so it's not just glazed tiles one must be careful of in situations where tiles are likely to be wet a good portion of the time.

Many, if not most, tiles commonly used inside the home or business are not suited to the outdoors. Most of the burnt clay products offer good footing in wet conditions, but some don't. Certain quarry tiles can be very slippery when wet. Bricks, brick pavers and thin bricks are usually a good bet. There are quarry tiles and thin bricks that are specifically made to be abrasive. These are often intended for commercial and industrial applications, but that doesn't mean they wouldn't be a good choice for the front porch or stoop. I'll tell you, if you somehow fall in front of my door, you're going to get up with a little abrasion of your own. The thin bricks I installed there years ago have metal shavings molded into the clay.

So use caution when purchasing tiles for outdoor installations. Do not be tempted to compromise on safety for architectural or aesthetic reasons.

Frost Resistance: The ability to resist freezing is another factor that must be considered in tiles intended for outdoor use in areas other than the Tropics. If you get winter freezes where you live, you'll need tiles that are "frost proof" or "frost resistant." Generally speaking, the denser the tile, the more frost resistant it will be. Raw clay tiles such as Saltillos and terracottas are definitely not frost resistant and should not be used outdoors in northern climes.

Here's what happens. If enough water gets into and under the tiles prior to a sustained freeze, ice will form and expand, causing the tiles to "heave" up from the setting bed. Harder, denser tiles prevent significant amounts of water from being absorbed.

Hard fired quarry tiles, thin bricks and all true porcelain tiles are considered frost proof. Single-fired clay floor tiles are usually a good bet, depending on the density of the clay underbody. Suitability information, if not on the packaging itself, is obtainable where you buy your tiles.

Break Strength: And then there is break strength. How much pressure from above does it actually take to cause a floor tile to break into pieces? Break strength is measured with a specialized machine developed for that purpose. It will not be necessary to delve into the subject here. I mention it only so that you will be aware of the quality when you shop for floor tiles. The higher the rating the better. Your tile distributor will have this information for each floor tile he or she carries.

Tools of the Trade

In *Ceramic Tile Setting* I set out to cover most of the tools used in tile setting at the beginning of the book, but I don't think I want to do that this time around. All the tools aren't used all the time, and it will be better if new tools are introduced as new projects are brought up. Still, though, there are basic tools and equipment that no modern craftsman, tile setter or otherwise, can do without. And there are a few tile and masonry tools that are necessary in almost every job. It is these implements that will be discussed here.

Hammer: When Gherd's descendants discovered they could shape rocks by hitting them with other harder rocks, they became craftsmen, and since that time no craftsman or craftswoman has been able to get by without a striking implement, most commonly a hammer. Hammers come in all shapes and sizes, for all sorts of uses, but the one we'll most often use is the old garden variety carpenter's hammer, about 16 to 20 ounces in weight, with either curved or straight nail-pulling claws. The straight claws work like a mason's chipping hammer to break bricks and concrete blocks, but there are other ways of doing that, so just have a "claw hammer" around before you begin any tile or stone project.

Measuring Tape: I use a steel measuring tape to lay out my projects. Mine is 25 feet long and has a built-in spring that automatically rolls it up inside its case when it's not needed. A number of companies make this style of tape and I have no favorites. Price is often the determining factor, but I would never buy a cheap measuring tape. Buy one that a professional would use, not an import from the dollar store.

There are still some old-timers floating around the trade who won't use anything but a wooden folding rule for measuring and layout. They are wizards at layout with this ancient but accurate tool. But using a rule that is only six feet long makes it sort of tough to lay out anything that spans more than six feet. Get a measuring tape.

Pencils: Sounds pretty basic, not even worth mentioning, but it is worth mentioning. All pencils used to be made from wood, but not many are these days. I go to office supply stores to stock up on wood pencils. Number 2 hexagonal wooden lead pencils work best for me. You need a pencil that can be continually sharpened to a fine point. Carpenter or lumber pencils actually have too much lead in them and often the lead is too soft to hold a point. The pencils made from fiber bend too easily. The pencil may not break in half, but the lead ends up in short segments inside the pencil. When you try to sharpen it, the lead pulls out of the shaft.

Knife: I use my knife to sharpen my pencil because I don't want to carry a pencil sharpener around with me. The less baggage the better. Get a good quality utility knife, one that has storage for extra blades and has a quick blade change feature. Again, get a knife that a professional wouldn't mind being caught with. It will be used for a variety of chores besides sharpening pencils.

I also carry a pocket knife, but that's optional.

Knee pads: It won't take you long to develop a healthy respect for knee pads when doing tile work, especially floor work. There are many varieties available in many price ranges. If you are only going to be doing one small job, get inexpensive knee pads, but if you think you might do a large project or a series of projects, spend a little more money.

Level (Spirit Level): You will need a good level whether you intend doing only a small project or a more extensive one. A two-foot level is standard equipment and will be all that is needed for most projects. A four-foot level is a plus for many projects, and a small "torpedo" level, about eight to ten inches long, is very handy when doing shower work.

If you are going to buy a level, buy one that has "fixed" vials instead of one that has so-called "adjustable" vials. Adjustable levels are out of adjustment most of the time. Fixed vial levels usually cost more than the adjustable levels, but there is nothing worse than a level that is not quite level. There are no screws holding the fixed vials in place. If you see the screws, move over to the next rack.

Square: I carry around a large size "speed square." A carpenter's framing square will also work, of course, but it's much harder to store. In any case, you will need some sort of square for just about every tile project you contemplate.

Trowel (Primary Trowel): We use an assortment of trowels in our business, but every tile setter has one particular trowel that he or she cannot be without. For me it's a gauging trowel, which is used to butter thin set mortar onto the backs of tiles, for daubing mortar onto curbs, for laying concrete blocks and for a host of other things. Some folks like a margin trowel with slightly rounded corners, and still others carry a larger "tile setter's" trowel. A brick layer's trowel is too large (and too pointed), and a pointing trowel is of limited use. Pointed trowels are not usually used inside showers when working over a shower pan membrane. There is always a chance of making a hole in the membrane.

Notched Trowels: Notched trowels are used in nearly every tile project for spreading tile adhesive on substrates. There is no standard size, and there is currently quite a debate in the industry as to which notched trowels are best for which projects. So don't buy a notched trowel until you know what size tiles you'll be using and the condition of the substrate the tiles will be going over. It's enough now to say that you'll be needing at least one notched trowel.

Straight-edges: Straight-edges are used for a variety of purposes in tile setting. I use common wood boards as straight-edges, but more expensive aluminum ones are better. It will depend on how much work you intend to do, but I would start out with wood boards. Choose the boards carefully. Straight grained softwoods are best. Hardwood boards tend to twist when wetted, and the boards will be wet often. One-by-four boards make good straight-edges. Not long ago I came across a long, straight piece of Honduran (African) Mahogany that had been discarded on a job site. I scooped it up and made a couple very excellent straight-edges from it. I wouldn't buy mahogany, though. It's terribly expensive.

Tile Cutting Tools

Cutting Boards (cutters)

Almost every tile project is going to entail the use of a cutter. Tile cutting boards come in a number of sizes and shapes, but they all operate on the same basic principle: they have a scoring wheel that scores the surface of the tile and a mechanism for breaking the scored tile in two. Prices for cutters run from around $30 to upwards of $300, depending on the cutter's capacity and sophistication. For a small project you can get by with a fairly inexpensive cutter, but for larger projects, or multiple projects, you should spend a little more money. Most novice tile setters should not spend more than $100 for a cutter and probably considerably less.

It is possible to rent or borrow a cutter.

Nippers (biters)

Nippers, which resemble pliers, are one of the handiest pieces of equipment a tiler can have. The tool is used for cutting or "biting" around obstacles, for trimming irregular cuts and for cleaning up cuts made on cutting boards. It is hard to find quality nippers nowadays, and I would not buy the most expensive tools, which are in the $30 to $40 range. I have found that biters costing under $20 dollars last just as long and do the same work.

Grinders

A 4-inch grinder equipped with a dry diamond cutting blade is invaluable for making "pocket cuts" such as openings for electrical outlets and switches. The tool will also come in handy for cutting large format tiles around toilet flanges and other obstacles. Switch over to a sanding disc and the tool can be used for profiling the edges of marble tiles. And, of course, it can also be used for grinding.

Tile Saws

There are big saws, little saws and in-between saws, and I seem to have one of each. My large saw will cut small marble slabs. It will diagonally halve 2-foot square tiles with room to spare. My saws happen to be made by Felker™, but there are many other brands. The intermediate saw cuts everything from 18-inch tiles on down and is my primary saw. Besides the two larger saws, I have a couple smaller tools I'll tell you about.

I have a Plasplug™ saw that costs about $80, Plasplug being the brand name. There are several brands of the same essential tool, some of them selling for around $50. I recommend buying one of these small and cheap tools if you need a saw for one or two tile projects and don't mind going a bit slow. They will do the job. With just a little imagination you can cut any size tile on the market with one of them.

The Plasplug has a tiny motor which turns a 5-inch diamond encrusted blade which in turn runs through a water reservoir in the base of the tool. The blade throws water upward where it is supposedly captured by a small hooded blade guard. Bring your raincoat or rig a sheet of plastic across your front. The water control system is anything but efficient. The first time I used my Plasplug I came away looking as though I had wet my pants after only one cut.

Many tile pros own the little saws but won't own up to the fact. The tools are invaluable for doing a small repair where only one or two cuts need to be made. You can set the saw up in a minute – it weighs only a few pounds – and when you've finished you can walk away with the tool tucked under your arm. Try that with a mid-size, 100 pound monster of a tile saw.

I also have a Felker TM-75, which I have done a review on. You will find it at the back of the book as Appendix IV.

Finally, I own a 4-inch circular saw that is equipped with a water cooling system which hooks to a hose or to a tile saw pump. The only thing this saw is good for is cutting tiles that have already been installed.

For an in-depth article on the functions of tile saws and their motors, please refer to Appendix III in the back. The article was written especially for this book by my friend Andy Lundgren, a recognized authority on the subject. Andy is products manager for Target/Felker Saws in the United States.

There are numerous other tools that will be needed, but we'll discuss them further along. I don't see a lot of sense in getting all geared up when many of the tools might not be needed for your particular project. I know, I know, you want to start cutting tile, but please be patient – take it easy. We'll get there.

Taking it Easy

It may be appropriate at this point to discuss tempo. For the professional tile setter, speed is a definite consideration. Slow pokes don't last long on the job. Good tile setters develop a combination of speed and precision that makes them desirable workman and keeps them in demand.

But since you won't be getting paid, speed is less important. In fact, it shouldn't even be a consideration. Don't start a project if you think you are going to be pushed for time to get it finished. An example of what not to do would be tearing your only bathroom out on a Friday night, hoping to have it all back together by Monday. You probably won't make it, and everyone, including your neighbors, will be impatient with you, and this will cause frustration. Do not become frustrated. It's not good for the spirit, and it makes for sloppy tile work.

The neighbors? Well, how long do you suppose they'll be amenable to you and yours popping in each time someone needs to use the bathroom?

It's much better to plan your work in stages, allow plenty of time for each stage, and preserve your sanity. Know exactly what you will need to do before you take anything apart. Trust me. I've been through all this.

Since I've entered my sixties (young sixties), I've become acutely aware of how hard I'm working as the day progresses, and the work day seldom exceeds seven hours — six and one-half hours are even better. I know how long the job will take when I begin it, and I pace myself. There is no time-keeper. The work day ends when I start getting "the attitude." When the attitude sets in it's time to quit, because nothing will go right if you remain on the job. You may want to stand around a little, but then get out of there.

Remember, as a tile setter you are a cool customer, much too cool to get caught up in a frenzy. Consider that you are about to attack a project that not too many people will even attempt. You are a member of a very exclusive clique of daring home craftsmen and craftswomen. You are on the cutting edge, a weekend warrior with a purpose. When the project has been completed, you will experience a personal satisfaction that is indescribable and not often duplicated. You will be somebody special, having done something special. It is crucial that you maintain your composure throughout all of this.

I'm getting so excited for you I can hardly contain myself.

I know I've inspired you to get at it forthwith, but please allow me to tell you about a couple of tile industry institutions whose resources may be of benefit to you along the way. I promise it'll only take a minute, and then we can jump right into the projects feet first.

Tile Council of America

Located at Anderson, South Carolina, the Tile Council of America (TCA) has become a sort of umbrella organization for various segments of the tile industry. Its members are tile manufacturers and makers of tile related products. There are also affiliate members such as the National Tile Contractors Association, the Ceramic Tile Institute of America, and other industry and trade groups.

The TCA, a non-profit group, operates a modern and fully-equipped testing lab that it shares jointly with Clemson University, which is located just a few miles down the road. Clemson, by the way, is one of only five schools in the United States that offers degrees in ceramic engineering. The lab's current director, Noah Chitty, is a Clemson graduate. (Figure 7)

In addition to testing materials for its members and others, the TCA publishes a handbook which covers standards and procedures approved by the American National Standards Institute (ANSI) and the American

Figure 7: Noah Chitty, TCA Tile Lab Director.

Society of Testing and Materials (ASTM). Geared for professionals, the handbook is also a worthwhile reference for the novice tile setter. It can be purchased directly from the TCA.

The president of the Tile Council is chosen annually from among its members. The current executive director of the organization is Bob Daniels.

You can access the TCA at its web site: http://www.tileusa.com/ index.html or you can write or email for more information.

Tile Council of America, Inc.
100 Clemson Research Blvd.
Anderson, SC 29625
Phone: 864-646-8453 • Fax: 864-646-2821
Email: literature@tileusa.com

Ceramic Tile Education Foundation (The Tile School)

The CTEF is located at Pendleton, South Carolina, only a few miles from the TCA. The tile school's current director is my friend Dave Gobis, who has graciously contributed the foreword to this book. The school provides hands-on instruction in several basic tile setting procedures to professional and novice tile setters alike. In fact, the school is open to anyone who wants to gain a better understanding of tile setting techniques. Courses are of varying lengths and are available throughout the year. People who are involved in all aspects of the industry, including manufacturing and marketing, attend the school.

When Dave is not actively running the tile school and teaching courses, he is on the road giving seminars and specialized courses in nearly every part of the country. As I write, he is in Mexico conferring with members of that country's tile industry. "Dave G." is a valued member of the JB Forums on the Internet. He is a walking encyclopedia of tile knowledge.

It is not necessary that you attend any courses or seminars, but if you have the mind to do so, I most emphatically recommend the Ceramic Tile Education Foundation. You can contact the school at its web site: http://www.tileschool.org or at its offices in South Carolina.

The Ceramic Tile Education Foundation
5326 Highway 76
Pendleton, South Carolina 29670
Tel: 864-222-2131 Fax: 864-222-1299
Email: info@tileschool.org

Terrazzo Tile and Marble Association of Canada
L'association Canadienne de Terrazzo, Tuile et Marbre

The TTMAC, located in Concord, Ontario, is Canada's counterpart to the Tile Council of America. The organization has been in place since 1944 and has contributed significantly to the standardization of tile, stone, and terrazzo installation techniques. Membership is composed of contractors and manufacturers. Visit TTMAC at www.ttmac.com.

TTMAC
30 Capstan Gate, Unit 5
Concord, Ontario L4K 3E8
Tel: (905) 660-9640 (800) 201-8599
Email: association@ttmac.com

CHAPTER TWO

CERAMIC TILE FLOORS

Gravity is Good

Fired clay tile floors have been around for about 8,000 years. Rude pavers have been uncovered in areas of the Middle East that go back at least that far. The pavers were set in dirt or sand in loose fashion. Mud or clay was used to more or less keep them in place. This is how things were done in the poorer sections of town. If you lived up on the hill, you got marble slabs on your floors, and they were set over a real sand substrate.

Things have definitely changed in the past eight millennia, and modern ceramic tile floors are well within the reach of the average person. True, tile is still expensive, but not so when you consider that you will be supplying your own labor force. Labor amounts to at least half the cost of a tile job and often more. Have I mentioned that you won't be getting paid for this work?

Why start on floors? It's a good place to start, for one thing, and floors are usually less difficult than walls. You lay a tile or anything else on a floor and it'll stay there until you move it. As everyone knows, that's not the case with walls. Putting things on walls requires a little more "style" than putting things on floors, and right now style in setting tile is probably not one of your strong points. You may rest assured, though, that by the time we've finished, you will be one stylish person indeed.

In acquainting you with the processes necessary to complete a tiled floor in any room of the house, I will focus on the kitchen. If I can provide you with the informa-tion that will enable you to do an outstanding job on a kitchen floor, you'll be able to handle anything that comes your way. The kitchen, unlike the living room or the den, is cluttered with cabinets and appliances. Laying out and cutting around these obstacles will challenge your skills. You don't just start in the middle of the floor and work your way toward the walls, because there is no middle. (Figure 8)

The kitchen floor usually consists of a number of connected rectangles. Every once in a while,

Figure 8: Kitchen floors are not simple rectangles.

someone will throw in a portion of a circle or a triangle just to make things interesting. It all boils down to basic high school geometry. If you made it through your junior year in high school, as I did before I got smart and dropped out, you'll have no problems understanding what we are about to discuss. If you didn't make it through your junior year, there is still hope for you with a little tutoring. If, on the other hand, you messed up and graduated from high school, we've got work to do, but I'll be patient with you. It's going to be really tough, though, if you went on to college. You didn't do that, did you? Higher math and all that?

Geometry is the branch of math we'll be using more than any other, and I will acquaint or re-acquaint you with a few basic processes as we go along. Before we arrive at that stage, however, there are a number of other factors that must be discussed.

Sub-floors

In homebuilding, the sub-floor is something that is certain to be covered up, as opposed to the "finish floor," which everyone will see when the house has been completed. Sub-floors can be concrete, as is the case in my part of the country more often than not; they can be plywood sheathing over wood joists, the norm in many parts of the country and in Canada; or in older homes the "sheathing" or planking on the floor might be softwood boards laid either straight or diagonally across the joists.

And then there are the modern "engineered" sub-floors. These might consist of wood or metal trusses which span distances that conventional joists would not be capable of spanning, covered by plywood substitutes such as particle board and oriented-strand-board (OSB). You may find that your floor consists of some or all of these components. You might have wood trusses covered with conventional plywood or OSB, or you might have wood joists covered with plywood, particle board or both. The best wood floors I have worked above are those consisting of trusses covered with plywood that is one and one-eighth inches thick (Sturd-I-floor®). If you are building a new house, and you can afford this method, I recommend it. You can install any type of finish flooring with no worry about structure. A membrane material or a thin layer of cement backer board over the Sturd-I-floor and you're ready for ceramic tile or stone. Similarly, if you are using conventional joists, the addition of the thick Sturd-I-floor is well worth the added expense.

Concrete Slab Sub-floors (Slab-on-Grade)

Homes are built over concrete slabs in many parts of the country, particularly throughout the southern states. Essentially, a "pad" is built up from fill dirt and aggregate, and reinforced concrete is formed and poured on top of it. There are perimeter "beams" or footings which support the perimeter of the building. There will also be areas of the slab's interior that will be thickened to support interior bearing walls. Well done house slabs will contain "control joints" which will help eliminate cracking in areas that might cause problems with direct bonded flooring. In my part of the country, control joints are seldom used — to the detriment of tile and stone flooring installers. More on concrete slabs in general will follow.

Floating Mortar Beds

The best possible technique over a concrete slab is the "floating floor" or "floating mortar bed." When the slab is poured, it is poured a couple inches lower than the intended finish floor. A slip sheet (moisture barrier) of construction felt (tar paper) or plastic sheeting (poly) is first laid over the slab. The slip sheet is also known as a

Colleen Staton

Seth Frankel

Ryan Kitchen

Trask Bergerson

Colleen Staton

John Koessler

Jerry Nebel

Wayne Chism

Barb Freda

Denise Kober

Dave Ashton

"cleavage membrane." Expanded metal lath or reinforcing mesh is laid over the slip sheet with the edges of the reinforcing overlapped to make a continuous armature. Good quality galvanized chicken wire (poultry netting) might also be used for the reinforcing. Finally, dry pack mortar (deck mud/floor mud) is placed over the reinforcing material, and the floor is screeded to a level plane.[1] Ceramic or stone tiles are then cemented to the mud with thin set mortar (also called dry set mortar or bonding mortar).

Once grouted and cured, the floor becomes a unit. If the slab below should crack or shift, it won't affect the floor above because nothing is attached. The floor system merely rests on the slab. Gravity holds it in place, and the walls prevent it from floating off into the sunset.

A floating floor is not feasible in an existing slab house. There is simply no room to raise the floor to the height necessary to create a cohesive system above the slab. It thus becomes necessary to install the tiles directly to the slab or over a thin membrane glued to the concrete. Although not the best of situations, floors done in this manner can last a long time, indefinitely if done correctly. There will be more on mortar substrates.

So we arrive at basically two types of tile installation: one over a wood subfloor, and one over a concrete slab (slab-on-grade). Before we begin installing the tiles themselves, we'll cover the two flooring systems in detail. As anyone who has been in the tile or flooring business for more than a week or two will tell you, most of the time and energy spent in coming up with a satisfactory installation goes into what's underneath. We cannot afford any shortcuts in this area.

Wood Floor Structures

Essentially, wood floor framing is used in three residential settings: over an open "crawl space," over a basement or cellar and on second and third story floors. The floors are usually constructed of dimension lumber, boards or timbers whose vertical measurement when installed exceeds their width or thickness. In the United States and Canada, the timbers or "members" are referred to as *joists*. The joists most often used are nominally 2 inches thick, and their height

Figure 9: Under side floor joists. OSB decking above.

can be anywhere from 4 inches to 14 inches. Actually, the boards are only 1-1/2 inches thick when leaving the mill.

The joist most often used is a "two by ten," a timber that is 1-1/2 inches thick by 9-1/4 inches tall when installed. The most common spacing for these joists is 16 inches from centerline to centerline. This spacing is referred to as 16 inches on center (16 in. o. c.). It happens that two by ten joists, 16 inches on center (2 x 10 – 16 in. o. c.) represent the minimum structural standard (in many incidences) accepted by the American National Standards Institute (ANSI) for floors which are to receive ceramic tiles. However, other joist sizes and other joist spacing can be adapted to tile installations

---

[1] *In the United Kingdom, as well as in Australia and New Zealand, dry pack mortar or floor mud is most often referred to as "screed."*

with additional shoring and bracing. (Figure 9)

Loads: Joists are supported by walls or by supporting "beams." They are also supported by foundation walls or perimeter beams. The distance a joist travels unsupported between walls or beams is called its *span*. The longer the span, the greater the deflection that will occur when pressure is applied to the member from above. The downward pressure on a joist or other flooring member is referred to as *load*. There are two types of load. *Dead load* represents the downward pressure exerted by the weight of the member itself, as well as the flooring and built-in structures above it. *Live load* consists of the weight of persons and objects that are movable. Both of these load categories will figure into the overall load a floor system is expected to support.

Deflection: The propensity for joists and sub-floors to bend downward under a load is called *deflection*. The joists and beams will be covered with a sub-floor that may be comprised of wood planks, plywood or other engineered wood sheathing. In addition to overall joist and beam deflection, we will be concerned with the deflection caused by loads on the sub-floor and finish flooring between the joists. This deflection will be caused by concentrated loads on the floor, such as human feet, table legs, chairs and a variety of other objects which do not span more than one joist space.

I know this sounds like a lot of information to absorb all at once, and it is, but you will not be required to remember it, I promise. You can return here at any time to refresh your memory. Keep in mind, though, that what we are talking about represents the *minimum,* and stronger floors are certainly desirable.

Maximum Allowable Deflection

According to ANSI, the maximum allowable deflection in a subfloor system designed to accept a ceramic tile installation is one-three hundred sixtieth of its overall span when subjected to a 300 lb. concentrated load (one heavy person or a couple of lighter persons dancing with each other). This is expressed as L/360. This standard applies not only to the overall span of the joists but to the sub-floor sheathing that stretches across the joists, since this sheathing is most often unsupported between the joists. In short, if you expect a ceramic tile installation to survive above a wood sub-floor, that floor must be very strong and "stiff." 1/360 of a span of, say, ten feet is about five-sixteenths of an inch, and that's not very much. Any more deflection than that and there's a good chance your tile installation will fail.

I have converted all this into the metric system for the benefit of all our friends abroad who no longer use the English Standard System of measurements. 1/360 roughly equates to 0.0028. Sticking to even increments, ten feet most closely compares to three meters. The maximum allowable deflection in three meters, then, would be a bit over eight millimeters (8 mm). I repeat that these are minimum standards and maximum allowable deflections. Greater stiffness, which means less deflection, is advisable if at all attainable.

I will also add that folks in countries other than the United States have developed their own sets of standards, and all countries do not completely agree in these matters. Efforts are being made on several fronts, however, to bring about a degree of universal agreement. As I write, Canadians and Americans are very close in thought, and the respective standards of the two countries are not too dissimilar. I have little knowledge of what's going on in other countries as far as building standards are concerned.

And I do not mean to infer that American standards are superior to anyone else's. It's just that these are the rules I am familiar with, and following them will certainly do you no harm. I would suggest that people in countries other than the U.S. check into local standards and codes before they commit to a project.

Deflection in Stone Floors: As I mentioned earlier in the book, some do-it-your-selfers have taken on projects that tax the abilities of many professionals, and installing a stone tile floor would fall into that category. You may be one of those spunky novices for all I know, so I had better tell you that the sub-floor requirements for a marble, granite, slate or other stone tile floor are exactly twice those for a ceramic tile floor. That's right, L/720, which means that the sub-floor mentioned above can have a maximum deflection of about 5/32 of an inch (4mm) when the dancers are on it. Put that in your satchel before you go getting froggy.[2]

It is important to know that in most cases the tile installation adds nothing to the floor structure. Various membranes, cement backer boards and even thin mortar beds cannot be considered when stiffness is being calculated. The stiffness has to be there before any of these products is installed. There are methods of constructing reinforced mortar surfaces that are somewhat structural, but it is better to have sufficient support underneath.

In most cases, the floor you intend to tile will have already been built. What if it's not up to standards? How can you fix it? Although we can't go into all the intricacies of floor framing, we can discuss ways that floors can be shored up to make them acceptable. For in reality, there are few floors that cannot be brought up to the standards necessary to support a tile installation.

The Jump Test

How can the average person measure the deflection in an existing floor? He or she can't without specialized measuring instruments that are not at all likely to be at hand. Besides visually inspecting the floor and its structural members, there is one test that is available to everyone. I should say it is available to every *two*. It's called the "jump test," and two people perform it. One person jumps as high as he or she can while the other person places both hands palm down on the floor and gauges the reverberation as the first person comes down on it. It is important for the person on the floor to keep his hands out of the way of the person doing the jumping, or the test results will be murky at best. It's hard to concentrate on deflection while at the same time trying to ignore excruciating pain.

The idea is to try to feel the deflection in the floor. The test is not scientific at all and certainly not sanctioned by the TCA, but if you sense considerable "bounce" when your cohort lands, there's a good chance the floor won't support a tile installation. If, on the other hand, the floor feels solid to you, it's an indication the installation will hold up. I can just see the tile gurus gritting their teeth over this one.

A short piece directed toward engineers is contained in Appendix II at the back. It is written by Bob Campbell, a mechanical engineer who is "Chief Engineer" of the John Bridge Forums. In Appendix VIII, you will find an informative article on subfloor deflection by Keith T. Bretzfield and Frank E. Woeste (Virginia Tech University).

Sistering (Partnering): Suppose your floor joists are only 2 x 8 instead of the recommended 2 x 10 size. And suppose those joists are over-spanned. This is often the case in older homes, those built prior to the 1960s. You are not going to abandon your tile project because of this. You are going to cope with the situation by shoring up the floor until it reaches the stiffness required to support a tile installation. "Sistering" the joists is one of the ways this can be done.

Essentially, you will screw or nail additional joists or other members alongside the existing joists. Increasing mass in this manner will increase stiffness along the length of

---

[2] *froggy – prepared to leap like a frog, overconfident.*

the joist in question. As each joist in a floor system is thus stiffened, the entire floor gains the ability to better support a load, which is what we are concerned with — live and dead load, including the weight of the tile installation itself.

In many instances you won't be able to add sister joists of the same dimension as the originals because of wiring, piping and air handling ducts running through the joists and through the spaces between them. Smaller members may have to be used instead. A 2 x 6 securely screwed to the side of a 2 x 8 joist will stiffen it significantly, for example, and even a 2x4 will add some strength.

Blocking or Bridging: Installing solid blocking between joists stiffens the overall floor considerably. Instead of the entire load of the 300 lb. couple being concentrated on one joist, the weight will be distributed farther out in the floor by virtue of the blocking. "X"-bridging accomplishes the same thing as solid blocking. X-braces can be inserted into areas where solid blocking might not fit.

Support Beams (Girders)

In crawl spaces or basements it is often feasible to shore up the floors above by adding beams under the joists and thus reducing their span. The beams or girders can be made up of two or more joists screwed together side-by-side, or they can be solid timbers. In short spans the new members might be supported on their ends by brackets or ledgers attached to the foundation walls. In longer spans you might need to add intermediate supports under the beams in the form of piers into the ground. Steel I-beams might also be considered.

How much shoring will be necessary to bring your floor up to standards? It's impossible for me to say, and it will be your responsibility alone to design and calculate your improvements. Employing the services of a structural engineer would certainly be worthwhile. The professional fee paid will be returned a hundred times in peace of mind.

Or, you can log onto the JB Forums and ask the advice of our professional engineers. As I write, this advice is given *free of charge* and free of obligation. By this I mean that no one offering advice on the forums can be held responsible for outcomes resulting from that advice. There are no guarantees. Find the forums at: http://johnbridge. com/vbulletin/index.php

I said earlier that it's possible to tile almost any floor, but I did use the word "almost." In some cases, the subfloor will be so under-built, or so dilapidated, that it will not be feasible to consider a ceramic tile floor above it. The situation comes up occasionally at the JB Forums. We reach a point where we have to advise people to consider an alternative floor covering, one that will flex as deflection works its treachery. Laminate and wood floors will work well where ceramic tile and stone floors will fail. There are also solid vinyl tiles and vinyl linoleum. There is also carpeting.

Trusses and I-Joists: An increasing number of residential floors are being constructed using engineered trusses which are composed of wood and metal parts. Trusses can support heavier loads over longer spans than can solid wood members, and for this reason they can also be spaced farther apart. As far as floor rigidity is concerned, trusses are good and bad. Although they may support greater loads per unit, they may bend (deflect) farther than solid wood in so doing. This, of course, is due to the longer spans. There is also a phenomenon called the "trampoline effect" in which a floor reverberates excessively when people walk or run across it. Constant and intense up and down movement plays havoc with a tile or stone installation.

I have found, however, that trussed sub-floors are completely suitable for tile installations if a sufficient thickness of sub-flooring is used. I've mentioned 1-1/8 in. Sturd-I-Floor and that it should be used in new floor construction, but that will hardly ever be the case in remodeling. It is not unusual, for example, to run into situations where trusses have been spread up to two feet apart and covered with a layer of 5/8 in. plywood. A floor such as this would not be acceptable for a tile installation in my opinion, but it could certainly be reinforced with another layer of plywood glued and screwed to the original. One and one-eighth inches of plywood will make just about any framing system complete when it comes to a tile floor.

I-Joists are composed of top and bottom rails with a webbing of plywood or OSB between them. I-Joists have a couple advantages over conventional solid timber joists: They can span greater distances for their weight, and they tend to afford a smoother floor — the tops of the I-Joists are more in line with one another than are conventional joists. Depending on their spacing, I-Joists can deliver a very solid floor structure.

Sub-flooring Panels

Although the stiffness and integrity of the flooring structure is important in the sense that deflection of any sort is always a factor to be considered in a tile floor installation, deflection rates in the sub-flooring panels themselves will prove to be critical. It is this deflection *between* the joists that often causes the most problems, and thus it is imperative that good quality flooring panels be used.

Plywood, specifically flooring grade plywood, is the best available material for subfloors. There are many grades of plywood that are not acceptable. CDX or exterior sheathing used primarily for roof decking and wall bracing is not considered structural when it comes to sub-floors for ceramic and stone tiles. There are too many voids in the various "plies" of the boards to make them of value for our purposes. Cabinet grade plywood is also unacceptable for floors. The panels are extremely soft even though they might be described as "oak" plywood or "birch" plywood. The hardwoods used in these panels are in the form of extremely thin veneers, and they are only on the surface of the panels. What's inside is not very sturdy at all.

Luan (Philippine Mahogany) plywood has lost favor not only in the tile industry but in the flooring industry in general. Luan is extremely unstable, and oils in the wood cause it to shrink and swell after installation. Additionally, the panels do not hold glue particularly well. If you find a layer of luan on your existing sub-floor, it's best to remove it.

Particle board can be used in floors that are not exposed to moisture in any way. I say this only because a great many existing floors have particle board in their composition. If it can be kept dry, it will work. If, however, it becomes wet, it can swell to nearly twice its original thickness. Particle board should never be considered when you are planning a new floor. Use plywood.[3]

OSB

Oriented Strand Board (OSB), also called "chip board," is being used extensively in new home construction in the United States and Canada. OSB is very strong, and as long as it can be kept dry, it will do the job. Once again, though, plywood should be your choice if you are building a new floor. Additionally, there are certain grades of OSB that are weatherproofed on their surfaces. The process makes the surfaces unsuitable for direct gluing. As far as strength is concerned, though, OSB is rated the same as plywood by the American Plywood Association.

---

[3]*I am aware that the majority of new homes in Australia and New Zealand are currently constructed with particle board sub-floors and that tile is routinely installed directly to it. I suspect that American and Canadian versions of "particle board" are not up to the standards of our friends Down Under. I suspect also that we could be talking about entirely different materials.*

In 1997, Paul R. Fisette, Director of Building Materials and Wood Technology at the University of Massachusetts, produced a comprehensive article on the attributes of OSB. Mr. Fisette has kindly allowed me to reproduce his work here. You will find the piece contained in Appendix V at the back of the book.

Grades of Plywood

Plywood is graded by the number and density of its plies and by the condition of its surface. Usually two letters represent a particular panel. AD, for example, means that one side or "face" of the panel is top quality, usually without knots or other blemishes. The reverse side of the panel will contain knot holes and other flaws. BC would be the next panel down the list. B panels can contain small tight knots in the face but no out-and-out voids. C panels will contain sizable knots. CC Plugged is a C panel in which the knots on the face have been replaced with inserts of veneer. These "plugs" are usually in the shape of a football, an American football that is oval in shape.

When building a new floor, the minimum panel used would be five-eighths of an inch (15 mm) thick, and a three-quarter inch panel would improve things considerably. I personally would not bother with the thinner panels at all. As I've stated, panels of an inch or more in thickness solve most of the problems incurred in tile flooring installation. Because of their weight, however, the thicker panels are extremely difficult to handle, and it is possible to achieve nearly the same result by using two thinner panels which will be screwed together. More work, certainly, but it might be your only option, depending on your physical strength and the availability of helpers.

Cement Backer Board (Cement Backer Unit or "CBU")

Cement backer board was developed several decades ago as a substitute for cement mortar (mud) substrates. Are CBUs better than mud? No, nothing is better than mud, but CBUs do make suitable substrates for tile floors if they are installed correctly. We'll spend some time on this because it is an area in which there is much misunderstanding both inside and outside the tile industry.

In the first place, CBUs used on floors are not structural. They are not designed to add stiffness to the floor. They are instead intended to separate the tile field from the sub-floor and to provide a more stable substrate than the plywood or other panels below. CBUs offer a substrate that is closer to the expansion and contraction rates of tile and stone than does plywood, for example. While plywood will shift due to temperature and moisture variations, CBUs will hold still. And while all of the movement that occurs in floors might be considered microscopic, it is of crucial concern in substrates. It doesn't take a lot to cause a tile floor to de-bond or otherwise come apart due to excessive movement.

So although CBUs are fastened to the sub-floor, they are deliberately installed so that they can move laterally. The panels are not bumped tightly together. A space is left, which is later filled with thin set mortar. The panels are not nailed directly into joists or other framing members. They are instead fastened only to the sub-floor sheathing or decking, with their end joints staggered throughout the installation.

Cement backer boards are bedded in thin set mortar as they are installed. The mortar is spread on the sub-flooring with a notched trowel, and the backer board panel is laid into it and nailed or screwed. The mortar is not intended to bond the CBU to the sub-floor. It merely supports the panels by filling every void that is likely to occur between the panels and the sub-floor decking. For this reason, the very cheapest of thin set mortars can be used. Can you skip the thin set step? No. (By the way, say "thin set step" several times rapidly.)

And this brings us to an area where there seems to be a bit of confusion within the industry. I've just told you to use cheap unmodified thin set under your backer board when you lay it, and that is in fact the recommendation of the Tile Council of America. But certain backer board manufacturers specify that their products be installed with modified thin set mortar. These instructions could change at any time, but they may not. All I can tell you is that despite what I've said above, you must follow the recommendations of the manufacturer of the product you've chosen to use. If the manufacturer wants modified thin set, use it. The standards set forth by the American National Standards Institute (ANSI), which are supported and published by the Tile Council of America (TCA), are *voluntary*. They in no way hinder a manufacturer from determining how his or her products are to be used.

Most manufacturers of CBUs specify that their panels be "taped" at the joints with an alkaline-resistant fiberglass mesh tape that is sold where CBUs are sold. The tape is adhered to the joints in the panels with thin set mortar which is then flattened with a trowel or drywall knife. The backer board tape looks very much like drywall (sheetrock) joint tape, which should *not* be used. The drywall tape reacts adversely with thin set mortar, and this will cause the tape to deteriorate.[4]

More Controversy

The argument as to whether cement backer board is structural continues. I have found that the majority of installers believe that the panels improve the stiffness of the floor. "It just feels more solid" is a common phrase heard during conversations on the subject of CBUs. You may experience this feeling of solidity also.

But as I said earlier, don't be tempted to depend on any added stiffness that CBUs might contribute. In rigorous testing by the TCA and other agencies, CBUs have not come through as having added anything to floor structures. Their value is solely in providing a tile substrate that is more dimensionally stable than the wood subflooring below.

Vinyl Linoleum (Removal)

Many residential kitchen floors have been covered with vinyl linoleum or with vinyl tiles. In most cases this flooring should be removed or at least partially removed before a tile installation is attempted. You will hear an abundance of confusing opinions on this issue from people within the industry who should know better. You will be told, for example, that tile can be installed directly to linoleum and that the linoleum will in fact improve the installation. It will act as a crack suppression membrane, for example.

The fact is, vinyl is extremely unstable as a substrate for ceramic tile. Notice how vinyl linoleum tends to shrink and become brittle with age. Notice how it tends to open at the seams and pull away and curl where it abuts walls and cabinets if it's not held down by a molding. Imagine all of this going on under the tile installation that cost you a tidy sum even if you did do the work yourself. Nah, it's not worth it at all. Pull the stuff up and get rid of it. At least get the vinyl "wear layer" off the top and scrape up as much of the backing as you can. Small sections of backing that refuse to scrape up can be left in place.

It has been reported that certain flooring retailers in the United States and Canada have been selling cheap vinyl linoleum as a setting membrane to go under the ceramic tiles they sell and install. You might guess that the linoleum is not sold at cost and that the sale represents added profit to the retailer. He or she is not doing anyone any favors.

[4]*Sheetrock is called "gyp-rock" or "gyp-board" in Canada. In England it is generally "plaster board" or "wall board."*

The customer is told that the method is superior to other methods he or she might have heard about. In my opinion, these tile sellers (who are, fortunately, in the minority) ought to be run out of the business. Whether they are committing this sin through malice or out of ignorance, they should know better, and in many cases they do.

Linoleum and vinyl tiles may be left in place under cement backer board installations if the vinyl is not of the cushion type. Fortunately, cushion vinyl is no longer the trend and hasn't been for a number of years. If you do have cushion vinyl floors, scrape them up. Again, backer board manufacturers issue their own advice on this subject. Follow their directions when using their products.

Removing Ceramic or Stone Tiles

In some cases no matter how well a tile floor may have been installed, someone is going to come along and want to remove it. Maybe the color is not right for the new decorating scheme, or maybe the tile is "dated" as in the case of the pink tiles with black trim that were all the rage when I was growing up in the fifties. I still can't imagine why anyone would want to get rid of that beautiful combination, but people do. Other times, the tiles might not have been installed correctly. In any case, tiles will from time to time be removed.

If the tiles are installed over a concrete substrate or over plywood, it is usually necessary to chip them up individually either by hand with a hammer and chisel or by using an electric chipping

Figure 10: A hammer and chisel will work, but an electric tool is quicker.

hammer. In either case, be assured there will be a mountain of chips and shards and a thick layer of dust over everything in no time at all. It is important to wear eye and ear protection as well as a protective mask over the mouth and nose.

Getting under the edges of the tiles and working somewhat laterally is better than attacking the tiles with direct blows to the surface. In some cases, entire tiles can be lifted, but not often. Whatever the situation, it will not be an easy job. Prepare yourself mentally for an ordeal. (Figure 10)

There will usually be adhesive remaining on the floor when the tile has been removed. If this is a cement bonding mortar, the ridges may be ground down or in some cases chipped off with the hammer and chisel. At other times it may be acceptable to simply go over the residue with the new setting material. And then again, you may choose to skim coat the residue with a portland cement base patching compound or with stiff mixed thin set mortar.

If the tiles were installed over cement backer board or over thin plywood underlayment, it is better to remove that material along with the tiles. It is possible to pry up the backer board or other underlayment with the tiles still attached to it. It's not easy, mind you, but it has to be done. The backer will be of no value and will have to be replaced regardless of how the tiles are removed. Might as well get it all up at once.

Reinforced Mortar Beds

I am a mud man. I have portland cement coursing through my veins. Mortar is a part of me. I dream about it (for crying out loud). I don't know of a better medium upon which to set ceramic or stone tiles.

There are tile and stone installations done in Europe over mud screeds that date to well over a millennium ago. It was the Romans who invented the process for making cement mortar, and that process has changed very little since those times. The make-up of the cement has changed considerably but not how cement is used in masonry construction.

Over a wood sub-floor a mortar bed can do anything any other underlayment can do and do it better – if there is sufficient room for the build-up. In general, a 3/4 inch thick mortar bed should be considered minimum, although I have many times constructed beds as thin as 1/2 inch, these over extremely stout plywood sub-floors that would themselves support the tile installation were it feasible to glue tiles directly to plywood.

Cement Then and Now

The Romans used lime and sand as basic ingredients of their mortar. Blood, milk and animal fat were employed as strengthening additives. One of the first uses of cement was during the building of the Appian Way. The cement used was composed of pozzolana (volcanic rock from the Pozzuoli area of Italy) and lime. The material, in varying recipes, was also used to construct the Parthenon and the Coliseum in Rome and the Pont du Gard aqueduct in the South of France. These structures, or portions of them, survive to this day.

The product that evolved from the Romans' early efforts is called "natural cement." Natural cement is derived from limestone, gypsum and other natural elements. The making of natural cement depended upon finding stone deposits that more or less contained the correct amounts of the needed elements, so manufacturing the cement was sort of a hit and miss proposition. Natural cement is still used, however, in remote regions of the world.

And then came modern portland cement. The term "portland" derives from the town of Portland, England, whose building stone is gray, the essential color of portland cement. The material has been produced for well over a century, beginning it's evolution in Europe. The product was initially imported into the United States, as the means for making it were considered too labor intensive to accommodate the high wages then paid in the States. It was not until new methods of manufacture were developed that the material was produced in North America. Portland cement, or "portland," is made by combining limestone, clay, and other elements and "cooking" them in an oven or "kiln." The resultant "clinkers" are then pulverized into a very fine powder. When water is introduced, the particles tend to recombine and bond to one another, forming a mass nearly as hard as the original stone from which the material is produced.

Cement cures by a process known as "hydration." It does not need air in order to become hard and dry. In fact, the longer the material can be kept wet, the stronger it becomes. This is how it is possible to build concrete bridge supports and other underwater structures.

Besides increased strength, the advantage of portland cement is that it can be manufactured consistently. Its ingredients can be obtained from various points and assembled at the "batch plant." The art of making construction cement no longer depends on finding the necessary ingredients all in the same place.

Should you consider a mud job on your floor instead of a backer board job? Well, that will depend on your ability and whether you have room for the increased height. Keep in mind that a backer board installation, properly done, is more than adequate. (Figure 10A)

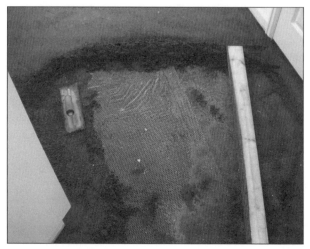

Figure 10A: Mud floor.

Creating a Mortar Bed Floor

We begin by ensuring that the subflooring is properly secured to the framing. If need be, re-nail or screw the floor boards to the joists. Remember,

Deck Mud/Dry Pack/Floor Mud

Floor mud is distinguished from other mortars most notably by it's dryness. It contains only enough water to allow the mix to hold together and to activate the hydration process. The mortar is prepared by combining 4 to 5 parts of clean concrete sand (sharp sand) to 1 part portland cement. My preference is for a leaner (weaker) mix, so I use the 5:1 ratio. This recipe will produce a cured mortar that will meet or exceed most requirements for tile subfloor screeds in general and all requirements for residential subfloors.

Combine the cement and sand by dry mixing until the sand particles are coated with cement. Then add water carefully, a little at a time. You want only enough water to cause the mortar to hold together when clumped in the palm of the hand. In properly proportioned floor mud you will not be able to see any water after the mud has been mixed, and when working the mortar, water will not rise to the surface as it does when concrete is tooled, for example. (Figure 11)

If you only need a small amount of mortar, you can mix it in a wheelbarrow or in a mud mixing box. Use a mason's hoe as your mixing tool. A garden hoe will work also, although it will work slower. 10 shovels of sand would constitute a small batch of deck mud. Observing the 5:1 ratio you would add 2 shovels of portland cement.

Figure 11: Blend the sand and cement.

The tricky part is the water, and the amount you add will depend on the water content of the sand when you begin. If your sand has been out in the rain, it's possible it has already absorbed too much water. You could allow it to drain and then add the cement to it. No water would be added. On the other hand, if the sand is completely dry, you might add a gallon of water to the ten-shovel batch. I would add a half-gallon to begin with. Add more water in small amounts as needed. (Figure 12)

Using the hoe, you chop the mix back and forth in the mixing container. You will be finished when the mortar is consistently damp throughout. You can also mix the mud by forming a pile on a concrete slab (garage floor, maybe) and tossing it with a shovel. Be sure to rinse off the floor when you've finished. (Figure 13)

The mortar can best be described as "sand-castle material." You want enough water to cause the mix to hold together but not so much as to cause it to slump. You have made sandcastles, haven't you? (Figure 14)

Deck mud when properly mixed will be fluffy. It is packed down with a wood float or a flat trowel after placement, hence the term "dry pack." After the mortar has been leveled off it is gently smoothed with a flat trowel in order to embed the loose particles of sand on its finished surface. Do not expect the surface to resemble troweled concrete. Finished deck mud will appear sandy and grainy. (Figure 15)

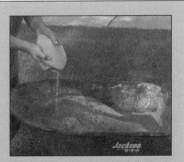

Figure 12: Add water carefully. Keep the mix on the dry side.

Figure 13: This mud is about ready to use.

Figure 15: Deck mud is sandy and grainy.

Figure 14: Clump the mud in your hands. It should hold together.

for thin screeds, most of the ultimate strength is derived from the subfloor itself.

A moisture barrier of either sheet plastic (poly) or tar paper (15 lb. felt) is installed over the subfloor. It is only necessary to tack it in the corners to keep it from sliding around while the lath is nailed over it. The primary purpose of the moisture barrier is to keep the dry wood subfloor from prematurely drawing moisture from the mortar. Its secondary function is that of a water inhibitor to protect the wood.

The moisture barrier also acts as a "cleavage membrane" or slip sheet. It allows the completed mortar bed to move about over the subfloor as the forces of nature – moisture and temperature – work upon it. This ability to move about is extremely beneficial to a successful tile floor installation. Since the tile installation itself is not tightly bonded to the subfloor, the movements of the subfloor can't cause problems. (Figure 16)

Expanded metal lath is nailed or stapled over the moisture barrier. Sheets are over-lapped a minimum of 2 inches, and fasteners are placed approximately 6 inches apart in both directions for mud beds that are less than an inch in thickness. In thicker beds it is not necessary to nail the reinforcing securely. I usually just tack it in a manner that prohibits it from moving around. The weight of the mortar will hold it down.

Good quality galvanized chicken wire (poultry netting) can be used in place of the lath. Other forms of reinforcing mesh can also be used. Metal lath and poultry netting can be obtained from masonry supply stores and home centers. Many lumber yards also carry masonry supplies. (Figures 17, 17-2, 17-3)

Figure 16: Tar paper or plastic sheeting is placed over subfloor.

Figure 17: 2.5 lb. metal lath is nailed or stapled to the floor.

Figure 17-2: Seams are overlapped a minimum of two inches.

Figure 17-3: Lath is extended into doorway.

Mud Screeds: Mortar is placed around the room against cabinets and walls. The mud is packed with a wood float or flat trowel and leveled off at the desired height – at least 3/4 in. (18 mm) thick. Use your level to get the screeds on grade. Smooth the screeds with the flat trowel and cut away the surplus mortar that accumulates against walls and cabinets. If areas of the room are wider than about five or six feet, intermediate screeds must be built in the center of the floor. (Figures 18, 18-2)

The areas between the screeds are filled in, and the excess mortar is raked off with a straightedge. Pack the mortar down and use the screeds as guides. Be very careful not to dig the straightedge into the screeds as you rake. When a section has been screeded and raked level, lightly trowel the surface to embed the loose particles of sand. The surface will not look

Figure 18: Mortar is packed around edges of room.

like that of a concrete slab. The deck mud will instead appear to be quite sandy. Don't let it worry you. That's how it's supposed to be. (Figure 19)

Remember to plan your moves so you'll be able to back out the door. When the mud work is complete, allow it to set at least 24 hours before walking on it. Screeded mud floors should be tiled as soon as possible. The mortar is not intended as a surface to be walked upon indefinitely. (Figure 20)

Figure 18-2: Mortar is raked off level.

Tiling Over Concrete Slabs

In my neck of the woods concrete slab homes are the norm. This is a mixed blessing. Slab-on-grade construction is cheaper than having to build a house on a pier and beam foundation with wood floors. But at the same time, concrete slabs tend to crack, especially in southern coastal areas. We are afloat on a sea of mud. The nearest rock beneath us is a couple hundred feet down. But even in areas where the soil is more stable and rock exists, the installation of ceramic and stone tiles directly to a concrete slab must be carefully considered.

There are several ways we can approach the installation. We can bond the tiles directly to the concrete, and in fact that is usually what is done. If the slab manages to stay intact as the years go by, the installation will usually survive. If minor cracks are discovered prior to installing the tiles, the floor can be spot treated with crack isolation/anti-fracture membranes. These are pliable materials that are glued over the cracks to separate the tile installation from

Figure 19: Mortar is packed and smoothed into areas between screeds.

Figure 20: Close-up of finished mud surface.

the concrete below. If there is future movement in the slab, it is hoped the membrane will buffer the tile installation and keep it from cracking as well. There are no guarantees, though. (Figure 21)

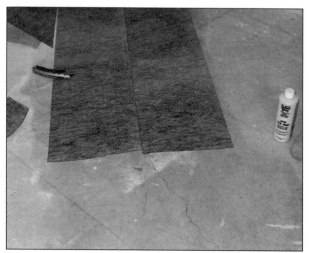

At first inkling it might seem that a concrete slab would be the best of all possible substrates for ceramic and stone tiles, but that's not really the case. A concrete slab does not present the deflection problems associated with a framed wood floor, but there are problems in other regards.

Figure 21: Anti-fracture membrane is placed over cracks.

Cracking is inherent to concrete slab construction in general. As concrete "cures" after it is poured, it tends to shrink. This shrinkage can impose great internal stress, and the stress can cause cracking which is referred to in this case as "stress" cracking. For this reason concrete must be reinforced. Reinforcing can include the use of steel reinforcement rods called "re-bars," metal reinforcement mesh that resembles cattle wire and glass fibers which can be mixed into the concrete. Additionally, you may possess a "post-tension" slab, one that contains little or no re-bar but instead has taut cables running through it from side to side. Whatever the case, you will have some form of cracking to deal with.

Curing Fissures: Small intermittent cracks that do not go all the way through the slab will usually cause no problems when tile floors are installed above them. These cracks occur on the surface of concrete as it cures under certain conditions, most notably in extremely hot regions. Fissures will appear as hairlines and will not be continuous. You will not be able to insert a fingernail into the crack.

Stress Cracks: Cracking from the stress of curing can usually be prevented by incorporating expansion and control joints within the poured slab. Expansion joints are complete separations of the concrete into segments which are divided by boards or other isolating materials. The segments are, however, connected to one another by means of the reinforcing that runs through the slab. Control joints are simply controlled cracks that are planned within the slab. Usually they will be covered by long walls and partitions in the finished house. If no control or expansion joints are used in the average residential slab, you will have stress cracking elsewhere. Unfortunately, many builders do not employ control or expansion joints in residential slabs, so this type of cracking will have to be considered when planning tile and stone floors.

Structural Cracks: Cracking that occurs as a result of improper construction or from ground movement after the fact is called structural cracking. This type of cracking is common in many areas of the country where soils are expansive and where there is little or no rock near the surface. The entire Gulf Coast Region of the United States, stretching from Mexico to the Florida Keys, falls into this category. Structural cracking is more severe and is thus harder to deal with than stress cracking, but in most cases it can be handled with applied membranes which are used directly on the concrete prior to the tile installation going in.

Vertical Cracking: There is one category of crack that may preclude a tile installation altogether, and that is a vertical crack. A vertical crack is one in which one side is appreciably higher than the other. There may be an eighth of an inch difference from side to side, for instance. There is no feasible method for bridging such a crack with a tile floor installation. Something caused one portion of the floor to rise higher than the other, and that "something" could continue or even reverse itself at any time.

A floating floor might be the answer to vertical cracking, but as I stated earlier, a floating floor entails a considerable increase in height – an inch and a half to two inches. It is usually not an option in an existing house. The house would have to be completely re-built to accommodate a mortar bed that deep. In the end, if you discover vertical cracking in your slab, you should probably not consider ceramic or stone tiles as flooring.

Anti-fracture Membranes (AFMs)

Stress cracks and structural cracks that are not vertical in nature can be treated with an array of membrane products, some better than others but none guaranteed to completely eliminate future cracks in tiled floors. There are basically two types of AFMs: mat type membranes and liquid applied membranes. Mats are glued to the concrete, and liquid membranes are brushed on or rolled on. Liquid membranes might also be applied with a flat trowel. There is a great deal of debate as to which type of product is best. I usually use a mat product to treat the cracks I run into in

Figure 22: A double width of anti-fracture membrane is used to bridge a crack.

Houston. I prefer not to be bothered with liquid products in this instance. (Figure 22)

In my opinion, the best available crack isolation membrane is Ditra from Schluter Systems. Ditra provides for more lateral movement between the tile field and the substrate than any other membrane or mat I am aware of. If the budget permits, it would not be an unreasonable course of action to cover the entire concrete area to be tiled with Ditra, whether there are apparent cracks or not. Do I use Ditra routinely on the jobs I do for others? No. It's expensive, and people would rather run the risk of minor cracking in the future. You will not be paying for labor, however, which contributes about half the cost of a Ditra installation.

For a more complete, in-depth discussion of Ditra and the principle of uncoupling in general, please see Appendix I at the back of the book. It contains an article written by William M. Carty, Ph.D., New York State College of Ceramics at Alfred University, Alfred, N.Y. and by my friend Peter Nielsen, Technical Director, Schluter Systems, L.P., Plattsburgh, N.Y. While the article will be useful to the novice tile setter, it will be of particular interest to the pro. It clears up a bit of the dogma surrounding the use of various uncoupling systems.

Membranes for Crack Isolation and Waterproofing
by Todd Groettum

It seems as though every tile job presents something out of the ordinary that must be dealt with. Perhaps it's the inability to use a standard shower pan material due to various conditions, or maybe it's a case of fine cracks in a cement floor. Or, heaven forbid, you could even have a large crack. Manufacturers of tile installation products realize that the world is not a perfect place and that your substrate probably isn't either. For those in this imperfect world, membranes may be the answer.

There are four basic types of membranes used in ceramic tile applications:

1. Sheet material. PVC and CPE membranes along with composite sheet membranes fall into this category. Uncoupling membranes would also be included here.
2. Liquid membranes. These include any rubber or latex polymer membrane that is used by itself and applied with a brush, roller, sprayer or trowel.
3. Combination membranes. Included in this category are products that combine liquids with fabric or mesh reinforcing.
4. Membranes comprised of portland cement products combined with liquid latex.

Sheet and Composite Membranes

Although PVC and CPE shower pan liners are the primary membranes used in the construction of tile showers, I won't be discussing them here. My main thrust will be toward anti-fracture membranes.

Composite anti-fracture membranes (and sound deadening membranes) come in rolls of varying widths. Many have self-stick backing, and are rather thin, which is a plus in direct-bond tile applications. There are other products which are adhered to the substrate in various ways. All of these products are designed to cover horizontal cracks in the substrate. Vertical cracks, those which exhibit a different height from one side to the other, should not be treated with a membrane. In fact, vertical cracks in a concrete substrate will usually preclude the installation of ceramic tile in a direct-bond application.

Generally, the membrane is glued to the floor over the area of the crack. The tile is laid directly over the membrane and soft joints (flexible caulking or sanded caulking) are installed on either side of the crack area. You need to cover the crack so that an entire tile and two grout lines occur over the membrane.

Composite products are excellent for dealing with concrete expansion joints and saw cuts. A properly installed membrane will go a long way in assuring that structural cuts and or cracks are kept to a minimum. There is no guaranty, however, from manufacturers or anyone else that the installation of a membrane will preclude cracking of the tiled surface. Installation of the membrane is simply the prudent thing to do.

Liquid Membranes

The first project that comes to my mind when using this type of product is a handicap or roll-in shower. Without a curb and door or curtain to contain it, water can find its way outside the shower area. This can lead to serious water damage to substrates and to living areas below the installation.

The liquid membrane is truly friendly to the do-it-yourselfer. It is a surface-applied membrane that can be painted on with a brush or rolled on with a roller. Each manufacturer has its own instructions on the use of its product. One criterion, however, seems to remain constant from brand to brand: two coats are required. Read the directions for the particular product you have and follow them. Liquid membranes also have a limited anti-fracture ability and can be used to cover small hairline cracks – spider-webbing in a concrete floor, for example.

Combination Membranes

A combination membrane pairs the easily used liquid membrane with the added strength of a fabric or mesh. An initial coat is applied into which the fabric is embedded. This is followed by an additional coat of liquid. The system affords additional strength in areas where it's needed — where you change planes, for example.

Portland Cement-base Membranes

A cement-based membrane, as its name implies, is a flexible waterproof cement product. Some of these products can be skim coated onto a substrate to act as a moisture barrier, and others can be used as the actual adhesive into which the tiles are set. The membrane generally consists of a thin set mortar and a liquid admix. When the two are combined, they form a very strong membrane with flexible properties. At one time these products were used almost exclusively where a waterproof skim coat was required, but with the advent of the more modern membrane products, cement-base products have lost favor.

Membranes Applied with Thin set Mortar

There are a small number of membranes that can be applied with thin set mortar, including Schluter Ditra and Kerdi mats and others. The advantage to using products in this range is apparent to professional tile installers. Thin set mortar is always at hand on a tile job site. No other adhesives are needed.

Summary

Membranes used in the tile industry accomplish three major functions: waterproofing and moisture resistance; crack suppression and isolation; and sound deadening. It would take an article much longer and much more comprehensive than this one to completely instruct you on membrane use. I can't over-emphasize the importance of reading and following the instructions which accompany each product.

Todd Groettum is proprietor of Tilewerks (sic) Tile and Stone Contracting, Warba, MN. He is also a moderator of the John Bridge Forums on the Internet. Mr. Groettum's email address is lesabre@uslink.net

Preparation

Floor preparation for a concrete slab is similar to that for a wood sub-floor insofar as cleanliness is concerned. Existing linoleum must be scraped up, along with any paint that was left on the slab during the course of construction. The idea is to get as close to the original concrete as possible with the setting material. Small patches of stubborn linoleum backing can be left in place. And many of the glues used for soft flooring products are not water soluble and can be gone over. Anything that is water soluble must be removed. Give it the water test. Make a small puddle of water on the floor and let it stand for half an hour. If the material emulsifies or loosens, remove it.

"Cutback" adhesive, a black tar-like glue, was used for years to hold down vinyl, vinyl-asbestos and asbestos floor tiles. In most cases, the tiles will release quite easily when pried upon. The adhesive itself should be scraped up as much as possible. It is then possible to install tiles over the remainder with high-flex thin set products that are rated to go over "cutback." This ability will be listed on the back panel of the thin set bag.

Asbestos

There is little danger from asbestos when removing floor coverings and adhesive that might contain the substance. Asbestos represents a hazard when it becomes airborne and is drawn into the lungs. The danger is readily apparent in insulation and other products composed of loose fibers. However, asbestos in floor tiles, linoleum and glues is held "captive" by the material in which it resides. It is not loose and not likely to become airborne. And even if particles of asbestos were to become airborne, you would not become ill by removing one floor. Asbestosis, the disease, develops over the course of many years of continued exposure to airborne fibers.

Having said that, I still urge you to wear a face mask when removing old flooring and glues like "cutback," which may contain asbestos. Additionally, you might want to sprinkle the area with water to help keep dust down. And also, there is no reason to have children or other non-workers on the premises when floor removal work is being done.

Floor Leveling

Tile installations demand a subfloor that is reasonably flat, and unfortunately many subfloors are not flat. You can correct inconsistencies with various floor patching compounds that are compatible with thin set mortar, which means the patches will be done with portland cement base products. You might also want to consider using a self-leveling cement (SLC). Jim Buckley explains the process.

Self-leveling Cement
by James P. Buckley

There is no question self-leveling cements or SLCs can be useful in tile projects. This is especially true when skills are lacking in other means of floor leveling. Basically, SLCs are portland cements that have been modified by adding polymers and other ingredients to them. The additives cause the cement, when mixed with water, to flow with a consistency similar to pancake batter. Accelerated curing times are also attainable with the inclusion of certain ingredients – all very hush hush stuff. Self-leveling cements can be used to increase the elevation of floors, to prepare old ceramic

Figure 23: Self-leveling cement can be mixed with a drill and mixing paddle. (Credit Doug Swallow)

tile floors for new tile installations and to resurface (and
level) old chipped concrete,
terrazzo or even wood surfaces.

The upside to SLCs is
that when properly done
they will provide a smooth,
flat floor very quickly and
with minimal effort. The
downside is that they are
somewhat expensive.

Another factor that must
be considered is the
increase in floor elevation.
While high spots will retain
very little material, the lower
points might rise considerably. Clearance under door-

Figure 23-1: Begin in the area furthest from your exit. (Credit Doug
Swallow)

ways, thresholds and appliances must be taken into consideration.

Key to a successful installation is proper preparation of the substrate. Oils,
grease, adhesives and non-cementitous patches must be removed. Seal off all
areas where you do not want the SLC to flow. A piece of scrap lumber tacked into
the substrate and caulked where it meets the substrate will act as a dam, preventing flow into adjacent rooms. Any large openings can be sealed with a non-
expanding foam. You may want to cover sheetrock or other wall surfaces with
plastic, paper towels or even newspaper to prevent spattering. After the floor has
been cleaned and sealed, primer must be applied and broomed into the surface. A
primer is essential to bond the SLC to the substrate. Use the SLC manufacturer's
primer.

When pouring over wood, most manufacturers require that 2.5-diamond lath
mesh be installed. Lay the lath out so that it is perpendicular to the seams of the
wood. Fasten with staples every six inches, overlapping the edges two inches.
Insufficient stapling will permit the mesh to float when you pour the SLC over it.
The metal has sharp edges so wear work gloves to protect your hands. Prime the
floor twice before installing the mesh. The wood will very quickly absorb the first
primer coat.

Set up your work area in advance. Have a large clean container, a reservoir,
filled with all the water you will need for mixing and another container for the
actual mixing. The mixing container should be sturdy and have handles for easy
lifting and pouring. You will be lifting and carrying 100 lbs of wet SLC. New plastic garbage pails are recommended. You will need a one-half inch electric drill
with a jiffy mixing paddle to do the mixing with. You will also need a tool called a
"smoother" for distributing the cement and blending the edges of each pour. A
plastic drop cloth in the mixing area will help with clean up. You will also need a
bucket for pouring the mix water into the mixing container.

Check the manufacturer's instructions on the bag for the correct amount of
water to be added to the powder. Pour a measured amount of water into the
bucket. After the water has settled, mark the high point with an indelible marker.
You might even drill a few holes in the bucket at these points to prevent overfill-
ing. The purpose of this is to avoid adding too much water to the mix. The correct amount of water is critical; even a half pint can make a big difference. Mix
two bags at a time and always remember to add the powder into the water. Do

not dump the powder and then try to add water.

Mixing in extremely hot weather, 85°F (29°C) and above will reduce the set up or working time of the material. To avoid this, simply add ice to your reservoir of water. Block ice works best.

The actual mixing and pouring will go very quickly. You shouldn't have to spend much more than three minutes per bag. Try to have at least two other people working with you. They will mix and carry while you spread the material. Start in the area furthest from your exit

Figure 23-2: Back out of the room and allow the SLC to set. (Credit Doug Swallow)

and work your way back. Blend-in successive batches by pouring gently into the edge of the previous pour. After each pour, use the smoother to help get a uniform height and eliminate any minute bubbles. Do not overwork the material; one or two passes with the smoother will be quite adequate. Once the material begins to set up, do not attempt to trowel or smooth it. Any high spots can be taken care of with a sander after the material has set.

Most important, don't panic. Each batch needs at least 10 minutes to begin to set, so you'll have plenty of time to mix and pour again. Many times when the material is very wet, you may think you see irregularities in the surface. Most of the time this is caused by light reflection. Resist the urge to trowel the material. Let it do the job it's designed to do. We have walked many DIYers through this process on the John Bridge Forums and haven't lost one yet. (Figures 23, 23-1, 23-2)

Jim Buckley, who lives in Long Island, New York with his wife Kathleen and dog Mikey, is a self-leveling cement specialist and a moderator at the John Bridge Forums. He can be reached by email: cmentpro@optonline.net

Ditra from Schluter Systems

Ditra, as mentioned earlier, is a plastic matting that is designed to go over both wood and concrete sub-floors to "uncouple" the tile installation from what's underneath it. It is glued to the sub-floor with modified thin set. Modified thin set is that which contains latex or acrylic polymers to give it a high degree of flexibility and "cling." Ditra incorporates a special fleece backing that allows it to attach itself to the thin set.

The top face of the product can be compared to an inverted waffle iron. It is a series of tiny squares that are molded into the plastic surface, the sides of which are angled under in a dovetail fashion. Tiles are installed to Ditra with thin set mortar, which flows into the tiny squares and hardens. The thin set adhered to the tile backs and locked into the Ditra surface is what holds the tiles down. The mortar does not actually adhere to the mat itself. (Figure 24)

The combination of fleece and semi-rigid plastic surface allows a considerable amount of lateral shifting between the tile installation above, and the sub-floor below the Ditra matting. It is all-in-all a most excellent means of installing tiles over problematic substrates.

In most cases, Ditra can be substituted for cement backer board over wood subfloors, and in certain circumstances it can be used instead of reinforced cement mortar. When I work in new homes that have been constructed with thick Sturd-I-Floor plywood over well-designed trusses, I no longer float mud beds. I use Ditra instead. There is a slight increase in material cost, but it is more than made up for in labor savings. (Figure 25)

Ditra is especially attractive when height is a consideration. The product is about an eighth of an inch thick. This can be very important when matching up with adjacent floors is a consideration and when built-in kitchen appliances cannot be raised enough to accommodate backer board or a mud bed.

Figure 24: Ditra installation — Schluter Systems.

Figure 25: Ditra over wood subfloor.

Installing Ditra on Subfloors

As previously mentioned, Ditra by Schluter Systems works well over both wood and concrete subfloors. It is also recommended over the leveling screed when radiant heat is incorporated into the floor. The constant movement caused by the heating and cooling cycle is effectively neutralized with the addition of Ditra between the screed and the tiled surface. And Ditra will not hinder heat transfer to the floor surface.

Installing Ditra is a snap if only a couple of things are kept in mind. The material must be tightly bonded to the subfloor, no ifs, ands or buts. It is essential to obtain complete coverage when spreading the adhesive, which will be modified thin set mortar in most cases. It goes without saying (but I'll say it), the floor must be clean and free of paint, grease and other "bond breakers."

Over plywood and smooth concrete I like to use a 1/4 by 1/4 in. square notched trowel. You will also need a utility knife with which to cut the product. A straightedge and a chalk line will also be of use. Your measuring tape should already be clipped to your belt or pocket. And while not absolutely essential, large scissors or shears might come in handy. Is your pencil still tucked behind your ear?

I suppose it's not absolutely necessary, but I think it's a good idea to make a chalk line on the floor to delineate the area where thin set needs to be spread. That way, when you get your piece of Ditra spread out, you won't be wallowing in excess thin set. You should, however, allow enough thin set to extend a half inch or so beyond the edge of the sheet. This is simply to make sure you achieve total coverage underneath. (Figure 26)

Figure 26: Modified thin set mortar is spread with notched trowel.

You can pre-cut the pieces of Ditra if you like. Begin near the wall furthest away from your point of exit and work your way out. Lay the largest pieces first and then come back and fit in the smaller pieces. This will ensure that you get the most efficient use of your material. Walking on the material you've just installed does not present a problem.

First spread the modified thin set with the back, flat side of the trowel and "burn" it into the substrate. Make sure it reaches into all the tiny depressions and crags of the concrete or plywood. Then switch the trowel around and use the notched side to add material and comb it into uniform

Figure 27: Kerdi-band is used to waterproof the seams of the Ditra.

ridges. The ridges will reach out and grip the fleece backing of the Ditra as you lay it down.

Lay your piece of Ditra into the fresh mortar and, beginning in the middle, force the material down with the flat side of your trowel or with a wood float. Getting the material as close to the subfloor as possible is important. Occasionally, lift the edge of the piece of material you've just installed to check the coverage you've attained. Joining individual pieces of Ditra is easy. You just butt them together and flatten them out. Scrape the excess thin set from the surface and return it to the bucket. Likewise, if you need to remove a small section of the material, say you discover an air pocket, you can simply cut it out with a knife, apply more mortar and reinstall the piece.

Ditra seams are normally just butted, but if a waterproof installation is needed or desired, you apply strips of Kerdi-band® over the seams of the Ditra. Bed the strips in thin set and smooth them down tight with the flat side of the trowel. (Figure 27)

To waterproof the edges of the floor, apply strips of Kerdi-band and fold them up onto the walls, securing them to both wall and floor with thin set. Allow the pieces to overlap at least two inches (5 cm). Leave a tab of material in each corner to overlap around the corner onto the adjacent wall. Remember, for complete water-tightness the laps must be at least two inches. (Figure 28)

You can begin installing tiles over your Ditra as soon as you have it installed. There is no need to wait for the mortar under the matting to cure. You go about laying out your floor in the usual manner, striking chalk lines on the surface of the matting.

This brings us to about the only drawback I can think of to using Ditra. The stuff absolutely hates chalk. It's very difficult to get a chalk line to stick to its surface. Installers around the globe have come up with ingenious ways of preserving their lines once they get them right. You can spray over the lines with cheap hair spray or with clear spray paint. You don't have to worry about breaking the bond because the setting material will not bond to the Ditra anyway. You can also smear liquid latex additive onto the Ditra and allow it to tack up before you strike your lines. I like the hairspray idea better. Use blue chalk. It shows up nicely over the orange color of the Ditra. (Figure 29)

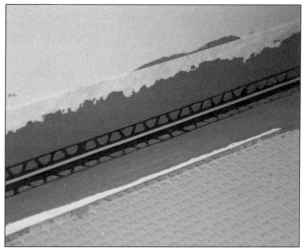

Figure 28: Kerdi-band overlaps the Ditra and folds up the wall. The EKE corner profile is optional.

Figure 29: Tile is installed over the Ditra.

Ditra Hands

While working over Ditra there is a tendency to rest oneself on one's idle hand, and it is not long before the heel of the palm takes on the grid-like attributes of the matting. And it is not much further beyond that point that the hand begins to burn and itch. I suggest that when working over Ditra for extended periods you slide a small block of wood around the floor with you and rest your hand on that. Remember the small block of wood? What did you do with it?

Ditra Outdoors

Balconies have always been problematic for tile setters inasmuch as they need to be waterproofed, either to keep water from getting into living spaces below or to keep water from penetrating the structure and causing problems within. Ditra solves both problems.

Traditionally, balconies have been waterproofed and then mud beds have been laid over the waterproofing. Tile is laid over the mud. The whole installation becomes saturated with the first rain and seldom dries out completely. The moisture works on the mortar and on its reinforcing. It also affects the waterproofing itself and eventually causes it to fatigue and give way.

Since Ditra does its waterproofing trick on the surface, it effectively eliminates all moisture from the substrate. The small amount of water that penetrates the grout joints and reaches the matting easily dries out between rains. There is no chance for mold to grow and accumulate, and there is no chance for water to damage the reinforcing in the setting bed, if a mortar bed is used. A complete range of edge and gutter extrusions is available for balcony overhangs.

Over concrete, Ditra acts not only as a waterproofer, protecting the reinforcing within, but it also isolates minor cracking of the concrete as discussed previously. For these reasons, I strongly recommend its use over exposed patio slabs prior to the installation of tile or stone.

There are certain considerations that must be taken into account when using Ditra in wet areas or outdoors. If modified thin sets are used, they must be of the type that is not affected by continuous exposure to moisture. Some modified thin sets can emulsify under these conditions. It is extremely important to read the back panel of the sack your thin set comes in. As to bonding the tiles themselves, it is recommended that a premium quality unmodified dry set mortar be used when installing over Ditra. Even very dense porcelain tiles can be installed over Ditra using unmodified dry set mortar. Dry set is not adversely affected by repeated wettings.

Baseboards (Skirting)

It is best if tiles go under baseboards. This, of course, entails removing the baseboards and re-installing them after the tiles have been installed. The procedure represents sizable costs in time and in material, and you may not wish to do it. Certainly in new construction, though, the baseboards should not be installed until after the tile floors have gone in.

If you choose to leave your baseboards in place, you will provide for an expansion joint throughout the tile installation wherever it abuts the baseboards, under-cabinet toe boards and other fixed obstacles. The joint should be no less than 1/8 inches, and it must be filled with flexible caulking, not grout. (Figure 30)

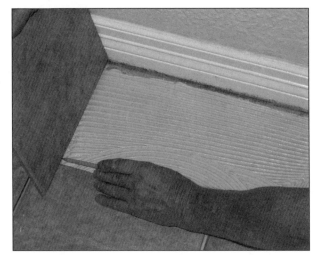

Figure 30: If baseboards are left in place, allow for a 1/8 in. expansion joint.

Door Frames

Proficient and conscientious floor layers always undercut door frames and jambs so that the flooring materials go under them. This is particularly true with ceramic and stone tile installations. There are specialized power tools (jamb saws) that will do the job with ease, but the weekend warrior will seldom have access to one of these. There are hand saws specifically made for this work which are available at tile stores, but an ordinary hand saw will also do an admirable job of it. I often use a rather cheap short blade saw along with a piece of the tile to be installed. Place the tile alongside the frame or casing. Add a thin layer of cardboard and place the saw on top of that. The cardboard plus the thickness of the saw blade will allow for the build-up of setting materials that will attach the tiles to the substrate. (Figures 31, 32)

Floor Layout

The importance of layout, that act of placing lines and marks on the substrate in preparation for the installation of tiles, cannot be over-stated. It is at the layout stage that many novices and some so-called professionals "lose it." There is no way to know how a job is going to look upon completion unless a considerable amount of time is spent in completing this all-important operation. Do not be tempted to commence tile setting until the layout has been completed, checked and double checked.

The first step in floor layout is determining the space that each tile will consume. Since there are no standard sizes in ceramic and stone floor tiles, the most practical way to determine spacing is to lay a few tiles on the floor, line them up with the appropriate grout spaces between them and measure them. You will need to determine the measurement of only the number of tiles you will be able to reach comfortably while on your knees. In the case of 12 in. or 13 in. tiles, this space will incorporate only two tiles and two grout spaces. It is difficult to reach further than about two feet while working on your knees. If the tiles are smaller, you may want to set them three or four deep at a time. Very large

Figure 31: Most weekend warriors won't have access to a jamb saw.

Figure 32: The hand saw will do the job.

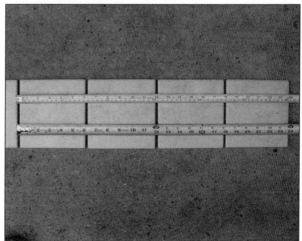
Figure 33: Tiles are measured.

tiles will be laid in rows of one tile only. (Figure 33)

Do not simply lay out two or three tiles and measure them. Tiles, especially very hard and durable tiles, vary considerably within the boxes. You should perform the measuring exercise on several different sets of tiles taken from several different boxes. Make your calculations based on the largest tiles you find. Remember that each tile needs an accompanying grout space.

Layout Schedule

When the amount of space your reachable tiles (and their grout spaces) will consume has been determined, it is then necessary to create a layout schedule. The schedule, which can be written on a piece of scrap paper or even on the flap of a tile box, will tell you where and how far apart to place your layout lines once the main reference lines of the layout have been established and marked on the floor.

Let's say, for example, that we are laying 12 in. or 13 in. tiles and that we'll be reaching across two rows of tiles in the process. One increment on the layout schedule, then, will equal the space that two tiles and two grout joints consume. I could make it come out in even, easy to follow numbers, but even numbers will seldom occur on an actual job. So let's be realistic about it. A 12 inch tile is almost never exactly 12 inches across, even when a grout space is considered. Let's say the tile actually measures 11-7/8 inches and we want to incorporate 1/4 inch grout spaces. That means that one tile and one grout space will equal 12-1/8 inches, and two tiles and two grout spaces will equal 24-1/4 inches. The 24-1/4 inches will become an increment.

At the top of the piece of paper, write down 24-1/4. Then double it and write 48-1/2 below the first figure. Then triple it (treble it) and write 72-3/4 below the other figures, keeping all the figures in line on the paper. I think you can see what's happening here. You can continue adding increments until you have enough to stretch across the area to be tiled or until you reach the maximum extent of your measuring tape. This is where a fairly long tape comes into its own. 97-, 121-1/4, 145-1/2, etc.

If you live in one of those countries that has abandoned the English Standard System of measurements, you're on your own. Actually, though, you may have it easier than we Americans, because most of the floor tiles produced in the world are produced in countries that adhere to the metric system. When I describe a 12 x 12 tile, for example, I am more likely referring to a 30 cm by 30 cm tile. Increments in the situation above would span something over 60 centimeters.

When your layout schedule is complete, check your figures. Check them twice, backwards and forwards. Have your helper check the figures.

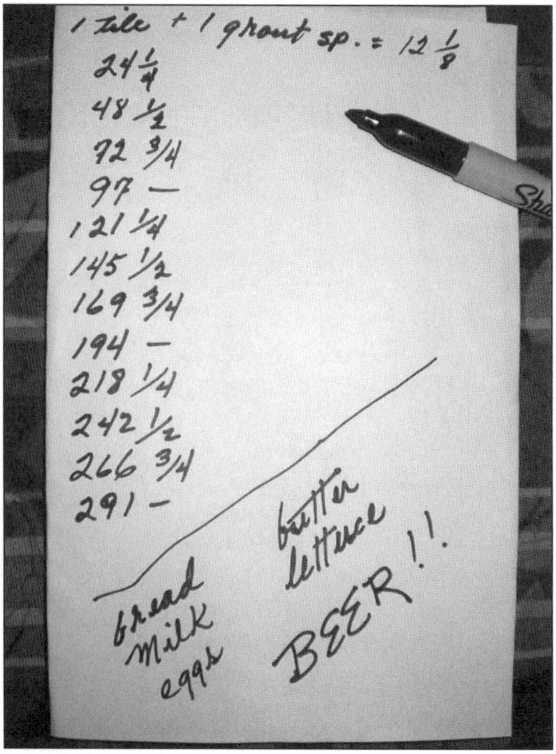

Figure 34: Don't lose this. It's important.

Walk across the street and have your neighbor check them, too. I can't stress enough the absolute importance of having no mistakes in your arithmetic. When you are positive there are no mistakes, set the schedule aside where it won't become lost. (Figure 34)

Squaring the Floor (Layout)

Rooms are square, right?

Wrong. Rooms are seldom absolutely square. Homes are built by humans, and humans make mistakes. Some humans fix their mistakes when they discover them, and some don't. Some humans don't discover their errors at all, and some simply don't care. In any case, it is good policy to assume that the walls of the house are not at right angles to one another, not exactly so, anyway.

Exactness in floor layout is crucial. Ceramic and stone tiles are square and must be laid square to one another in straight lines. There is no way to "hedge" or "fake it." It has to be, so we can't simply use the walls as reference points. We must develop our own "square" lines on the floor.

"We," by the way, means you and I. We are going to do this thing together. I'm going to lead you by the hand. Wait, what do you look like?

We will use a bit of that 10th grade geometry I spoke about earlier to check the square of the floor before we begin laying out. The system we'll be using is called "3-4-5." The 3-4-5 method is based on the Pythagorean Theorem we all learned in Plane Geometry. Pythagoras, a sixth century B.C. Greek philosopher, developed a very tricky way of creating right angles on a flat surface or "plane." The Pythagorean Theorem states roughly that the sums of the squares of the two shorter sides of a right (90 degree) triangle are equal to the square of the longest side, which is called the hypotenuse. The way to determine the square of a side of a triangle or any other shape that has straight segments is called square root. I have learned how to do square root twice in my life, once in school and once when I was an apprentice. I have forgotten it both times.

This is where the 3-4-5 method shines. It just happens that these lengths will create a right triangle every time, and they are the only combination of lengths that will come out even. If one side of a right triangle is 3 feet, for example, and another side is 4 feet, the longest side or hypotenuse will always be 5 feet. It works the same way in meters or any other unit of measurement. Instead of 3, 4 and 5, for instance, we could just as easily use 6, 8 and 10, which are multiples of 3, 4, and 5. In larger rooms we could use 9, 12 and 15. The larger the triangle, the greater the chance for accuracy.

On very small floors, a small entry or bathroom, for example, the 3-4-5 method may not be necessary. A carpenters framing square will probably do the job just as adequately. But on larger areas, I suggest you take the time to use the 3-4-5 method.

Reference Lines

A helper is nearly indispensable in the layout operation. You will be making chalk lines on the floor, some of them quite long. It's possible to complete the process solo, but it's certainly no fun, and accuracy will suffer. You will need a pencil, a measuring tape and a chalk box.

We begin by making a chalk line parallel to the longest wall in the room. This line is arbitrary and does not have to be a specified distance from the wall so long as it is parallel to the wall. At an open area in the room we will construct a right triangle along the line using the 3-4-5 method. Measure out a segment of the line that is 4 feet long and mark the segment with tick marks, using a sharp pencil. Label the first tick mark "A" and the second one "B." Using the measuring tape as a trammel, trace an arc 3 feet away from the line using "A" as a pivot. The arc must be perpendicular to "A" at some point. Now, from "B," trace an arc 5 feet away that will intersect the first arc drawn. The intersection of these two arcs (we'll call it "C") will be exactly perpendicular to "A," the first tick mark on the line. The line, by the way, will now be called a reference line.

By drawing a line through "A," the first tick mark, and "C," the intersection of the two arcs, you can create a line that is perpendicular (at 90 degrees) to the first reference line. This is done with the chalk line. This second line will also be used as a reference line. All subsequent lines made on the floor will be parallel to one or the other of these two reference lines. (Figure 35)

There are other ways in geometry of constructing intersecting perpendicular lines, but there is often not enough space in the room to employ them. But certainly if you are aware of these procedures and have enough space for them to work, you may use them. The 3-4-5 method, however, will work every time and in any size room, regardless of its shape. It is worth mastering.

If you are interested in how far out of square the room is, you can measure the distance of the second line from a supposed parallel wall at both of its ends. Usually, the error will be less than an inch — a quarter-inch, perhaps, or maybe a half-inch. But occasionally the error will be quite dramatic. It's still amazing to me after thirty years in the business that things can become so far out of whack when homes are constructed.

Layout Lines and the Grid System

It is now time to recover that scrap of paper on which you made your layout schedule. You don't remember where you placed it? Oh, I surely hope you do. You do remember how long it took to make and check it, don't you?

With the layout schedule before you, measure the width of the largest area of the floor. This will often be in the breakfast area of kitchens which incorporate breakfast areas, or it may be in the food preparation area of kitchens which do not adjoin breakfast areas. Looking at the layout schedule, determine how the tiles should be spaced across the floor. It is desirable to have cuts at the walls that are larger than half a tile. It's not always possible, but it's the best way to do things. With the tape measure butted against a wall on one side, you will be able to determine the space left near the opposite wall after full tiles have been laid across the floor. You can do this by merely finding the last increment on the layout schedule that will fit in the distance between the walls and then measuring the remaining space.

Using 12-inch tiles, let's say the space remaining after the last increment is 10 inches. In this instance you would probably want to move the tiles closer to the opposite wall by an inch. That way you would have cuts along both walls of about 11 inches, which would be very acceptable from a layout and design standpoint. If the distance remaining after the last increment were less than half a tile, the full tiles (the "field") would be shifted in the other direction. Let's say the remaining distance is only 5 inches, less than half a 12-inch tile. By shifting the field it would be possible to end up with cuts that are approximately 8-1/2 inches in width. It would be less desirable to split the 5-inch remainder and have 2-1/2-inch cuts at both walls. This should never (almost never) be done.

When you have arrived at the placement of tiles in this first area, make a tick mark on the floor that will represent the edge of one of the increments. You may decide to shift the tiles further in this area, but you'll need to remember what you've done so far in order to continue.

That takes care of one area in one direction, but what about adjoining areas or rooms which may be equally important when it comes to achieving cuts at the walls

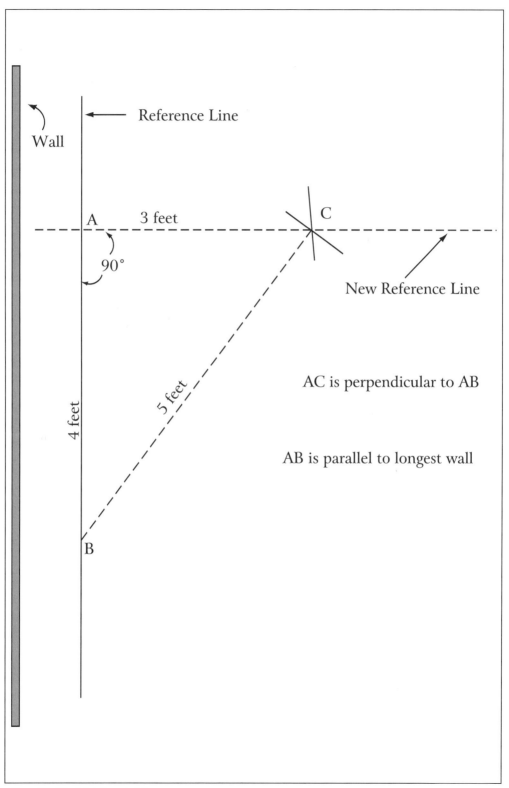

Reference Line

Wall

A   3 feet   C

90°

New Reference Line

4 feet

5 feet

B

AC is perpendicular to AB

AB is parallel to longest wall

Figure 35: The "3-4-5 method."

greater than half a tile? Positioning the end of the tape measure on the increment mark you made in the first area, stretch it out into the adjoining area, glancing at the schedule to determine what the cuts are going to look like in that area. You may find you want to shift the field slightly to avoid having very narrow cuts ("skinnies") where they will be noticeable. By shifting back and forth while studying the layout schedule, you can arrive at presentable cuts in most areas. Skinnies should be reserved for areas that are less noticeable — under cabinet overhangs at toe spaces, for example, or in broom closets or behind the fridge.

You will often find it necessary to relocate your tick marks, and it's not hard to do. Carefully measure the distance from the reference line to the tick mark and transfer the measurement along the line to where it's needed. Make a new tick mark, snap a new chalk line and off you go.

Obviously, you will not be able to center the field of tile in all of the areas. You will probably not even be able to center the tiles in one area. Again, what is important here is making the overall layout presentable.

One of the few instances in which a perfectly centered and balanced layout will occur is when the room is a rectangle. But even then, don't fall into the old trap of automatically starting in the center of the floor and working to the four walls, the method often outlined in short magazine articles and in some books. The method hardly ever produces cuts of pleasing sizes at the walls or at the perimeter of the area. It may be necessary to begin with a tile that covers the center point of the rectangle, for example. Always do a complete layout before laying the first piece of tile. And in a single rectangle or square, remember that it is *always* possible to end up with cuts at the perimeter which are larger than one-half a tile.

When you have developed a general idea of where the field of tile should be located in one direction, make a mark at one of the increments and scratch out any previous marks you've made. Measure from the reference line to the mark and note the measurement. Then transfer the measurement to both ends of a new line that you will make on the floor. This new line will be an actual layout line, meaning the edge of a row of tiles will be placed along it. You should now mark the layout line with a large "L." Mark the original reference line with an "R." This will help you to avoid confusing the reference line with the subsequent layout lines you will be making. You can now measure out and snap all your remaining layout lines, using your layout schedule to locate them on the floor. Remember that all layout lines are parallel to the reference line and thus parallel to each other. Check the locations of the lines by reversing the measuring tape and measuring from the other direction. If you are still not sure the lines are correct, go through the procedure again. There is no room for error here.

When the lines in one direction have been made and checked, you repeat the procedure in the other direction, keeping in mind that cuts, no matter where they fall, should be pleasing to the eye. By snapping all the lines in the new direction you will create a series of squares on the floor that we'll call "grids." In each of these grids you will be placing four 12-inch tiles. And you can now see at a glance what the cuts are going to look like at every wall and at every other obstacle in the room. When you have checked this layout thoroughly, you will be able to begin laying tile anywhere on the floor and at more than one location if you so choose. As long as you keep the tiles within the grids you can't go wrong. If the lines are correct, the system is foolproof – or nearly so. (Figure 36)

There are other systems of floor layout that professionals use, but none is as complete and forthright as the grid system. I urge you to take the time and effort to lay out

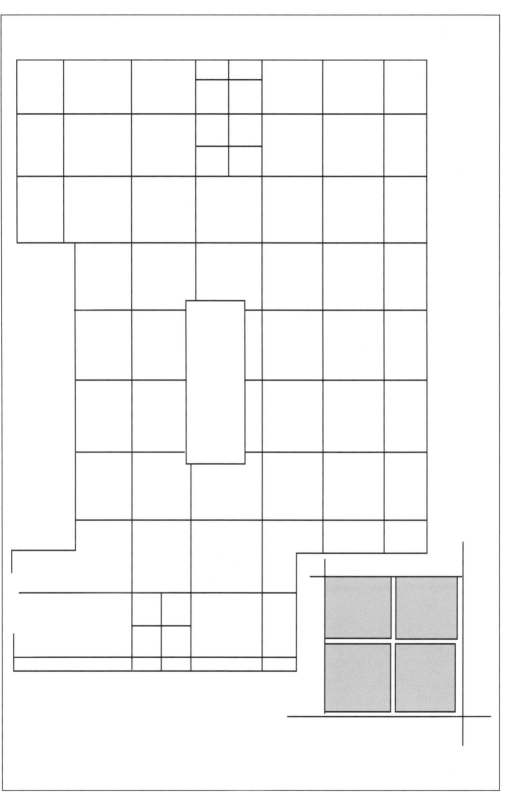

Figure 36: This grid is laid out for four tiles in each square.

your floor in this manner. You will never be sorry you did.

I know you made sure you had created an exact set of perpendicular reference lines at the onset of the process, but why not check to be sure? It's easily enough done at this stage by measuring diagonally across one of the grid squares from corner to corner. Note the distance and measure the other diagonal. The measurements should be equal. If they are not, go back to square one and start checking. Check your original 3-4-5 plotting to make sure your reference lines are in fact perpendicular. If they are perpendicular, begin checking the layout lines nearest the reference lines. Check in both directions. If the lines all fall on the increment measurements at both ends as noted on the layout schedule, the schedule itself is wrong (blame your neighbor). Whatever it takes, the layout must be square, and four tiles must fit within each grid square, meaning the distance between all the lines must be equal.

Do not be tempted, even for a moment, to go on without correcting a problem in the layout. I simply can't over-stress the importance of this. If it is determined that all the lines or most of them must be redone, it is best to use a different color chalk for the new lines. In some cases, it is desirable and advisable to erase all the lines with a damp sponge and start over.

Open Areas

In many modern homes, kitchens and breakfast areas are not separated from other rooms of the house by walls. Homes tend to be open with breakfast areas, for instance, flowing right into family rooms and other living areas. Making transitions between tile and carpeting and between tile and wood floors deserves some discussion. Larger pieces of tile, if not full tiles, are desirable at these transitions. Cuts which are less than half a tile should be avoided, even if this means making less attractive cuts elsewhere. If your rooms are separated by narrower, more traditional openings – doorways and cased openings – the size of the cuts is less important.

Symmetrical Rooms

As I mentioned earlier, there are times when actually centering the field of tile in a room is desirable. Occasionally, breakfast rooms are symmetrical, at least in one dimension. They often have a window or windows centered in the outside wall of the room. Although it is not always feasible to do so, an effort should be made to make the floor layout symmetrical as well. Play with the layout in this situation. If it works, great, but if centering the field will create unpleasantness in other noticeable areas, abandon the plan. It's not that important.

Movement Joints

In addition to the expansion joints that you will provide around the perimeter of the tiled floor, intermediate movement joints will also be necessary once your floor reaches a certain expanse. The maximum distance a tiled floor can travel without a movement joint (soft joint) in the field is 30 feet, but that is stretching it a bit. I like to include joints when the expanse is greater than 20 feet if the joints can be accomplished in an unobtrusive manner, such as in doorways or other narrow areas. In extra large rooms there is often no alternative to placing a movement joint in the middle of the floor.

Movement joints are nothing more than grout joints that are filled with a flexible material such as caulking instead of grout. Colored (sanded) caulking is made in most of the colors that grouts are produced in. You will find the caulking wherever sanded tile grout is sold. (Figures 37, 38)

What can happen if you do not provide for expansion in large tile floors? Well, you

Eric Rattan – Santa Fe Design Studio, Madison, Wisconsin

Emily Tholberg – Pagosa Springs, Colorado

Emily Tholberg

Sheila Little/Michael Moore

Michael Burne

Linda Fahey

Fred De Baugh

can lose the whole installation to "tenting," for one thing. Tenting occurs when a sizable portion of the floor delaminates from the substrate because no provision has been made to prevent it. Tile usually expands and contracts at a slightly different rate than the substrate. This movement is microscopic, but it is enough to cause serious problems, including tenting and cracking. I have examined tented floors where the tiles have raised nearly two inches off the substrate. People sometimes report hearing a sudden loud cracking noise as the tenting occurs. It can happen that quickly.

Figure 37: Matching sanded caulking is inserted into movement joint.

Layout Patterns

Although most ceramic floor tiles are either squares or rectangles, possible layout arrangements are almost limitless. My friends at Daltile have kindly allowed me to reproduce some of the layout images they have developed through the years. The folks at Daltile have been very imaginative, but they, of course, have not exhausted the possibilities. There are hundreds more.

Figure 38: The joint is wiped clean with a wet sponge. Wring the sponge frequently.

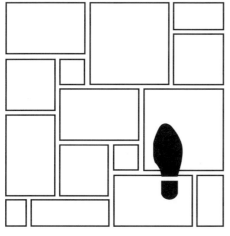

18-12-6

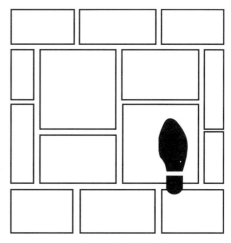

Alternating Vertical

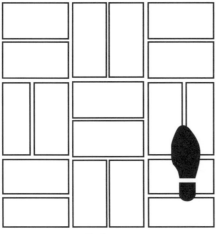

Basketweave

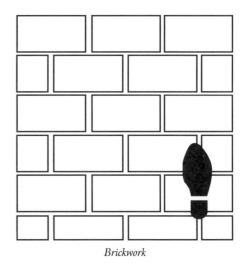

Brickwork

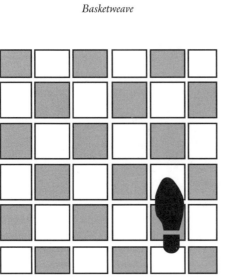

Checkerboard

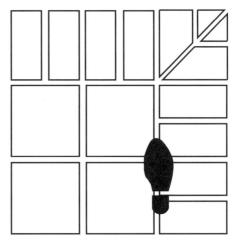

Corner Cut

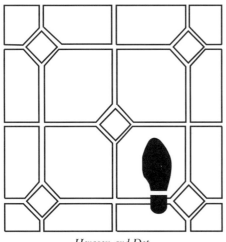

Hexagon and Dot

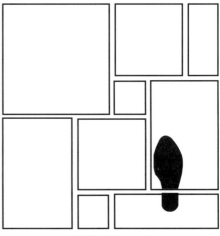

Modified Hopscotch

Pinwheel

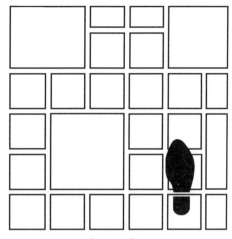

Stepping Stone

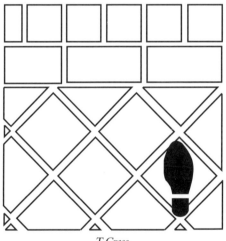

T-Cross

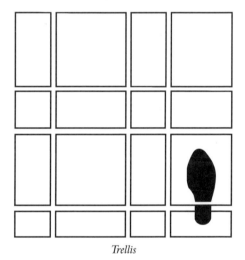

Trellis

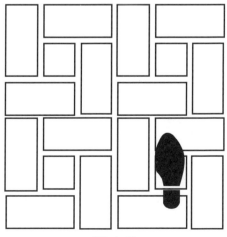

Windmill

Zigzag

Laying the Tiles

At last we have arrived at that most pleasurable of events in the completion of a tiled floor, the actual installation of the tiles. I am so happy for you now... well, words fail me, and I'm a wordy guy.

Thin Set

There are dozens of thin set mortar products on the market. Some of these are called bonding mortars or tile and marble mortars, and some are called dry set mortars. When I wrote *Ceramic Tile Setting,* "thin set" was a method of installing tiles with "dry set mortar" as opposed to "thick set," which incorporates the use of portland cement screeds. But in the ensuing years, "thin set" has come to mean the setting material itself, and that is how the term will be used here.

We will be using a "modified" thin set mortar. Modified mortars are those that have been fortified with dry latex or acrylic polymers to make them stronger and more flexible than traditional dry set mortars. An alternative would be to use unmodified dry set mortar but mix it with liquid latex admix. I prefer using modified mortar.

Each modified mortar is formulated for a different task. There is no "one size fits all" product that can be used for everything. I do not have the time and the space to go into all the mortars that are available. They are all the same in two respects, though: they are made with portland cement and they are mixed by adding water to them.

There are approximately a dozen major companies that produce thin set mortars in the U.S., and there are any number of smaller regional companies that do the same. I ask you to check with the manufacturer of the line of thin set mortars that are available in your area. All manufacturers publish detailed instructions for the use of their products; all have full-time technical support people at your disposal and most have web sites.

Mixing: Place a couple inches of water in a large plastic bucket and then add part of a sack of thin set. Mix with a long, wide stick or with a long margin trowel, depending on the amount you intend to make. You should never attempt to mix a full 50 pound sack of thin set at once. The most you will be able to use at one time will be about half a sack, and you should probably mix even less than that until you get a feel for things.

Professionals often use heavy-duty electric drills and special mixing paddles to mix their thin set, but usually the novice will not have a drill that large available. Smaller, home-duty drills should not be used. The strain of mixing will ruin light-duty tools. If you are contemplating a large floor, though, having to mix quantities of thin set and grout may offer a needed excuse to add to your collection of power tools. The cost of a drill capable of mixing at that level, however, will often approach $300 (U.S.). (Figure 40)

Figure 40: Heavy-duty drill and mixing paddle.

Mix the thin set to a smooth, semi-fluid paste. To test the mix, spread some on the floor and comb it with a notched trowel. The ridges created by the trowel should remain erect with only the slightest amount of sag. If the ridges collapse, the mix is too thin and additional dry material should be added. Conversely, if the mix is too stiff, it will be very difficult to spread with the notched trowel. More fluid should then be added. The finished product should be "creamy" and not runny. It will have substance, but it will be easy to apply.

Figure 41: Thin set is semi-fluid, yet the ridges stand up.

"Buttery" is the best descriptive term I have ever heard used, and it was used by a lady who wrote a how-to book years ago. I can't remember the book, and I can't remember the author's name, but if she ever reads my book, I want her to know I tried my best to give her credit. She was actually describing how to mix brick mortar, but that's close enough for our needs.

When you are satisfied with the consistency of the mix, allow it to rest or "slake" for about ten minutes and then re-stir it. Slaking allows time for all of the dry ingredients to soak up the liquid, rendering the mix consistent throughout. (Figure 41)

Notched Trowels

The size of the notched trowel you use will be determined by only two factors: the condition of the backs of the tiles you are setting and the condition of the substrate. Now I must tell you, the sizing of notched trowels is one of those areas in the tile industry that seems to generate a considerable amount of controversy. Thin set manufacturers often specify trowel sizes on the back panels of sacks, and certain trade organizations have published guidelines on the matter, specifying trowels with up to 3/4 by 3/4 inch notches for large format tiles. I've even seen monster trowels with notches measuring an inch by an inch peering out of display cases at tile stores.

But tile size has very little to do with the matter, and I have never used trowels larger than 1/4 by 3/8 inches (1/4 by 1/2 at the absolute most). What is pertinent is flatness. If your tiles are nearly flat on their backs, and your substrate is smooth and level, you should probably use a trowel with notches that measure 1/4 by 1/4 inches. The larger 1/4 by 3/8 size should be used if the ridges on the backs of the tiles are pronounced. Using a larger size trowel when it is not needed will most likely only cause thin set to accumulate in the joints between the tiles. Since this excess material must be scraped away and washed out of the joints, it makes a lot of sense to me to avoid the excess to begin with.

Smear the thin set down in one of the layout grids and "burn" it in with the straight side of the trowel – make sure the material is forced into the pores of the substrate. Then reverse the trowel in your hand and comb the thin set as you form ridges. Keep the trowel angle as close to 90 degrees as you can, making the ridges as high as possible. Cover the entire grid square, paying particular attention to the corners. Smear right up to the lines, but do not cover them. This takes a little practice, but it will come to you. (Figures 42, 43)

Placing the Tiles

It is important to get the tiles onto the thin set as soon as possible after the material has been spread, otherwise, air causes the thin set to partially dry on its surface. Surface drying is often referred to as "skinning over" or "over-glazing." Tiles set in thin set that has skinned over will not completely bond.

Move each tile around slightly to help bed it in the thin set. When all the tiles have been set in the grid, pry one of them up and check the back for complete coverage. You can readily tell whether the tile has made complete contact by examining the ridge pattern on the back of the piece. There should be thin set ridges on all parts of the tile. If you find voids, spread additional thin set on the back of the piece with your margin trowel or buttering trowel. Then lift the remaining tiles up and check each of them. Doing this at the beginning of the installation ensures you are using the right tool and the right technique. You should check random tiles throughout the installation to ensure that complete coverage is being attained, certainly not in every grid square but every now and then. (Figure 44)

The process of applying adhesive to the back of a tile with a buttering trowel is called "back buttering." Back buttering is usually a secondary procedure, the main method of applying adhesive being the spreading of it on the floor with the notched trowel. Back buttering can be frequent, however, if the substrate is not completely smooth and flat. The tool I use for this and other incidental functions is called a gauging trowel. This tool is never far

Figure 42: Thin set is "burned in" with the flat side of the trowel.

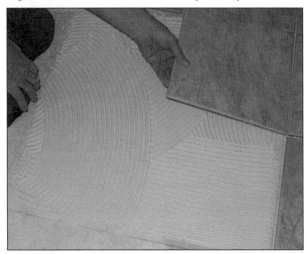

Figure 43: Thin set is combed with the notched side of the trowel.

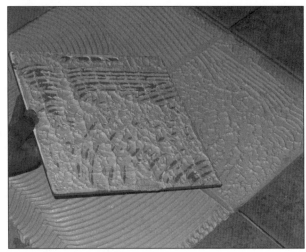

Figure 44: Fairly good coverage here.

from me. In fact, I refer to it simply as "my tool." (Figure 45)

The weakest parts of a square tile are its corners. Particular attention must be paid when placing tiles on the floor to getting complete support under the corners of each piece. Voids often occur at the edges of the grid. If there is any question that a corner might not be supported, remove the piece and make sure that it is. It is also possible to push thin set under the edges of tiles facing you. Strike all excess adhesive from the joints and wipe them with the sponge before you move on to the next grid.

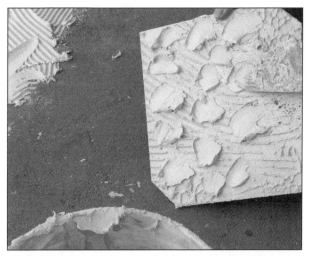

Figure 45: Additional thin set is "back buttered" onto a tile.

Tiling Sequence

I mentioned earlier that the grid system makes it possible to set tiles in different areas at the same time. Suppose you have a closet or two you would like to tile and get out of the way before you begin tiling the main floor? This is, in fact, a good thing to do. Go ahead and tile the closets. Also, it might be convenient to begin tiling in two different areas of the main floor and work toward the door or your planned avenue of retreat. You can do whatever you want as long as you keep the tiles

Figure 46: I like to pre-cut and fit tiles into doorways.

in the proper position within each grid. Sooner or later, the entire pattern will come together. This convenient approach is not possible (or practical) when using most other layout systems. (You do have a plan for backing your way out of the room, don't you?)

I often find it convenient to make a grouping of cuts in doorways or closets before I begin spreading thin set. The procedure also works well in small toilet rooms where freedom of movement is somewhat restricted. It is much easier to mark and make cuts with no previously set tiles to get in the way. Employing the grid system, it's a simple matter to lay tiles on the floor to mark them for cutting. Just stay with the grid lines, and you can't go wrong. (Figure 46)

As you move from one grid to the next, look back over the work you've done. You may want to re-align a tile now and again as you progress. Unaligned tiles are sometimes difficult to notice at close range. For this reason you should take a break occasionally. Back off and stand around a bit so you can scope out your work.

Standing Around

It takes years to develop a passable approach to goofing off while making it look as though you're doing something useful. In *Ceramic Tile Setting* (McGraw-Hill, 1992) I passed along a method of standing around that fools people most of the time, and during the ensuing years I've improved the technique considerably. Please feel free to use my experience as a basis for the development of your own unique routine.

There are, of course, many ways to stand around, but if you're going to do it right, you've got to consider it the art form it is. I mean, don't just stand there like a ninny; do it with flare and with *style*. Spread your feet apart a comfortable distance while focusing on the project. Contrive a facial expression that is contemplative but nonchalant as well. The idea is to let on that while you're very serious about the work you're doing, it's really not much of a challenge to a person of your technical ability. Taking a deep breath and exhaling audibly while staring intently at the work tends to impress anyone who might be looking on. Propping a hand under your chin while mumbling technical-sounding but otherwise unintelligible word fragments works even better.

An important component of the standing around routine is the ability to deter onlookers from asking you embarrassing questions on practical points you might not fully understand, so it pays to prepare yourself in advance. For example, you should develop a condescending look and practice it frequently in front of the mirror. Should someone dare ask you a question while in the course of your standing around, flashing the look usually suffices in place of an answer. I must warn you, however, that occasionally, you'll be confronted by a particularly inquisitive and grating person, and the look won't be enough. Should you determine this is the case, revert immediately to the mumbling sequence. It'll be your best defense.

Making Cuts

On a floor this size you'll almost always have a tile saw available to you. If you don't want to buy one outright, you can rent one at a rental yard and at many of the large home-improvement stores. Saws are used when cuts have to be made around cabinet corners, in door-ways – wherever a straight cut won't do the job. Straight cuts are usually made on the cutting board (cutter), although some super-hard tiles will require the use of a saw for making all cuts, straight or otherwise.[5]

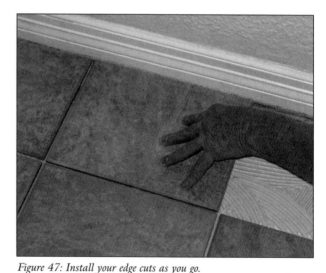

Figure 47: Install your edge cuts as you go.

For a detailed and authoritative discussion of electric tile saws, please see Appendix II in the back of the book. It contains an article written by my friend Andy Lundgren, a fellow who lives and breathes tile saws.

Make your cuts as you go. As you set the full tiles in grids near the edge of the layout,

---

[5]*It is my understanding that in countries other than the United States one might "hire" a tile saw instead of "renting" one.*

set the cut tiles, too. It is much harder to return and do the cutting after all the full tiles have been set over the entire layout. (Figure 47)

L-Cuts: Cuts that go around corners are often called L-cuts. Making them is not difficult with the use of a tile saw. Marking them, however, takes a little finesse, since the object you are cutting around is often not at right angles to the room. Oh, it's supposed to be, but it probably isn't. You'll need to create cutting lines on the surface of the tile that conform to the object. (Figure 48)

Figure 48: L-cuts are made with the tile saw.

U-Cuts: Cuts in the shape of a "U" are sometimes necessary under door frames, depending on how you laid the floor out. There was a time when I was almost always able to avoid having to make U-cuts by employing creative layout techniques, but then those crafty tile manufacturers began making floor tiles larger and larger and the trend caught on. Nowadays I just assume there will be U-cuts to make. Mastering this type of cut is one of the things that separates the pros from the wannabes in our trade.[6]

Figure 49: U-cuts ready for installation.

Take your time when marking and making U-cuts. If you ruin a piece, don't let it deter you. Take a break and then start over. You will be so proud of yourself when you have successfully mastered this skill, you'll want to run out into the street and tell all your neighbors. Don't do that, though. It's very bad form. (Figure 49)

U-cuts are one good reason to set all your cuts as you tile the field. It is often necessary to remove one or more full pieces in order to slide the U-cut under a door frame. It would be impossible to do this with hard set tiles in the way. You would have to either get out the hammer and chisel and remove a tile or two, or compromise your craftsmanship by splitting the U into segments. Ugh!

Back Mitering: Maybe you have a sunken living room you're heading into, or maybe your breakfast area is on a different level than the kitchen. You have a step to deal with. You can overlap the vertical tile (riser) with the horizontal tile (tread) if you have tiles whose edges will not stand out when exposed. Or you can "back miter" both pieces and eliminate the raw edges altogether. (Figure 50)

---

[6]*Wannabes are folks who want to be tile setters but who are not. They only "wannabe."*

Please keep in mind, however, that mitered edges tend to be hard on small children. Until the kids are old enough to keep themselves right side up most of the time, it might be a good idea to protect the edge with a rubber or plastic corner piece or "stair nosing."

Bullnose

Some floor tiles, not many, come with matching surface caps or "bullnose" pieces that will work well on steps or other changes in plane. Even at that, though, there may be times when back mitering presents a more pleasing "look."

Figure 50: Mitering is best done with the tile saw.

Occasionally, "stair tread" tiles are available which match the floor tiles, but often these are only used in commercial and industrial settings. You may not like the look in your home.

Layout Options

Who says you have to put your tiles in straight? I mean, who says you have to put your tiles in straight to the walls? You don't, you know. You might prefer a diagonal pattern, or you might want to try something random. How about a few "spots" or "dots" incorporated into the scheme? A border, perhaps. A few decorative tiles (decos). The possibilities are nearly limitless, and you can let your creative juices flow – if you know one additional thing, and that is how to turn your square grid layout on the diagonal — forty-five degrees to the walls of the room.

Let's revisit the original reference lines we made at the beginning of the layout process. We used the longest wall we had available to us, and we made a chalk line parallel to it. We then constructed an intersecting perpendicular line employing the 3-4-5 method. From that point you simply snapped a series of evenly spaced lines in two directions which were parallel to those two intersecting reference lines.

If you were able to turn those two original reference lines one-eighth of a full circle or 45 degrees, you would expand your layout horizons instantly. That's what we're going to do. We're going to *empower* you, you lucky person.

Note that the two intersecting perpendicular lines form four quadrants streaming out into infinity. At any point from the intersection, you can make a mark on one of the lines. Let's, just for the sake of arbitrariness, make a mark 4 feet from the intersection. Now make a similar mark 4 feet out on the perpendicular line. Using these two points as fulcrums, trace intersecting arcs 4 feet away from each point. By drawing a line through the intersection of the arcs and the original intersection of the lines, you can create a "diagonal," a line that is exactly 45 degrees to the original lines. By doing this in one other quadrant, you will have constructed intersecting perpendicular reference lines – "on the diagonal." From this point it is merely a matter of following the same procedures discussed in the square grid layout. You now possess diagonal style, and your layout capabilities are unchallenged. (Figure 51)

Unless you want to do something at 30 degrees...

Sometimes, 30-degree layouts are used in buildings. Why? I don't know. I only

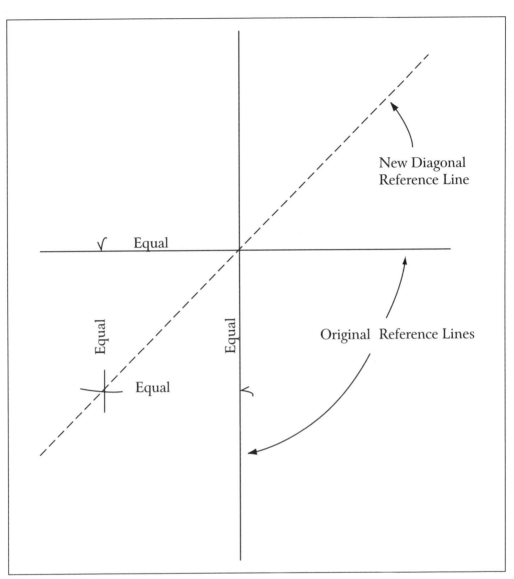

Figure 51: Creating diagonal lines.

know that 30 degrees is traditional. If you find something in a building laid out at, say, 27 degrees, there's a better than even chance it's a screw up.

Coming up with thirty degree angles is a bit trickier than achieving 90 and 45 degree angles, but it's really nothing for a layout person of your talent. Here's what you're going to do.

Cheat.

There are, of course, procedures in geometry for construction of 30-degree angles, but they would entail making numerous marks and lines on the floor, and it would get quite confusing. So I've come up with an approximation for you, and it really won't make a difference if you're off a fraction of a degree. 30 degrees is arbitrary just as 29 degrees, 58 minutes, 41 seconds is arbitrary. No one *cares*. On a large commercial building, certainly, but in your little castle, no.

Instead of the 3-4-5 method, we're going to use the secret John Bridge 47-81.5-95 method. Along one of your perpendicular reference lines mark out a segment that is 81-1/2 inches long. From one of the points trace an arc that is exactly 47 inches away and roughly perpendicular to the point. From the other point trace an intersecting arc that has a radius of 95 inches. Snap a line through the second point and the intersecting arcs. The line will be so close to 30 degrees off the reference line that not even Pythagoras would know the difference.

Who needs higher math, anyway?

If you have a supposed 30-degree angle in your home or some other angle dreamed up by an architect or designer, simply follow it by measuring out and snapping a reference line parallel to it. Tile cutting will then follow the lines. Lay the pieces on the floor and trace the cutting lines on them with a straightedge lined up with the layout lines. The feature may have been originally depicted by the draftsman at exactly 30 degrees, for example, but there is a great chance that the carpenter didn't hit it exactly right.

Circles and Arcs

Circles and portions of circles called arcs have been incorporated into buildings throughout recorded history. The Greeks and Romans made great use of the concept in constructing many noted buildings of their times – the Amphitheater in Rome is one classic example.

Houses also sometimes contain circles or portions of them in their architecture, and installing floor-coverings other than carpeting in them presents a unique challenge both in application and in estimating materials. In addition to high school geometry, you'll have to recall something even more mystifying – seventh grade math.

In tiling arcs it is often feasible to simply lay the tiles to be cut on the floor and trace cutting lines on their surface, using a trammel or measuring tape. A trammel can be made by driving a nail through one end of a stick or narrow board and holding a pencil fast against it at some point along its length. By trial and error you can determine the approximate radius and center point needed to form the arc or circle. Often the edges of the tiles will be covered with baseboards or skirting and will not need to be perfectly accurate.

But what if the circle or portion thereof is something you want to create from scratch? Suppose you would like to form a medallion in the middle of your entryway, for instance. A limitless number of original creations are possible when using broken tiles of different colors and when using a number of tiles of differing colors. Making the cuts is, of course, tedious and time-consuming, but you can't even get started unless you are able to draw and lay out the pattern on the floor.

When estimating materials for floor areas contained within circles there are two basic methods. One has to do with the seventh grade math I mentioned, and the other is called a "wild guess." Let's review the math.

Pi, represented by π, is a transcendental or infinitive number: 3.1459265 and so on. In seventh grade we usually settled on 3.14. To find the area of a circle we use the formula πr^2 which means Pi times the radius squared. Thus we take 3.14 times the square of the radius of the circle. To square the radius, multiply it by itself. If the radius is 5 feet, for example, the square is 25 square feet (I know you already knew that). 3.14 times 25 equals 78.5, and from this we could say we need about 80 square feet of tile to tile a circle with a radius of 5 feet.

Say we need a special tile to form a border around the circle. The formula for finding the circumference of a circle is πd or Pi times the diameter. Since the radius is 5 feet, the diameter is 10 feet. 3.14 times 10 equals 31.4 lineal feet. Purchase 32 lineal feet, and you'll have enough.

Pi (π) is the sixteenth letter of the Greek alphabet and is translated to English as the letter P. I provide you with this information only so you'll be better able to impress a friend, relative or neighbor as you show off your completed tile medallion. Tile setters are good at making impressions on people. The conversation might go something like:

"Wow, that's some medallion. How did you do that?

"Well, as you know, Pi, the sixteenth letter of the Greek alphabet, is the symbol for the transcendental number 3.1416. Pi, by the way, is translated to English as the letter P..."

I think you get the idea, and you can imagine how enthralled your visitor will be.

Outdoor Tile Setting — The Small Concrete Porch

My plan was to stick to projects inside the home, primarily, but I recently did a small front porch in conjunction with a larger tile job inside a home, and it occurs to me you might have a need for the little bit of know-how that distinguishes an outdoor tile job from an inside one. I will also show you pictures of a larger elliptical patio we completed with slate tiles and an exterior balcony covered with cobblestone-looking porcelain tiles.

I spend much more time when working outdoors making sure I have total coverage with the thin set. Where I live it doesn't matter as much as it does further north, but freezing weather has to be taken into account when you work outside with tile. Water can get under the tiles if you leave voids, and water freezes and becomes ice. Ice expands as it forms and exerts a great deal of pressure in all directions, enough to pop tiles up off the substrate.

The other factor to consider when working outdoors is that the rate of expansion is going to be much greater than it is indoors. Temperature swings will be much more dramatic, from zero degrees to over ninety in some parts of the country. And when sun shines directly on a clay tile installation, the temperature of the material can rise to 120 degrees and higher. So even for a small porch it is best to provide plenty of room for expansion. I recommend you form expansion joints wherever your tiled field abuts walls or other obstructions. Also, where the porch joins the sidewalk there can be no solid connection. I usually just leave that joint open, but you might want to fill it with flexible caulking.

Expansion joints in terraces, patios, sidewalks and other larger areas should be no farther apart than 10 to 12 feet (3 meters or so) in my opinion. I have seen too many cracked driveways, patios and walkways in the area where I live to ever consider stretching things further than that.

The Porch

When working with the types of tiles that would normally go on a porch, you will usually not be able to find a matching bullnose. It's not really a problem because

Figure 52: Use a tile to gauge the overhang.

you can almost always find tiles in your stock that have one or more edges that have been painted over at the factory. Pull enough of these out ahead of time to run the length of the step. When the time comes you can simply lap these tiles over the vertical tiles on the face of the step or "riser." I like to install all the horizontal tiles, including the edge tiles, and then suspend the vertical "riser" tiles with tape while they take hold. (Figure 52)

The layout on this particular porch is centered on the door. Shift the field so that you get the largest cuts possible on both sides. Remember, there are two ways to center a field of tile: tiles can be placed on either side of the center-line, or a tile can straddle the center line. (Figure 53)

If the porch happened to be open on one end, you would probably want to start from that edge and work your way toward the wall. You would do the same on the front edge. If the layout becomes a problem due to "skinnies" over by the wall, you might consider running a "soldier course" or square border on both open edges and then turning the

Figure 53: The tiles are centered in the doorway.

Figure 53A: Completed porch. Tiles in doorway go under the threshold.

field on the diagonal. A soldier course is simply a row of rectangular or square tiles that run in a row and frame some other pattern. The term "soldier course" is used frequently in brick work where a row of bricks are lined up side-by-side instead of in the usual broken joint fashion. Since I'm a mud man and essentially a mason, I feel no regret at all for having stolen the term and transported it over to the tile trade.

The installation of the tiles is precisely the same as that which we have already covered inside the house. Don't start this project, however, if there is the least possibility of rain. Murphy's Law will almost certainly catch you.[7] (Figure 53 A)

When the installation has cured for a few days it should be sealed with a penetrating sealer. Do not allow the sealer to build up on the tiled surface. Have rags or paper towels handy to keep things wiped off. The sealer will help prevent water from migrating into the interior of the installation.

It is also important to note that all outdoor tiled surfaces are sloped slightly so that water does not collect on them. Use your level to make sure you have a slope before

---

[7]*Murphy's Law states that if there is the least likelihood of a mishap or of disaster, it will most assuredly occur.*

you begin laying tile. One-eighth of an inch per running foot is adequate if your surface is perfectly flat. One-quarter inch per foot is much better.

It should go without saying, but I'll say it. Choose tiles that are not slippery. Enough said.

Also make sure the tiles you choose are rated "frost-proof" or "frost-resistant." What this means is that Yankees cannot put Saltillo tiles out on the front porch – not on the back porch, either.[8]

The Balcony

A balcony is really nothing more than an elevated porch, but this particular balcony has a radius feature that I want to show you. It would have been possible and feasible to simply ignore the feature and cut the tiles at the edge as needed, but following the curvature with the tiles in a cobblestone manner added a bit of style to the project, I think. (Figures 54, 55, 56)

Figure 54: A batten (bent stick) is used to align the tiles.

The Slate Patio

I want to say at the onset that I did not have the opportunity to design the concrete work on this project. By the time I was called to perform the tile work, the concrete had been poured (without a single expansion joint). I made the owners painfully aware of the problems that might occur down the road and proceeded to do the work. I provided movement joints in the tiled field and also where the patio abuts walls and columns. (Figures 57, 58, 59, 60)

Grouting Tiled Floors

Inside the house or outdoors, applying grout to tiled floors (or tiled walls) is an art in itself. While the work is not high-tech by any means, it does take a little know-how. A grout job absolutely makes or breaks a job. It is possible to ruin an otherwise perfect installation with sloppy grouting procedures. The cardinal rule for a beginner is to start with very small areas and work your way into larger areas as you pick up the technique. Do not begin by smearing grout over a large area and expecting to have it cleaned up before it hardens on the surface.

Yes, I said "smear," because grouting is the art of making one huge mess and then cleaning it up. Having not seen the process, many people think that grout is somehow inserted into the joints with something like a caulking gun, but that is not the case at all. An operation like that would take longer than installing the tiles themselves. No, grout is smeared onto the surface of every tile as it is forced down into the grout joints.

---

[8]*Yankees are Americans who live anywhere north of Texas.*

The tool used is a rubber grout trowel or "float." Grout floats can be purchased at tile stores as well as at home centers and some hardware stores. There are many styles, brands and grades of floats. The one you choose will depend on the amount of tile you will be grouting. If your floor area is small, you can get by with a cheaper tool, but if you are doing a larger floor, say, a kitchen and breakfast area, or you anticipate doing more tile work in the future, you should buy a good quality tool.

There are highly specialized tiles that cannot be grouted in the normal manner. For these there are "grout bags" that work exactly like cake decorating bags. Very fluid grout is loaded into the bag and squeezed through a nozzle into the joints. Do not consider using a grout bag for normal grouting. The process can be slow and frustrating, as stated above.

Figure 55: Just finished grouting. Tiles are still wet.

Mixing: Since our grout spaces are approximately 3/16 to 1/4 inch in width (4 mm to 6 mm), we'll be using "sanded" grout as opposed to unsanded. The sand in the grout is actually silica and can be hazardous when breathed in. You should wear a dust mask when mixing the grout.

If this is your first time at grouting, you should start by mixing a small amount of grout. The open time of the material is about an hour, and then it will begin to hydrate to the point that it won't be usable. So start out with a small amount, and then mix more as you progress. It is crucial, though, that you use the same recipe for each successive batch. Measure carefully the amount of water and grout powder used. Once you have achieved a workable mix, write the formula down. As you improve with experience, you'll be able to make larger batches and cover vaster areas, but take it easy for now. Don't get in a hurry.

Grout manufacturers place instructions for using their products on the packaging. Please take the time to read the directions. If the manufacturer tells you to mix the grout with water only, don't use an additive. Most grouts nowadays are "modified," meaning that polymers have been included at the factory. A very few grouts, however, still require the use of a liquid additive.

Mix the grout, let it stand for about 10 minutes and then re-mix it. This is referred to as "slaking." During this wait time the dry ingredients of the grout have ample time to absorb the liquid and thus produce a thorough and uniform blend. Once again, don't get in a rush. The slaking of the product is important.

Application: Apply the grout to an area you know you will be able to clean in the space of a few minutes. If you are a newbie, this area will probably encompass no more than fifteen to twenty square feet or two square meters. Using the float at a rather low angle to the floor, force the material into all the joints. Two or three passes over the joints will ensure complete penetration. (Figure 61)

Figure 56: Same tiles used on front porch. Broken tile mosaic step risers.

Figure 57: Slate tiles are cut into soldier course edge.

Figure 58: The grid system of layout lines is used.

Figure 59: See how the edge flows.

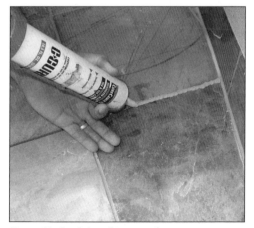

Figure 60: Sanded caulking is used in movement joints.

Then turn the float to a higher angle, as close to ninety degrees to the floor as you can get it, and rake the excess grout from the surface. Do not try to thoroughly clean the floor. Leave a little grout on the surface. If you see a joint that looks different from the rest, go back and smooth a little more grout into it. Pick up the remaining grout and stir it back into the remainder of the batch in the bucket. (Figure 62)

Now would be a good time to fetch a pail of water and a sponge if you haven't done so. You will allow the grout to remain on the surface at least five minutes. I would not recommend leaving it there longer than ten minutes if this is your first attempt at grouting. You may find it necessary to let the grout rest a bit longer, but don't assume that at the onset. It's much better to screw up a grout job by washing too soon than it is to botch the job by allowing grout to harden on the surface of the tiles. Yes, I've been there more than once.

Wring the sponge out thoroughly and wipe across the surface with a swirling motion, keeping your eyes on the grout joints and not on the surface of the tiles. As you wash, you will notice the

Figure 61: As he pushes the grout across the tiles, Albert is forcing it into the joints.

Figure 62: With the float at a higher angle, excess grout is raked from the surface.

joints begin to smooth and straighten. Rinse and wring the sponge frequently, and continue to wash until the joints are straight and eye-pleasing. Stop. You're done. (Figure 63)

As the surface of the tiles dries, you will see a film or haze begin to develop. When the surface is totally dry, you may be able to wipe the haze away with a clean dry cloth. A towel or a tee-shirt will work best. If when you try to wipe the surface, grout pulls out of the joints and smears the edges of the tiles, stop what you're doing and wait an additional few minutes. Try it again, but if the joints continue to smear, give it up. Instead, use clean water and the sponge to wipe the surface again. Wring the sponge out tightly and make only one pass over the surface.

Allow the surface to dry thoroughly. If a haze remains it can be cleaned off after a couple of days have elapsed using white vinegar and water mixed half-and-half.

Continue grouting by smearing another section and repeating the process. As your confidence and technical ability grow, you can cover larger and larger areas. But don't ever get a big head and decide you are Mr. or Mrs. Grouter Supreme. Never take the chance of letting the job get ahead of you, and never forget that grout is cement. Cement is a material with which you get only one chance.

Using a Grout "System": For large floor areas it makes sense to invest in and use a better system than the bucket and the sponge. Several manufacturers have come out with rolling buckets that are equipped with various ringer and roller devices. Sponges are special made to attach to large tools that resemble grout floats. The idea is that you can cover much larger areas at a pass than you can with a sponge held in the hand. Furthermore, having the sponge attached to a stiff platform keeps it on the surface of the joints as they are washed. Your grout joints will be fuller and flatter than those washed with a conventional sponge. (Figures 64, 65, 66)

Grouting Problem Tiles: The trend in floor tiles, as I write, is leaning toward the natural look; the "stone look" is the descriptive term I most often hear. Some of the tiles are so authentic looking that they actually have deep pits and crags molded into their surface. While these features are desirable from the style standpoint, they are absolute murder when it comes to grouting (and routine cleaning). If you have used a tile like this (and there's a good chance you have), I suggest you do a test grouting run on the surface of a spare tile before you begin grouting the floor itself. If you are not able to wipe the grout from the depressions in the sample piece,

Figure 63: Move the sponge diagonally across the tiles. Rinse the sponge and wring it after each pass.

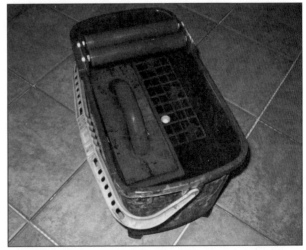

Figure 64: Roller-type grout washing system.

Figure 65: Push the sponge holder across the rollers several times.

you certainly won't be able to do it on the floor itself.

Grout Release: You may want to use a "grout release" on the surface of the floor tiles to aid in washing up. Grout release is a gooey, semi-liquid substance that is smeared on the surface just prior to grouting. It inhibits the grout from attaching itself firmly to the surface of the tiles while at the same time allowing it time to firm up in the joints. The "release" is for the most part washed away as the grout is cleaned up. You can buy grout release at the places where ceramic tiles and tile related products are sold.

An alternative to grout release is pre-sealing the tiles. You can do this either before you install the tiles or after they have been laid. Do not apply sealer to the vertical edges of the tiles nor to their back sides. Certain sealing

Figure 66: Wash with a circular motion. Rinse the sponge frequently.

products are considered "bond breakers – they will prevent cement products from properly adhering to tiles.

Many of the modern tiles will not accept a great deal of sealer, and you should never let sealer dry on the surface of tiles. Wipe it on, let it stand for a minute and then remove it completely with a dry cloth.

My preference between the two methods is grout release, but other pros lean toward the sealer. It's six of one and half a dozen of the other. The important thing is to be aware of the pits and crevasses in your tiles and treat them before you apply grout. It is a sinking feeling to realize that you have created a mess on the surface of your tile installation and that it will take hours of drudgery to clean it up, if clean-up is possible at all.

Even having pre-sealed the tiles, you can still have a terrible time trying to wash up the grout. Sometimes, grout gets into deep, tight depressions and cannot be removed with the sponge. In that case, a sharpened stick is handy for gouging the grout out of the pits. Hardwood dowels work well. Buy the diameter that will fit into your pencil sharpener.

An easier route is to not buy tiles that will be difficult to clean. It's not just a matter of the one-time grout cleaning process. You'll have problems cleaning the tiles for as long as you have the floor.

Acid Cleaning

There are a number of acid based products on the market that can be used for cleaning problematic tiles. I shall explain them in their order of progression – the mildest products first.

White Vinegar: Vinegar is a mild acid, and it would be my first choice for removing stubborn grout haze or cement scum after the fact. As with all acids, you should wait a couple days after grouting to use it. You may need a scrub brush to agitate the vinegar. Start with a mixture of vinegar and water mixed half and half. Vinegar can be used full strength, though. It should not be used as a day-to-day cleaner, nor should anything else that contains any form of acid.

Phosphoric Acid Cleaner: Phosphoric acid can usually be found where tiles and tile products are sold. It is diluted with water and used in the same manner vinegar might be used. You must read and follow the safety precautions printed on the label. Allow for plenty of ventilation and avoid breathing in the fumes. Rubber gloves and eye protection are advised. Saturate the grout joints with clean water before you begin. This will help prevent the acid from infiltrating the interior of the joints where it is not needed and where it might actually weaken the structure of the grout. Rinse thoroughly with clean water and allow the floor to dry.

Sulfamic Acid Crystals: The crystals are added to clean water. You cannot over-concentrate the resulting solution because excess crystals will merely settle to the bottom of the bucket and will not dissolve. Sulfamic is a fairly strong cleaner. Precautions must be taken to protect yourself from fumes and mild burns. A very severe case of dishpan hands can develop if rubber gloves are not worn. Do not inhale the fumes.

Muriatic Acid: Muriatic acid is swimming pool acid, and it is sold wherever pool supplies are sold. I do not recommend you use muriatic acid, as it is harsh and can damage grout and some tiles, too. If you do use it, dilute it 10 to 1. That's 10 parts water to 1 part acid. Always add the acid to the water and never the reverse. Thoroughly saturate the grout before application, and do not allow the solution to rest on the surface any longer than absolutely necessary.

There are a variety of masonry cleaning products available that contain acid. These have been developed mostly for cleaning brick work and other masonry surfaces. Some of the products are used on tile by certain professionals, but I recommend that you stick to products which have been developed specifically for tile installations – products which have been thoroughly tested on tiles.

Never, ever, use any type of acid, including vinegar, on marble or marble-like stone such as travertine and limestone. Even household cleaners containing citric acid can permanently damage this type of material. There are special products that can be used instead. Find them where marble and other stone tiles are sold.

Sealing the Tiles

When I wrote *Ceramic Tile Setting,* sealers had not reached a very high state of the art, and I considered sealing tiles and grout very close to a complete waste of time. During the ensuing ten years, however, sealer technology has accelerated to the point that I now recommend sealing virtually all tile installations. There are high-tech sealers for every situation and every material. I suggest that they be used.

Since there are so many good products on the market, it would be impossible to do them justice here. Ask the advice of the people selling you tile and other tile related products, and do follow the instructions printed on the various labels. There is no longer a "one-size-fits-all" product. Find the one that suits the material you have installed.

General Care and Maintenance

Caring for a quality ceramic tile floor is easy. For the most part, tiles wash off with water. In cooking areas where grease is likely to be on the surface, a little mild detergent will be required. As you probably know, there are hundreds of cleaning products purported to be for tile, but many of these contain acids. Do read the labels of all cleaning products and avoid those whose list of ingredients contains acid of any sort. On the other end of the spectrum are cleaners which are highly alkaline. These should be avoided also. The best cleaner for tile and stone will be completely neutral. Look for terms like "pH neutral" on the label.

You will not want to wax your ceramic tiles, ever. Wax will only clog the grout and cause it to gather more dirt than it normally would, and the surfaces of modern floor tiles are a hundred times more durable than any wax could be. Why apply something that will eventually have to be stripped off? A ceramic tile floor is the most maintenance-free surface possible. Why make it otherwise?

Although ceramic tiles have become durable indeed, it is still possible to scratch them with metallic objects, and these include the tips of chair and table legs. Check all your furniture for anything metallic that might contact the tile and replace it with plastic or rubber. Metal file cabinets and other metal fixtures that reside directly on the floor should be elevated off the tile, as rust will stain the tiles over a period of time. Placing a small piece of scrap carpeting under filing cabinets is one effective way of handling the problem. Check also the legs of your washer and dryer to ensure the rubber pads are in good shape. New pads are available at home centers, hardware stores and appliance centers.

The Feeling

I don't think there is anything as satisfying and as *exciting* as having created something beautiful and durable with one's own hands. If you have completed your project, you have earned the right to do all the standing around you want to do, but don't make it too obvious. And by no means should you do any boasting, as that is considered extremely unprofessional by everyone in the tile industry.

Do maintain your tile setter's composure, that certain aloofness that separates you from ordinary people, the smug awareness (if you will) that tile setters might just be a breed apart. But keep it to yourself.

Welcome to the club.

CHAPTER 3

TILING WALLS

Gravity is Not-so-good

So you want to build and tile your own shower, do you? Well, you are about to get your chance. Although I am not from your government, I am nevertheless here to help you. Prepare yourself for a relatively lengthy project, one you can't abandon once you begin. Although nothing in our trade is high-tech (except for some of the materials), a ceramic tile shower is probably the most complex project one will encounter. Ceramic tile shower work is not for slackers. It takes real hand blistering, knuckle busting work. Plus, you have to be able to think on your feet and manage several operations simultaneously.

I see you're still here. What are you waiting for? Get out your tools and let's get moving.

As I mentioned earlier in the book, I have given up trying to discourage weekend warriors from taking on challenging tile projects, and instead I simply try to help them avoid the pitfalls associated with the work. Accordingly, in this chapter I will acquaint you with every way a tiled shower can be done – every feasible way, that is. We will begin with the ancient and honorable system that I and other mud men (and women) employ – the mud method. It's not for everyone, but it certainly won't hurt anyone to learn about it. Certain aspects of this method, i.e., the floor, the curb and the seat, will be incorporated into the other methods we will discuss later. And tiling a wall over cement mortar is very similar to tiling a wall over cement backer board or over a membrane covered substrate. So even if you don't intend to use the mud method to build your shower, please read through this section.

And even if you only want to tile a wall which is not part of a shower, I encourage you to read on through. Shower walls are only walls, and the processes for tiling them are not unique to showers.

Mortar

Mortar (mud) is generic. There are many styles, types, colors and blends of mud. When people hear or see the word "mortar," they most often associate it with the brick mortar that is used in masonry construction, but that is only one use for mortar. It is also used in plastering, in topping off, in patching and in a host of other construction techniques, including tile setting. In tile setting, mortar or "mud" is used in constructing walls, floors, ledges, seats, shower curbs, window and door jambs and sills, steps, ramps, slopes – well, it goes on.

Mortar is also tile grout and thin set adhesive. Thin set is often referred to as "thin set mortar," "bonding mortar" and "dry set mortar." There is also a "medium bed mortar" which is used in situations where a regular thin set won't create enough height or build-up to do the job.

There are many mortars, suffice it to say. We'll be using several of them for the mud shower, and I'll explain them to you as we progress. Get used to using the word "mud." We'll be wallowing in it before we're finished. You'll love it.[9]

Tear-out, Framing and Drywall

A tile setter is not always simply a tile setter. He or she is often a carpenter, a plumber, a jack-of-all-trades. In the type of work I do, I normally tear-out, re-build, re-plumb and then re-tile the showers I work on. That's how it is in remodeling, and that's how we will approach matters here. We will begin with demolition, i.e., breaking things.

Before you do anything else, plug the shower drain. I usually do this by removing the hair strainer and stuffing a rag down the drain pipe. You can then remove the trim from the faucets or shower valve, to include the shower head. Remove any other fixture that might be attached to the tile. It is also a good idea to remove pictures and other hanging objects from the opposite sides of the walls that will be affected.

Additionally, be aware that there are definitely pipes that need to be avoided, and there may also be electrical and telephone wires running through the walls you are about to break into. Be very careful when using saws, knives and other implements that can go deep into the wall.

No matter the method used to construct the shower, all tile showers contain tile, and ceramic tile when broken is treacherous. It is super sharp, and it can cut deeply. Wear a heavy pair of gloves, and be careful not to grab onto sharp edges. Wear eye protection and a dust mask as well. (Figure 67)

Figure 67: This shower is definitely ready for demolition.

Tearing a shower out can be fairly easy, or it can be really tough work. Showers that were originally tiled with nothing more than wall board (sheetrock) behind the tiles are simple to take apart. You cut the sheetrock all the way around the edge of the tiled surface and remove it, tile and all. It is a good idea to first chip off the edge trim (bullnose) and make your cut in an area that will be covered by the new tile installation. That way there will be no need for drywall finishing when the new shower is completed.

On showers that were constructed with cement backer board, it's often possible to pull the tile and backer board off in sections. There will be a need for a pry bar, a hammer and maybe a chisel. (Figure 68, 69, 70)

Showers that were built with the mud method are going to require a little more effort to remove. In fact, mud showers are a chore to take apart. A heavy maul (about 3 pounds) comes in very handy, as does a heavy-duty pry bar or wrecking bar. A claw hammer will be used as well. Tin snips are used to cut the old lath or other reinforcing so that sections of tile and mortar can be detached from the framing.

It is best to break the walls into sections that can be easily lifted and carried out of

---

[9]Brick and plaster mortar might be called "render" in some places, and the mortar we use for building floors and decks might be called "screed."

Figure 68: There is nothing more than sheetrock behind these tiles.

Figure 69: A combination of mold and dry rot. This wall was never waterproofed.

Figure 70: Backer board and tile are removed in one operation.

the room. Mortar and tile are heavy, and you won't be able to remove an entire wall at once. Most walls will be broken into three or four smaller pieces. Use the maul and a chisel to bang through the tile and mortar in roughly straight lines. Don't forget the goggles or safety glasses and your dust mask.

There are two ways of building mud walls. One entails a layer system that creates a mortar wall over an inch thick. We'll call this the two-coat method, and the installations are extremely heavy. If your walls are thick, you'll need to break them into rather small pieces in order to get them out in good order.

The other method is the one I use and the one I'll explain to you in detail as we get into re-building the shower. It's called the one-coat method, and the layer of mud you'll be tearing out is much thinner than with the two coat method. There will be a sheetrock or plaster wall behind the single layer of mortar, and it is usually possible to pry the mortar away from the sheetrock or plaster. In the case of sheetrock, it doesn't matter whether you destroy it or not, because it will be replaced in the course of things. However, a plaster wall should be retained if at all possible. Plaster is a much better base than sheetrock hands down, and plaster, of course, is much harder to repair.

Take the shower floor out by chopping it into sections with the maul and chisel. Most tile setters use no reinforcing in residential shower floors, and the mortar will break up. It will take some doing, though. Begin by chipping around the drain and isolating it so that it won't be damaged as the rest of the floor is removed. Do this whether or not you intend to replace the drain. Needlessly prying on the drain can damage the plumbing below that you will want to retain.

The curb or dam might be constructed with a core of framing lumber, or it might be built from bricks or masonry rubble. Hitting it with the maul or hammer will knock it away if it's built from masonry, but you should be careful if the curb contains wood members. Chip the tile and mortar away from the wooden curb. Repeatedly banging it with the maul could ruin adjacent framing or flooring that is not slated for

Figure 71: Bricks and mortar were used to form the curb in this shower.

replacement. You can discover what's in the curb by chiseling into it.[10] (Figure 71)

When all the tile and mortar have been removed from the shower, it'll be time to inspect the framing to determine whether any of it will need to be replaced due to water damage. In some cases only minor carpentry is needed, but it is not unusual to completely remove and replace a section of framing. For example, I can't remember when I haven't had to tear out a knee wall (low bulkhead) in a shower that contained one. I usually just re-build them as a matter of course. (Figures 72, 73)

Often the sole plate (sill plate), the lowest horizontal member of the wall, will be completely destroyed by dry rot and will have to be replaced in sections. It's usually impossible to replace the sill exactly as it was installed originally without further destroying the house. For this reason I often shove pieces of sill under the studs, and where that's not possible, I screw blocking between the studs instead.

It is often not feasible to pull out and replace entire studs, the

Figure 72: Not much remaining of this knee wall.

Figure 73: A completely re-framed knee wall.

vertical members that rise from the sole plate. In cases where only the lower portions of studs have rotted, it is sufficient to sister a new piece of stud to the old. The new member, or portion thereof, should overlap the good portion of the original by about two feet. The sisters can be nailed to the original studs, but screws are twice as good. Screws draw the members together and tighten the overall frame, whereas nails simply hold things together.

If removing slightly rotted portions of framing members will cause damage to areas not intended for rehabilitation, it is acceptable to leave them in the wall when sistering them. Dry rot, like mold and other living organisms, cannot exist or spread without moisture. Since you will be sealing off all sources of moisture in the wall cavity, there is no chance of future contamination.

Termites

In my part of the world, Houston, Texas, it is not uncommon to discover termites

---

[10][Footnote: A shower curb (dam) is often called a hob outside the U.S. and Canada.]

when tearing into showers that have been leaking for a while. And, of course, termites are no strangers to other areas as well. If you run into the little devils it's best to call a professional exterminator immediately and agree on a mutually acceptable course of action. All the affected wood and other material will be removed from the wall cavities, and then the termite person will do his or her thing, not only in the shower area but throughout the entire house and property.

How do you know that insects found in the wall cavities are termites? Well, sometimes ant larvae bear a striking resemblance to termite larvae, but you will see adult ants trying to save the young. Termites, on the other hand, seem to disappear as soon as they are exposed to air and daylight.

But, really, why attempt to make the call at all? It's better to call in the pro and have the problem, whatever it might be, eliminated.

Backing Blocks

I seldom find shower pan liner backing blocks in the showers I tear out. This is not strange when you consider that I often don't find shower pan liners, either. In any case, if the shower pan blocking is not there, you'll have to install it before the liner goes in. Shower blocking can be made from any board that can be fit between the studs and secured in place. It acts not only as a backer but as a nailer for the new shower pan liner you'll be installing. (Figure 74)

Figure 74: Backing blocks are added between the studs.

Curb Framing

The shower curb or dam can be built of stacked framing members, usually 2 x 4s, or it can be made of a single member installed on edge. I like the on-edge method because it allows me to build curbs considerably narrower than those in which the members have been stacked. The narrower curbs seem more attractive to me. Using the single member on edge, it is possible to build curbs that are modular to standard tile trim pieces such as the radius bull nose (A-4200). Radius bull nose pieces are also called mud caps. (Figure 75)

The stacked method, on the other hand, better accommodates shower openings that contain door jambs with their accompanying side walls. Since the walls

Figure 75: A single 2 by 4 laid on edge forms this curb.

are normally constructed from 2 x 4s, it makes sense to continue that width through the curb area.

Shower curbs can also be made from bricks or concrete block rubble, but this method is more time-consuming than wood framing. It is also a bit harder to ensure the shower pan liner will end up where you want it. Let's stick with the wood.

In all of my shower framing I use screws driven with an electric drill, and I recommend you give it a try. The screws I use are intended for drywall, but they work for framing as well. You will find that walls which have been screwed together are much stiffer than those which have been nailed. Nails can be used, but effort is needed to keep things from flopping around under the continual impact of the hammer.

Bent Studs

It is possible to correct badly bent framing members without removing them from the wall. This is often necessary because removing members might cause damage in adjacent rooms. If the stud is bent inward, or toward you, you can cut a narrow notch into its front edge, about two-thirds of the way into the stud. You can then push against it and at the same time screw a sister to the side of it to hold it in place. The sister or "scab" should extend at least a foot and a half beyond the saw cut in both directions. If the stud is bowed out, and you want to pull it in toward you, a single cut into the edge is all that is needed, once again, about two-thirds of the way into the member. You can drive a screw into the stud and pull on it with a claw hammer. Screw the scab in place while holding the stud straight, and you've got it.

It is not always desirable to straighten bent framing members in the foregoing manner. Doing so may damage the finished wall on the other side of the stud. In this case it is better to straighten only the edge of the stud that faces the shower. You can plane or sand down a stud that is bent inward, and you can install shims of wood to fill the hollow of a stud that is bent outward.. The mud method will accommodate studs that are only slightly bent, while showers built with other methods will depend on perfectly flat and true framing for their final appearance.

Plumbing

A certain amount of plumbing will be required in every shower remodel. At the very least the shower pan liner will be replaced, and often the drain fixture will be changed along with it. It may be desirable to relocate the shower drain. Now's the time to do it. You may also choose to replace the shower valve while you have the wall open. You may even want to install a second valve and shower head while you're at it.

How about a toe tester? You don't know what a toe tester is? It's simply a spout that comes out of the wall at the very bottom of the shower. It works off a diverter the same way a tub/shower spout works. When you turn the shower on, the water comes out of the lower spout until you divert it up to the shower head. This allows you to place a foot under the running water to test its temperature. I don't like the idea myself, but some do.

Shower Drains

In many cases, the existing shower drain can be re-used. All that will be needed is a new hair strainer, since that is all that is seen of the drain after the new shower has been built. In other situations the drain fixture itself will be replaced. In some cases the drain will be broken or rusted to the point that it is not worth re-using. And you may find that a proper drain was not used the first time around. I've found all sorts of drains in showers I've torn out, many of them designed and intended for laundry tubs or for floors not associated with showers.

The drain you'll need is called a "clamping drain" or "flanged drain," and it is sometimes referred to as an FHA drain. The drain will be composed of two or three pieces and will be made from metal or plastic. I like plastic (PVC) drains. They won't rust, and they are easy to install. Plastic drains incorporate metal hair strainers, and as I said, that's all you'll see of the finished job.[11] (Figure 76)

The clamping drain consists of a lower flange that is attached to the drain pipe or "riser" and an upper flange that is bolted on after the shower pan has been installed. Some drains have threaded inserts that allow the height of the hair strainer to be adjusted, hence the third part. How the lower flange is attached to the riser depends on the type of drain being used, the material that the riser is made of and the type of connector or glue used to complete the attachment.

Metal to metal connections might be made with lead, with screw threads, or with rubber couplings that clamp onto both parts with screw-tightened hose clamps. Plastic drains are mounted on plastic risers with the appropriate glue. If both parts are PVC, PVC pipe glue is used. If one part is ABS and one part

Figure 76: Flanged drain components: threaded insert with hair strainer; upper (clamping) flange; and lower flange with bolts.

Figure 77: PVC drain assembled and mounted onto riser pipe.

PVC, it is better to use a rubber coupling such as those made by Fernco™. It is also possible to mount metal drains on plastic risers and plastic drains on metal risers. It won't be possible to cover every drain situation here. If you are not an experienced plumber, you may find it helpful to acquire a plumbing manual. (Figures 77, 78)

And never forget that you can log onto the JB Forums for advice on plumbing and every other aspect of shower building. http://johnbridge.com/vbulletin/index.php.

Installing a New Shower Drain

Installing a shower drain, while it's not quite as easy as falling off a log, is a project that can be accomplished by just about anyone who possesses a basic knowledge of hand tools and understands that waste water runs downward. In fact, the larger drain problem in a shower remodel is usually getting the old drain off the drain pipe or "riser." Once the old one has been removed, installing the new one is a snap.

---

[11]*The Federal Housing Authority (FHA) sets forth standards for homes built that will receive government financing in the United States.*

One situation in which the drain will always be changed occurs when one wants to remove a bath tub and replace it with a stand-up shower. Tub drains are most always located at one end of the tub and very close to the wall. A tiled shower, on the other hand, requires a drain that is more centrally located. Trying to create a functional tiled shower floor when the drain is close to a wall is a challenge to say the least, and further, even if one does succeed, the result will not be eye-pleasing.

The scope of the project, then, is to cut out the drain and the trap below it and install new piping to a new centrally located drain. In this instance the sub-floor happens to be concrete, but wood floor plumbing is very similar. The piping in the concrete floor happens to be PVC Schedule 40. To break out the concrete it is best to rent (hire) a small electric jackhammer. I've tried it with a hammer and chisel, but I've never had a lot of success using that method. I suspect it's very similar to trying to dig one's way out of prison.

Cutting plastic pipe is fairly simple. A hack saw or even a short wood-cutting saw can be used, and an electric reciprocating saw will make short work of the procedure. There are also small cable or "wire" saws that can be wrapped around the pipe and pulled from both ends. The biggest problem in cutting any drain pipe is finding or creating the space in which to use the cutting tool.

Our existing drain goes into a short riser which is in turn connected to a water trap ("P" trap). From the trap a more or less

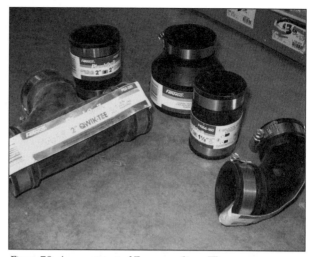

Figure 78: An assortment of Fernco couplings. There are many more.

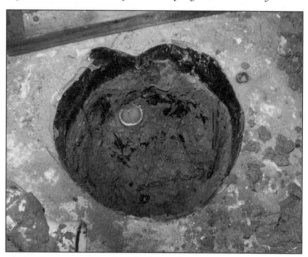

Figure 79: Old tub drain prior to breaking out the concrete slab.

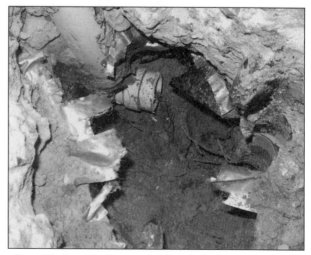

Figure 80: Slab is broken out and old drain line has been removed.

horizontal waste line goes down into a vertical waste/vent pipe. We will cut the entire assembly out right at the point it enters the waste/vent system. We will be careful to leave enough pipe projecting from the waste/vent to allow for the fitting of a new "elbow," from which all the new drain plumbing will proceed. (Figures 79, 80)

We'll connect the elbow and then dry fit all the remaining parts until we arrive at the new drain in its proper position. Some of the elbows in this installation are "eighth bends," fittings that turn 45 degrees (135 degrees in tile parlance). There is a "quarter-bend" or 90 degree turn installed onto the stub coming out of the waste/vent and another which forms a part of the trap. A collection of very short pipe segments or "nipples" completes the assembly.

It is essential that all horizontal pipe segments be pitched slightly toward the waste/vent pipe. A slope of

Figure 81: New drain line being assembled.

1/8 in. is adequate, but 1/4 in. is more prudent. Do not for a moment consider installing a segment with a reverse pitch. I know I shouldn't have to say this, and I know you would never consider doing such a foolish thing, but there's a guy looking over your shoulder who doesn't look too sure of himself. This is directed at him, not you.

Once all the pieces have been dry fitted, we'll take everything apart and lay the pieces out in their proper sequence. We will then begin assembling the pieces from the waste/vent pipe and work our way toward the drain. First, coat all the connecting sur-

faces with PVC pipe primer (purple primer). The primer ensures the connections will be free of contaminants that might prevent the glue from working properly. It also takes the smoothness off the surface of the parts, and this allows for better bonding.

After the primer has dried, begin assembling the parts by coating first one and then the other bonding surface. This means you'll not only coat the outside of a piece of pipe but also the inside of the connector into which it will be inserted. In plumbing terms, you will coat both the "male" and the "female"

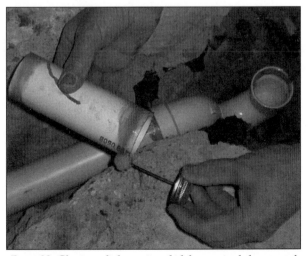

Figure 82: Glue is applied to a pipe which has previously been treated with purple primer.

surfaces to be connected. (Figure 81)

As you make each connection, hold it in place until the glue takes hold. This only takes a minute or so. In some cases you'll have to make two or more connections simultaneously. There is no problem doing this. The glue allows adequate time to get things in place before it takes hold. (Figure 82)

Eventually, the trap is fitted and finally the lower flange of the drain itself. It is advisable to disassemble the drain before cementing the lower flange. This will allow you to avoid the embarrassing experience of inadvertently gluing the upper and lower drain flanges together.

As you glue the lower flange, riser and trap together, hold the drain flange level until the glue sets. Because the horizontal sections of pipe are sloped toward the waste system, the vertical pieces or risers will tend to tilt out of plumb. It's therefore necessary to "tweak" the connections a bit in order to end up with a level drain. I use a small torpedo level to ensure that the assembly slopes toward the waste system and also to test the level of the drain flange itself. Hold everything in place for at least five minutes. I usually chock bits of rubble or small pieces of wood in place to hold things while the glue takes its final set. (Figures 83, 84)

Figure 83: Disassemble the drain before applying glue to the lower flange.

Figure 84: Use a level to ensure the drain is set correctly.

Back-fill the excavation up to within about four or five inches of the surface and fill the remainder with concrete mix or with mortar.

It is possible and advisable to replace old cast iron waste plumbing with PVC or ABS plastic. All that is needed is a rubber connector that will couple the old to the new. The Fernco fittings mentioned above will do the trick.[12]

Shower Valves

Shower valves have always come in various sizes and arrangements, but nowadays there exists an array of gadgets that have been incorporated into them. There are built-in temperature controls, sensors, diverters and other knobs, buttons, whistles and bells.

---

[12]*Among other places, Fernco does business in the U.S., Canada and the U.K. http://www.fernco.com*

Alex

Steven Kayser

J. Reynolds

*Vanessa Sorensen and
George Farnsworth*

Better Bench™

We won't be covering the entire field here. I can help you along with the basic connections, though.

Copper Pipes

Working with copper is easy once you understand how solder works. The pipes are "sweated" together using lead-free solder and flux. You will need a propane torch with a good nozzle on it in order to connect copper piping.

Turn off the water.

Cut the old valve out of the piping with a small pipe cutter which can be purchased at any hardware store, home center or plumbing supply. In some cases it becomes necessary to cut the pipes with a hacksaw due to space constrictions. There may not be enough room to "swing" the pipe cutter. In any case, we're going to cut the old valve out of the wall completely. It is not all that important where the pipes are cut, since it is a simple matter to join new pieces onto existing pipes. (Figure 85)

In many cases it's possible to re-use some of the fittings from the old installation, and we're going to do that. Our new valve is set up with pipe thread type connections that will require the use of copper pipe thread adaptors. The ones taken from the old valve are perfectly serviceable. We'll clean the pipe stubs thoroughly and then screw the adaptors into the new valve, one on the left or hot water side and one on the right, which is always the cold water side of a valve or faucet set. We'll wrap the adaptor threads with Teflon tape to ensure a good seal. Pipe joint compound can also be used, but it's much more messy. (Figures 86, 87)

Figure 85: Old valve is simply cut out of wall cavity.

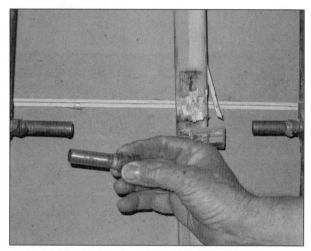

Figure 86: The old pipe adapters are cleaned for re-use.

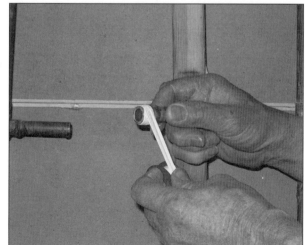

Figure 87: Teflon tape is used on the threads.

We'll be slipping straight couplings over the end of the pipe stubs, but before we do, we'll need to brush on a liberal coating of soldering flux. The flux paste can be bought wherever plumbing supplies are sold. Make sure you apply the flux all the way around the pipe, which has already been cleaned and burnished with fine sand paper or abrasive cloth.

Now, burnish the pipes in the wall that the new fixture will be attached to. It's important to get all the way down to new copper. (Figures 88, 89, 90)

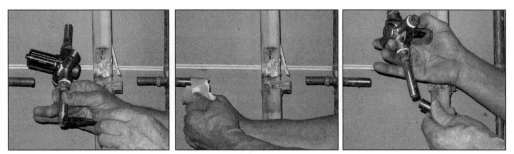

Figure 88: New valve is fitted with pipe adapters and flux is applied to ends.

Figure 89: Use sandpaper to burnish the pipes that will be joined.

Figure 90: Straight couplings are used to make the connections.

It will often be impractical to wait for the piping system to completely drain, and it is essential that no water, not even a drop, be present when the actual soldering is being done. Water when heated causes steam, and steam will cause pinholes in our soldered joint. An old plumber's trick is to stuff tightly rolled wads of white bread up the pipes in the wall to prevent water from dripping through during the soldering process. Make sure the bread fits snuggly. Push it up the pipe a few inches with a pencil or a screwdriver just prior to sweating the joint. Now let me give you a little tip here. Don't use whole wheat bread or any other bread that contains fragments of grains. The grain particles will block the new valve when the water has been turned on. This is another case in which I would prefer you not ask how I know this.

So with the water completely blocked, the ends of the pipes burnished and treated with flux, we'll install the valve in the wall by slipping couplings over the joints. Apply a liberal coating of flux inside the couplings also. Get the valve in place and prop it in the plumb position. A small torpedo level is useful in getting the valve in the right position. Either wire the valve in place or have your helper hold it with a pair of pliers while you do the soldering. Have a container of water on hand in case you light the wall on fire with your torch. Once again, please don't ask.

A trick is to line the wall cavity with aluminum foil. A couple layers will prevent the small flame from the torch from igniting the wood framing in the wall. Make sure you remove all insulation from the general area. You can re-install it after the pipes have cooled.

The key to successfully sweating copper pipes together is in knowing when and how much heat to apply to the joint. It is very worthwhile to practice making joints with extra fittings and spare sections of pipe. The parts are inexpensive.

Unroll about a foot of soldering wire. Ignite the torch and adjust it to run as hot as possible. A steady bluish flame is what you're looking for. Apply the flame to the pipe about a half inch away from the fitting and hold it there a few seconds. When you see the flux bubbling from the joint, try touching the end of the wire to the juncture of the fitting and the pipe, all the time holding the flame to the pipe. (Figure 91)

Figure 91: Heat is applied to a coupling. Try not to burn the house down.

If the correct heat level has been reached, you'll see the solder being sucked into the joint. If that doesn't occur, simply wait a few more seconds and try again. As soon as the solder is sucked into the joint, move the torch to the other side of the fitting and repeat the process. The solder will be taken into the joint in such a manner that it will completely encircle the pipe and fitting. When this has occurred, remove the heat. You've done it. Practice on several spare fittings before you attack the actual plumbing in the wall.

When the joints have cooled, you can screw in your shower "riser" and insert a temporary capped pipe where the shower arm will eventually be. Turn on the water and check for leaks. The leaks, if any, will be fine sprays of water and somewhat hard to see. Make sure you check very thoroughly. If a leak is detected, it's necessary to completely drain the system once again. You can undo the offending connection by applying heat

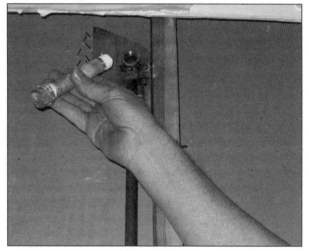

Figure 92: A capped nipple is inserted into the shower head fitting.

to it, but it's much easier to simply cut it out and replace it with a new one. Do not attempt to add more solder to a leaking joint. It just won't work.

When you have assured yourself you have no leaks, you can remove the cap from the "nipple" at the shower head and purge the bread from the pipes by turning the valve from hot to cold several times. Or, you can wait until the shower is complete. I would do it now just in case something gets caught in the system. It's much easier to purge the valve now that the new tile isn't in the way.

Now don't tell me you used that pumpernickel you had in the bread box. I told you to use white bread! (Figure 92)

It is important to protect copper pipes from nails and screws that could be driven into them as the wallboard is applied. Be sure to use the metal shields designed for this purpose. (Figure 93)

Galvanized Steel Pipes

Galvanized pipe is the old standby when it comes to household plumbing, and it's still a good choice but much harder to work with than copper. Pipes and fittings must be threaded, for one thing, and that usually presents a problem to the novice plumber who has no means of threading. Pre-cut and pre-threaded sections of pipe are available, though, at plumbing supply houses, hardware stores and at home centers. Also, pieces of pipe can be carted to the plumbing store to have them threaded, but careful and accurate measuring is crucial.

Figure 93: Pipe shields are installed where pipes pass through studs.

Shower valves installed in a galvanized system require "unions" on either side. In some cases, it's possible to install the valve with only one union. A union is a connection that can be undone without twisting the pipes on either side of it. (Figure 93A)

Shower Pan Installation

Shower "pans" have never been actual pans, and there has always been a great deal of misunderstanding as to what the "pan" does. Allow me to provide you with a little lesson in terminology. Shower pans are made from pliable material that is completely hidden from view when the shower is complete. Molded plastic shower bases are not shower

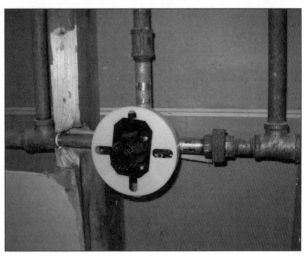

Figure 93A: A "union" is used to make the final connection in the galvanized installation.

"pans." They are bases or "receptors." The same goes for terrazzo and marble bases.

A pan might be formed from lead or copper sheeting, or it could be made up of layers of asphalt roofing material laminated together with molten tar. Most modern shower pans are made from plastic sheeting, either CPE or PVC. PVC pans are the more prevalent, and this is the pan we will focus on. The other materials are installed in essentially the same manner, except for the roofing material method, which is referred to as "hot mopped." Hot mopping, which is still widely used in California and a few other spots, is not a do-it-yourself process.

PVC pan liner material is produced in different gauges – 20, 30 and 40 mils. I recommend the 40 mil material, and as a matter of fact, it is that material that is required by the majority of local building authorities around the U.S. and Canada. I have been installing PVC pans for the 30 years I've been in the business, and they were in use at least a decade before I entered the trade. I have never known a PVC liner to fail if properly installed. Further, PVC material is easily found throughout the country. (Figure 94)

Pre-Slope: Once the lower flange of the shower drain is in place, the next step in the shower building process is to provide a "pre-slope" for the shower liner to rest upon. If the pan were to lie flat on the floor there would be dips in which water might collect.

That water needs to be channeled toward the weep holes in the drain. Water that is trapped in dips becomes brackish and is a contributing factor to mold growth.

The pre-slope is constructed from deck mud (also called floor mud), which is made with portland cement and clean sand. The ratio of the mix is about 5:1, that's five parts sand to one part portland cement. Water is limited to the amount it takes to moisten the mix and cause it to hold together when clumped in the palm of the hand. I refer to deck mud or floor mud as "sandcastle material." Too much water and it gets mushy and hard to work. Too little water and it's dry and won't hold together.

We are talking about the same deck mud that was used in the previous section on using mud screeds for tile floor applications. Oh, you didn't read that portion of the book? Back you go, my friend.

Figure 94: PVC shower pan material is sold by the lineal foot.

You can make your mud from the ingredients above or you can buy it pre-packaged. A number of companies sell mixtures of sand and cement. A common one in the U.S. is Quikrete™ Sand Topping Mix. I use the Quikrete product often, but I find it a bit "rich," meaning it contains too much cement to suit me. I usually add a little clean sand to the mix to get it closer to the 5:1 ratio that I consider ideal. You will eventually form your shower floor from the same mortar, so you could take this opportunity to buy enough to do the whole job. We are about to discuss how to determine the amount of deck mud you'll need, but I'll tell you now that if you decide to use the pre-packaged material, one 80 pound sack will usually do the pre-slope. Sand Topping Mix is also sold in 60 pound sacks.

Additionally, you can often purchase "floor mud" mix from tile supply stores. (Figure 95)

Determining the amount of material you'll need is not too difficult if you can once again recall a little of that old elementary school math. Let's say the shower floor will end up 2 inches thick overall – that's a pretty good guess. To come up with cubic feet you'll need to figure the area of the floor – length times width, remember? Say the floor is 4 feet by 3 feet. That comes to 12 square feet, each of them 2 inches thick. It will take

Figure 95: Quickrete Sand Topping Mix is simply a mixture of sand and portland cement.

6 of these 2-inch thick square feet to make 1 cubic foot. So a cubic foot accounts for 6 of our 12 square feet, and the remaining 6 feet will amount to another cubic foot, giving us a grand total of 2 cubic feet of shower floor material. I know you didn't need me to lead you by the hand through that exercise in basic arithmetic. I did it only to hone my own skills.

Manufacturers sell cement products by volume or by the pound. You'll need enough material to fill two cubic feet — plus a little reserve for inaccurate estimating. Maybe the floor will be 2-1/4 inches thick instead of 2 inches. You will be mixing only about a quarter of this material for the pre-slope. The rest

Figure 96: On wood subfloors metal lath or other reinforcing is nailed over a moisture barrier of either tar paper or plastic sheeting.

will be used to complete the upper portion of the shower floor after the walls have been attended to.

On wood sub-floors, a moisture barrier of either tar paper (roofing felt) or plastic sheeting is laid down. Over it a piece of expanded metal lath or chicken wire (poultry netting) is placed and stapled or nailed. Cut a hole in the reinforcing for the drain. (Figure 96)

On concrete floors the deck mud will be bonded directly to the sub-floor. No other reinforcing is necessary. I like to use thin set as a bonder. I sprinkle it on the concrete and then wet it by sprinkling water on it with a sponge just prior to dumping the mud. You want to get your bonder covered before it has a chance to dry out. Remember to plug the drain. We don't want any cement products in the trap.

Dump all of the mud at once and spread it around with either a flat trowel or a wood float if you are bonding your mortar to a concrete floor. It's important to get your thin set bonder covered before it has a chance to begin drying out. If you are working over a wood floor covered with lath, it's easier to pour mortar around the perimeter, build your screeds and then fill in the area between the walls and the drain.

Push the mud against the walls all the way around. Using your level, or your level in conjunction with a straight-edge, figure the amount of slope from the top of the drain to the walls and the curb. The ideal is1/4 inch per running foot of floor, but this will vary from wall to wall depending

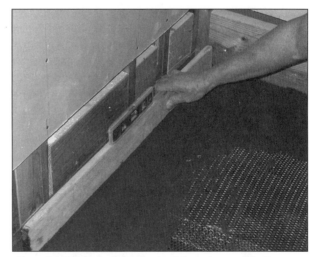

Figure 97: Form a level screed around the perimeter of the floor.

on the position of the drain. The important thing is that there is some pitch everywhere. Say the run to the longest wall is two feet. I would want at least a half inch of slope or pitch in that direction. Three-quarters of an inch would not be too much.

Keep the mortar level all the way around the perimeter of the shower no matter what slope that causes in the various quadrants of the floor. Use your level to create a mud "screed" near the walls and the curb. The screed is what will guide you as you smooth off the remainder of the floor and slope it to the drain. (Figure 97)

Figure 98: Use straightedges to shape the area between the drain and the perimeter screed.

When you have completed your screed at the perimeter, pack down the remainder of the mud and begin scraping it down and smoothing it out with a short straight-edge. You might also use a wood float, if you have one, to pack and smooth the mortar. If you have 1/4 inch per foot slope to your furthest wall, the slope to the shorter walls will be greater, but that's okay. Keep the perimeter level at all cost. (Figure 98)

Michael Byrne, author of *Setting Tile* (Taunton Press, 1995), has come up with the idea of using thin rippings of wood, cut to the height he wants the pre-slope to be at its perimeter. He nails the strips of wood to the floor or to the sole plates and uses them as "grounds" or guides as he shapes the floor. This, of course, eliminates the need for mud screeds. The rippings are left in place and covered by the shower pan material.

What you are looking for is a smooth and uniform slope from the walls to the drain flange. It's important to not have any depressions along the way which might invite pools of water ("bird baths") to form in the installed shower pan material. If you inadvertently build a bird bath, go back and pack in a little more mud and smooth it off.

When you are satisfied that your pre-slope is as good as it will ever be, smooth the surface with your flat trowel. (Figure 99)

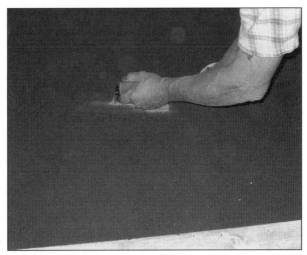

Clean your tools, and take a break. You may stand around a while, because you won't be installing the liner until morning. It'll take overnight for the mud to harden. Do remember to maintain your composure as you stand around. Pre-sloping shower pans really isn't much of a chore for a mud man/woman like yourself, but that's no reason to convey to others that the job can be done by just anyone. It might be a good idea to effect a short sigh of relief

Figure 99: When the floor has been shaped, use your flat trowel to smooth the surface and embed loose particles of sand.

that the job is finished and wipe a little imaginary sweat from your brow.

Pan Liner Installation:
You could draw lines on the pan material and measure it this way and that, but I never do it that way. I've found that simply having a piece of material the right size and folding it into the shower bottom works pretty well. You will need enough material to cover the shower floor, plus enough to go up the walls all the way around to a height that is about two inches above the top of your rough curb. This equates

Figure 100: Place the shower pan in the shower.

to a minimum of 6 inches of material going up the walls all the way around. A little more won't hurt.

So let's say, once again, that our floor is 3 feet by 4 feet. Adding 6 inches for the walls, we will need a piece of material that is 4 feet by 5 feet. On the curb side the material needs to come up and over the top to a point that will be outside the shower door or curtain. Six inches will handle it, but eight inches will handle it better.

Remove the rag or other stopper from the drain. Fold the edges of the material inward and place it in the shower. As you unfold it, you can center the liner in the shower, measuring the distance it travels up the walls. When you have the material centered begin stapling it or nailing it along the back wall. Be careful to nail only at the very top of the material. You don't want any holes down near the level of the curb. It is for this reason that some local building authorities specify that the liner end 3 inches above the curb instead of two. They reason that you'll be nailing in the top inch of material and that you'll still have 2 inches left above the curb when you've finished. (Figure 100)

You can now nail the material

Figure 101: Fold the corners carefully.

at the two adjacent walls but only toward the middle of the segments. You'll need some slack in order to make the corner folds. Fold the material in the corners so that there are no wrinkles or unnecessary gathers and staple or nail the folds at the top of the material. Many shower pan installers apply a little construction glue behind the folds to help hold the material flat against the blocking. (Figure 101)

Work around through the other corners, if any, or to the curb. The folds at the curb will depend upon whether you have jamb returns in your shower or whether your shower is of the three-wall variety with the curb going from wall to wall at the front. If you have the jamb returns you will slit the liner material alongside the jambs so that it will lay over the top of the curb. Then glue the dam corners in place with the special PVC liner cement. (Figures 102, 103, 104)

If your curb goes from wall to wall you will have to fold the material against the wall as if you

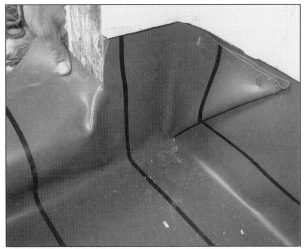

Figure 102: Cut the liner material so it will lay over the top of the curb.

Figure 103: Glue the dam corners in place with vinyl pan liner cement.

Figure 104: Each company that produces PVC shower pans also supplies adhesive.

were making a normal turn at a corner. Staple or nail the folded material against the wall and make a slit down to the top of the curb. You can then fold the liner over the curb and install the dam corners.

In showers that have wall-to-wall curbs you can install the liner without the benefit of dam corners when building a mud shower. It is possible to slit the liner further out at a point that will be well beyond where the door will be installed. In this case, the material is folded at the curb instead of against the wall, and it can then be stretched into position. The process places a slight bulge in the material at the wall, but there will be plenty of room to accommodate it. There would not be room for the bulge were you building a backer board shower directly over the studs. (Figure 105)

Bring the material over the top of the curb and down its front face as far as it will reach. The wood rough curb will have to be completely covered, but plastic sheeting can be substituted for liner material outside the point where the shower door will reside. Secure the liner only at the very edge or anywhere on the front outside surface of the rough curb.

You can now cut through the material over the drain hole. Careful here. Start with a small hole and enlarge it when you can see through to the interior of the drain pipe. The hole should be the exact size of the opening. Now notch around the bolts, again very carefully. (Figure 106)

When the drain has been cut in, lift the liner and make a bead of caulking all the way around the lower flange near its outside edge. It's hard to see under the liner, so take your time and make sure you get a continuous bead. Butyl or silicone caulking can be used. (Figure 107)

Place the upper drain flange over the bolts and tighten them gently. Do not crank down on only one bolt but work your way around the flange tightening them all as you go. Don't over tighten the bolts. Twist them down firmly, but don't place a lot of pressure on them. I would guess that you only want about 10 foot/pounds of torque. If you don't know what that means, just snug the bolts down and set them firmly. Then leave them alone. This is especially important on plastic drains. Over-tightening the bolts can actually warp the upper flange and cause the connection to leak. (Figure 108)

Observe the weep holes and make sure they do not become

Figure 105: It is possible to slightly stretch the material and omit dam corners on three-wall showers.

Figure 106: Carefully cut around drain and bolt holes.

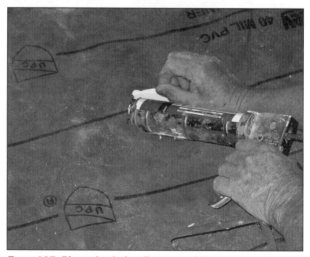

Figure 107: Place a bead of caulking around the perimeter of the bottom flange.

clogged with caulking. If they do, remove the upper flange and clean the holes out. It is crucial that the holes remain clear.

That's it. You have successfully installed your shower pan liner – maybe. I know you didn't make any holes in the material while you were working. I trust you, but you shouldn't trust yourself. You should fill the base of the shower with water and leave it overnight to make sure it doesn't leak.

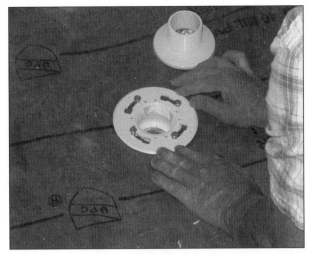

Figure 108: Install the upper flange.

You must plug the drain at a point that is below the weep holes. You can buy a special inflatable stopper at a plumbing shop, or you can use a child's party balloon. Inflate the balloon to just over the drain pipe diameter (2 inches in the U.S.) and ease it down the drain until it pops. Then inflate balloon number two and try it again. I usually get one in place on about the third try. Fortunately, you can't buy only one balloon. They usually come in packs of about a hundred. Don't worry about the burst balloons going down the drain. They will not cause a problem.

Figure 108A: Neo-angle curbs can be built from one member installed on edge or from 3 or 4 stacked members.

If you attempt to plug the drain higher up, the water will merely run through the weep holes and you will have proved nothing, so do get your stopper low enough. Now fill the base of the shower with water. A couple inches will do. Place a mark at the waterline on one of the walls. You can check the installation in the morning. I can almost guarantee you, though, you won't find a leak, so sleep tight. You are well on your way to becoming an accomplished plumber of the home-grown variety.

Extra-large Pans: Vinyl shower pan material is available in four-, five-, six-, and eight-foot widths, and the length can be what you want it to be, since the material comes on a roll. The eight-foot widths will have to be special ordered.

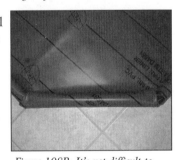

Figure 108B: It's not difficult to make reasonable folds for the neo-angle curb.

Additionally, it is possible to seam the material to make liners for larger showers by using the special seam glue that is made by the company producing the liner material. This is the same glue that is used to install the dam corners (above). You should follow the instructions on the glue can when seaming the material. It is not difficult work, but it must be done diligently.

Neo-angle Showers: Some showers have tile on only one or two walls and glass enclosures making up the

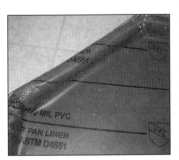

Figure 108C: Lath is pre-bent to fit the curb.

other sides. For these showers it is usually necessary to build a curb that contains more than one segment. The process is a bit more involved than that for a simple straight curb, but you can handle it.

Begin by framing the curb. As I've stated, I like a single-member curb, but you could make one with stacked 2 x 4s as well. The important thing is to get the segments square to the walls. (Figure 108A)

The shower pan is merely folded to make the turns. I know of no company that makes neo-angle dam corners. (Figure 108B)

Metal lath (or chicken wire) is pre-bent to fit snuggly over the curb. It is nailed only at the outside of the curb. (Figure 108C)

Plastic Shower Bases

Plastic bases are often used in tile showers where tile floors are not desired. Are plastic bases as good as tile shower floors? Of course not, but some people don't feel up to the rigors of doing tile floors, and others actually prefer the plastic base. I can't understand it, but it happens.

The bases are many times described as "acrylic" bases, and sometimes the term "fiberglass" is used. Fiberglass is only one element of the base, which is actually made from fiberglass reinforced plastic or "FRP." Additionally, acrylic is plastic, right? So let's just call the things plastic bases. The plumbing term for them is "receptors."

There are several very important things to check for when purchasing a plastic base, the least important of which is price. First of all, make sure there is a vertical "lip" going all the way around the wall sides of the unit. This lip or "flange" is there to keep water from going under the tiled wall and getting into the framing. The flange should end about midway across the curb area at both ends of the curb.

Make sure that the underside of the base is well braced with molded-in ribbing to help hold it firm when someone stands in it. It's also important that the plastic is thick enough to prevent excessive flexing, as this flexing will eventually lead to material fatigue and ultimate failure.

Now I mentioned that price is the least important of the things that need to be looked at when buying an FRP shower receptor. However, I would not buy the cheapest receptor I could find, and I would not buy one made by a company that no one has ever heard of. If you are going to build a very expensive and time consuming shower above it, it makes sense to use a quality receptor. Most of the major companies that produce bath tubs also produce plastic showers and shower receptors. I would spend that little extra and get my base from someone who is well-known in the field and who is likely to stand behind the product.

Not all shower receptors are made from acrylic or fiberglass, of course. The Swan Corporation of St. Louis makes high-quality bases from its own proprietary materials. The folks at Swan have been gracious enough to allow me to use the instruction guide they display on their web site. You will find it in Appendix VI at the back of the book.

Closing the Walls

Wake up! Rise and shine!

By installing the shower pan you have completed the rough plumbing portion of the shower. It is now almost time to become a mud man or mud woman who muds walls and not just floors. We've got a couple small chores to do before we engage in that most satisfying of occupations, though.

Replace any insulation that was removed during the course of demolition, and add insulation to outside walls where needed. Any insulation that has been water damaged must be removed and replaced. Fiberglass insulation is effective and inexpensive. Get either plain fiberglass batts or rolled insulation with the paper face. Foil faced insulation isn't needed, as you'll be adding a moisture barrier after closing the walls.

You will close up the open walls with sheetrock/plaster board/wall board/gyprock. You don't have to be particularly accurate in nailing the stuff up; just use plenty of nails or screws. The wall board performs only one function, and that is to support the metal reinforcing as it goes up. Don't bother taping and finishing the joints and angles that will be covered by the tile installation. It is, however, advantageous to finish the portions of the walls that will remain exposed when the tile work has been completed, but drywall taping and finishing can be done later as well.

It is important to note where your piping and wiring are located before you begin screwing or nailing your wallboard on. If you have any of the aforementioned within reach of nails or screws, be sure to use sheet metal stud shields over those areas. The inexpensive shields can be purchased anywhere building hardware is sold.

Layout for Mortar

Using a pencil and your level, mark off the area to be tiled. Keep the lines back from the edge of the area to be tiled by about half an inch. This is so the mortar won't interfere with the trim pieces you will later install. You can calculate how high your shower will be (if it's not going to the ceiling) by laying out a row of tiles on the floor and measuring them. Make sure the tiles are spaced the same as they will be when installed, and don't forget to account for the bull nose or other trim at the top. Have you provided space for the listello or liner?

Also remember that your shower floor will be about an inch and a half higher than the pan. Hold your top (level) lines down into the area to be tiled about 3/4 of an inch. These lines are merely intended as a limit for the mortar. You'll make much more precise measurements before you begin tiling.

There is one exception to the loose layout lines procedure, and that occurs in the instances when quarter-round trims are to be used instead of bull-nose pieces. Quarter-rounds have a very limited bonding surface which requires that about a quarter-inch of mortar protrude beyond where the field tiles will stop. If quarter-rounds are to be used you must figure your layout lines precisely. Too much mortar hanging out and you may end up having to chop it off, which is tedious; and too little mortar and you'll have nothing to bond your quarter-rounds to. You could, of course, add mortar to the edge, but it's not easy to bond it to the previously installed mortar, and it does impose additional labor.

Moisture Barrier

When your layout lines are complete, you must cover the entire area to be tiled with either plastic sheeting or tar paper (15 lb. roofing felt). This material will act as a moisture barrier behind the mortar. Install it right up to the lines you've just made, but don't go past them.

Obviously, the moisture barrier will not be waterproof, since you'll be making numerous holes through it as you attach it and the reinforcing that goes over it. The moisture barrier will, however, protect the wall board and prevent significant amounts of water from reaching it in the event that water penetrates behind the tile. I like to use plastic because it takes up less space than the roofing paper, and I can apply perhaps a millimeter or two more of mud. Every little bit helps. (Figure 109)

Waterproofing Knee Walls

Instead of using poly or tar paper as a moisture barrier on top of low walls, I use a piece of PVC shower pan material. The knee wall or bulkhead is, after all, merely a high curb. Fasten the material at the outside of the wall, well beyond where the glass enclosure with reside. Pull the material over and down the inside of the wall a few inches and tack it there. Make no holes in the horizontal portion of the material. Later, metal lath will be attached over the liner material in exactly the same fashion. (Figure 109A)

Figure 109: A moisture barrier is installed over the sheetrock.

Reinforcing

With the moisture barrier in place, begin installing metal lath or chicken wire. Begin at one extreme or edge of the shower and work your way around. On three-wall showers, it's best to work from both outside edges toward the middle of the back wall. You will be installing vertical pieces of wood lattice, called "float strips," about six to eight inches out from the corners of the shower. It's helpful to avoid overlaps in those areas, as the double thickness of lath or wire might prevent the float strips from being tapped in where you want them.

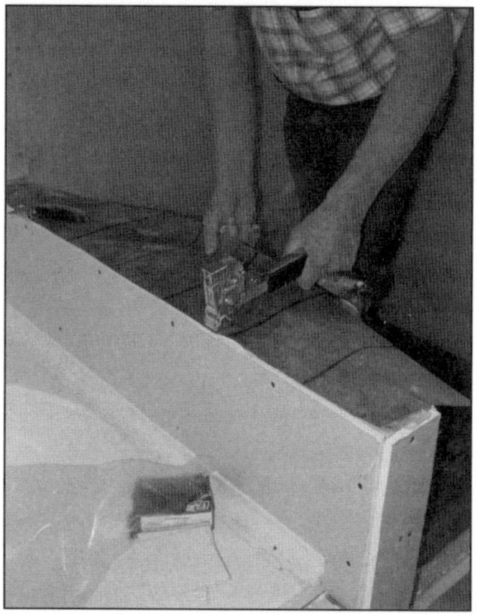

On showers that have door jamb returns, I usually begin lathing inside the shower and then do the jambs last. It's easier to bend narrow strips of lath around the jambs and overlap them on the walls than it is to bend full sheets of lath or wire.

Figure 109A: Fasten the material only at the outside edge.

The reinforcing must be overlapped a minimum of two inches at all joints. This allows for continuity in the completed armature. When finished, your mud shower will be a unit, a monolith that contains no joints whatever, at least not in the armature.

Staples or nails should be about six inches apart in both directions. It is not necessary to nail through the sheetrock into the studs, and staples are much easier to use than nails. I use staples that reach into the wall at least 3/8 of an inch. Most tile stores carry one-half inch staples. I prefer using a hammer-tacker, but the squeeze type staplers will do the job equally as well.

You can crease the lath or chicken wire to fit snuggly into the corners by using the head of your hammer or your snips as the creasing tool. This is done by nailing the lath to one wall and forcing it into the corner as far as you can. Then run the creasing tool up and down the material, making a straight crease exactly in the corner. Holding the material into the corner with one hand, begin nailing it to the other wall. You will have to use a few extra staples in the corners to hold the material flat against the wallboard.

And when using a hammer-tacker, I can tell you from experience it's not a good idea to get your fingers in the way. Ouch! (Figure 110)

You can cut small pieces of lath to be used at junctures where horizontal surfaces meet vertical ones. An example would be where the curb adjoins the walls or the door jambs. Lay the pieces over the lath that has already been installed and staple them to the walls, not to the curb top. Again, this allows for continuity. No two pieces of reinforcing are simply butted together. Everything is overlapped and thus made continuous. (Figure 111)

Do not drive any fasteners through the shower pan material below where you've tacked it into place at its top edge. The lath that extends beyond this point will not be attached at all. It will merely drape down to within an inch or so of the floor. Mortar will eventually hold the material against the wall portions of the liner.

Figure 110: Install the reinforcing.

The lath that covers the curb will be pre-formed and attached only to the front outside face of the curb. No penetrations can be made into the curb top or into it's inside face. All fasteners must be outside the point where the shower doors will reside. The pre-cut pieces of lath or wire can be bent over a straightedge or long level. Over-bending ensures the reinforcing will cling to the sides of the curb. (Figure 112)

Check the entire installation, adding staples or nails where needed to pull the material close to the wall board. You can also add fasteners after the mud process has commenced. I usually discover a loose area or two in the midst of the mud phase.

Mud Tools

I don't mind telling you I'm becoming so excited I can hardly control my emotions. I wish it were I instead of you who is about to have all the fun. Ah, well, I can't do them all. I'll go find a shower of my own to mud just as soon as you have finished yours.

You're obviously going to need some tools. You will need a flat plastering trowel, not a big one but one that is about 4 or 5 inches wide and about 12 inches in length. You will also need a medium size hawk. The hawk is the gadget with which you will hold the mud up with one hand while you try to capture it with the flat trowel held in the other hand.

Figure 111: Add reinforcing in the corners.

Using these two implements, you must somehow get the mud up off the mud board and onto the wall.

And that brings me to the mud board (mortar board). A piece of half-inch or five-eighths-inch plywood makes a fine mud board. It should measure about two feet (60 cm) by two-and-one-half feet (80 cm). A board this size will hold an ample amount of mud and will not take up any more space than necessary in the bathroom. By now I'm sure you've noticed that space is at a premium. (Figure 113)

Figure 112: Over-bending will allow the lath to cling to the curb. Attach it only at the front outside face.

Since space is also at a premium on the back of my truck, I don't carry a mud board stand, and you probably won't have one either. You can do like I do and stack up cartons of tile to support the board, or you can devise some sort of stand from scrap lumber. An overturned trash can will also work — anything to get the mud board at just below waist level. Position your board and "stand" where you can reach it without stepping out of the shower. This arrangement will often block you into the shower, which is fine if you have a helper. If you are working

Figure 113: I think you can tell my hawk has had some use.

alone, you will have to get around the board to dump mortar on it. I do hope you are not working alone. It's no fun.

You will need two float strips. These are lengths of wood lattice or rippings that you can make if you own a table saw. They are about an inch and a half wide by a quarter-inch thick. They must be long enough to stretch from the shower floor to the top of the shower walls.

You may also need a 1/2 x 1/2 inch "stop." The stop is merely a length of wood that can be tacked to the wall board at the edge of the shower. If the stop is plumbed with the level to get it perfectly vertical it can replace one of the float strips for that wall.

Straightedges are the next items. You will need several of different lengths. They will be used primarily to remove excess mud from the walls, so they'll have to fit horizontally inside the shower a few inches shy of the adjacent walls. If your shower has open walls without jambs, you'll need one straightedge that extends from just beyond the outside edge of the wall back to the corner of the shower. The straightedges can be cut from soft wood boards. (Figure 114)

The Little Wood Block: You will also need a piece of board that is about a foot long. This will be used as a beating block (explained later) and as a wood float for blocking off the mud walls after they have partially set. It will also come in handy for a number of other tasks. A piece of 1 x 4 – 10 to 12 inches long works well.

You can't be without your primary trowel which you will recall is a margin trowel or a gauging trowel. It is your general purpose tool that is used for all sorts of things that you shall learn about directly. Never start any tile project without your "tool."

Keep the hammer handy, along with a rubber mallet. You'll need the hammer to drive a couple nails, and the mallet is used to tap the level and float strips into the fresh mortar to get the strips plumb and straight. You will need your longest level, which will be hit gently by the mallet. Gently, I said.

Figure 114: (l. to r.) 1/2 in. wood stop, float strips, assorted wood straightedges. Notice the little block of wood near the bottom.

No tile project, and certainly no mud job, should be started without a bucket of water and a sponge on the side. Tools and hands need to be rinsed from time to time and spills need to be wiped up. A five-gallon plastic bucket is best, but a small version will work. You'll also need a couple buckets with which to transport your mud.

So much for inside the bathroom. Elsewhere you will need something in which to mix the mortar. A mixing box is best if you happen to have one, but a wheelbarrow will work also. In fact, there is no room for a mixing box on the back of my truck, so all our mud is mixed in the wheelbarrow. If you don't have a wheelbarrow, you should borrow one. It's possible to nail together makeshift mud boxes, but they really don't work well. If you've no other choice, though, do it that way.

A masonry hoe works best for doing the mixing. Masonry hoes have holes drilled through them to allow some of the mortar to flow through them as they are pushed back and forth in the mixing box. If you don't want to procure a mason's hoe, a garden hoe will do the job. It'll be slower, but it will work. A shovel will work, too, but not very well. Get a hoe.

A shovel will also be needed, though. A flat sand and gravel shovel works best for scooping sand up off the pile and for measuring out cement. A round digging shovel will work — not as well, but it will work. You will need another bucket of water at the mixing station. You will want to keep your mixing tools clean between batches.

Plastic Buckets: You cannot do even the smallest tile job without at least two or three buckets, and more are better. I know tile setters who pride themselves on the number of buckets they carry on the backs of their trucks. I usually lug around a dozen or so.

Although it is certainly possible to buy five-gallon buckets, it is much better to scrounge them whenever and wherever you can. I buy buckets only as a last resort. It's a matter of principle. Whenever painters are on the job, my helper is trained to follow them around, scooping up any buckets they might discard. The buckets must be washed out immediately if they are to be of much use. Clean buckets are especially hard to come by.

Three-gallon buckets are also very useful and coveted in our trade. Mastic comes in 3-1/2 gallon buckets, but I don't use mastic, so I don't have a ready source. Again, it is possible to buy the smaller buckets, and I have been known to do so, but I really hate it. The buckets just seem to work so much better when one has managed to scrounge them.

Guard your buckets, especially the really clean ones. They have a strange habit of walking away when you're not looking. I'm not saying anyone will steal them; they'll just move them when you're not looking. There is nothing worse than a bucket thief – I mean a bucket mover.

That's most of it. I may have forgotten a minor item or two but nothing important. I think it's about time to get some mud mixed and get on with it. The excitement within me is building to an unbearable level!

Mixing the Mud

Wall mud used in tile setting is often called "fat mud" in the United States and in Canada. In other countries it is referred to as "render." It is composed of sand, portland cement and construction lime. In certain areas fire clay is used in place of the lime. Fire clay makes the mud set up a little faster than when mixed with lime. I suggest you stick to the lime, as I doubt you are among the faster of the tile setting breed. Construction lime can be purchased in 50 pound bags at masonry supply stores and at some tile companies.

The mixing ratio for fat mud is somewhere between 4:1:1 and 5:1:1. That's four to five parts clean masonry sand to one part portland and one part lime. I give you approximate measurements because mixing fat mud is an approximate proposition. Cement can vary by brand, and the coarseness of the sand has a bearing on things as well. I would start out with about 4 to 1 and see how you like it. The mortar has to have some substance, but it also has to be workable. Mix small batches until you get into the swing of things – eight shovels of sand to two shovels of cement and two shovels of lime will do it.

In place of portland cement and lime you can use "masonry cement." Masonry cement contains lime. The only other ingredients you need are sand and water. I use masonry cement frequently because lime is becoming hard to find in the area where I live and work. Masonry cement comes in 70 lb. sacks. The ratio of sand to cement is about 16 shovels of sand to a sack of cement. You can divide the sack in half and mix only eight shovels of sand. Add one shovel of portland cement to each sack of masonry cement to make the mud strong. For an eight-shovel batch add a half shovel of portland.

Mix all the dry ingredients in the wheelbarrow with the hoe by chopping at the sand and cement with the blade of the tool. As you chop, the material will shift from one end of the mixing container

Figure 115: Bagged sand can be used. You can also buy sand at masonry supply stores and at top soil yards.

to the other. Walk around to the other end and chop it back toward you. Do not add any water until all the dry ingredients have been thoroughly blended. (Figures 115, 116)

Now for the water. Start with a gallon. Dump it into the mix and pull the dry ingredients into it, trying not to slop it around. It's not stylish to get the stuff all over yourself, so take it easy. After the water has been absorbed, you can again chop at the mud with the blade of the hoe. If the mix is stiff, add another quart of water and repeat the process. I know this sounds vague, but it's not an exacting art, as I said. A lot will have to do with the moisture content of the sand before you begin. Keep track of the recipe as you go, so you can make successive batches without experimentation. Keep adding water in small amounts until the mortar is workable. (Figure 117)

Figure 116: Masonry cement being added to the sand.

What is "workable"?: The mortar must be creamy but not runny. It must have some substance but not a lot. Remember the word "buttery." When you pick the mortar up in a shovel it will slump somewhat, but it will

Figure 117: Add the water in small amounts.

remain slightly heaped on the shovel. If you are familiar with the mortar used in brick laying, keep your mortar just a little stiffer. Not much, just a little.

Although the mortar must have substance, it must also be somewhat fluid, but not watery. I know this explanation might not be adequate, but it is the best I can do verbally. I hope the pictures will improve your understanding. If there were a way I could make some mortar and allow you to put your hands in it and feel it, I would do so. I would also have you smell the mud. It has to smell just so. (Figure 118)

Figure 118: "Workable" mud. It will mound on top of the mud board, but it is also fairly pliable.

Shovel your mud into the buckets and carry it into the bathroom. Don't fill the buckets completely. Half full is just about right. Before you dump a bucket on the mud board, wet the board with the sponge. Take a moment to do this, and make sure the surface of the board is saturated. If you don't do this, the wood will draw moisture from the mud as soon as it hits the board.

Mudding the Walls

Oh, but this is a glorious moment. You have the mud on the board. You have your hawk in one hand and your trowel in the other. You stare at the pile of mud. Should you attempt to pick some up?

Yes, yes! Lay the edge of the hawk on the surface of the mud board and push/pull some mortar onto it with the blade of the trowel. Raise the hawk up to a somewhat level position, turn around and face the wall. I like to start on the walls furthest from the mud board and work out toward the shower opening.

Figure 119: Apply the "pathway" of mortar about 6 to 8 inches out from the intersection of the walls.

To get the mud off the hawk and onto the trowel takes a bit of doing until you get the hang of it. You tilt the hawk toward you slightly and at the same time scoop a trowel-load of mud off it. Then quickly return the hawk to the level position while moving the trowel toward the wall. Believe me, this will take considerable practice, so don't feel badly when the mud slips off the trowel (and maybe the hawk, too) and falls on your shoes. I hope you're not wearing your Wing Tips or your toeless pumps.[13]

Pick the mud up off the floor, but not with the flat trowel. The trowel is sharp enough to make a hole in the shower liner. Instead scoop it up with the hawk and your hand. Don't be too concerned about style right now. Just get the mud back on the board. If your helper happens to be watching, you can scoop with a little flair and nonchalance, as if you intended that the mortar end up on the floor. With a little luck, the helper will be outside mixing more mud.

What you are attempting to do is make a pathway of mortar from the top of the shower to the bottom, about six to eight inches out from the corner. Into this mortar you will place a float strip. When you finally get the pathway made (conduct the mud to the wall by any means available at this point), moisten a float strip and press it gently into the mortar. Lay the edge of the level against the strip and tap the level with the mallet. I also sometimes tap the level with the butt of my "tool." Keep an eye on the bubble as you do this. Ideally, the strip will be plumb and straight when its face side is about a half inch out from the drywall, but this seldom happens. The walls may be a little out of plumb, and you may have a little more or less mud at top or bottom. What is important is to get the strip absolutely straight and as plumb as you can. (Figures 119, 120)

If you do not have a 4-foot or larger level, you can use a shorter one in conjunction with a straightedge that is 4 to 6 feet in length. Hold the straightedge against the float strip and the level against the straightedge. I'm not suggesting this method is easy. It

---

[13]*For the uninitiated, "Wingtips" is a style of men's dress shoe that contains a perforated leather toe.*

can be done, but a longer level will make life much more enjoyable.

When you are satisfied with the position of the strip, repeat the process in the opposite corner. This time you will have more success with the hawk and trowel. I guarantee it.

There is a limit to the amount of mud that can be loaded on a wall at one time. If you try creating a thickness much more than three-quarters of an inch (just under two centimeters), there's a better than even chance the mud will fall off or slide down the wall and then fall off. The weight of it will exceed its ability to "cling." If the mortar is a bit on the watery side, this can happen with a thickness of less than three-quarters of an inch.

If your walls are out of plumb, you have two choices: leave them out of plumb, or apply the mortar in more than one session. You can

Figure 120: Insert the wet float strip and lay your longest level against it.

apply a coat of mortar to the areas that will be the thickest and allow it to set up overnight. You will scratch the surface with a notched trowel or a scrap piece of lath after the mortar has partially set. The following day you can begin the mud process again, going over your "scratch coat" with new mud as you progress. Moisten the scratch coat with a damp sponge before applying new mortar over it. In cases where it won't affect the hanging of a shower door or enclosure, it is sometimes easier to leave the walls a little out of plumb.

I can imagine dozens of tile gurus around the globe gritting their teeth right about now. I would just remind them that we are talking about existing houses with existing walls. Certainly, if a person has an opportunity to build his own walls, those walls should be plumb. In an older home, though, it is not unusual to find situations in which it is not feasible to correct everything that is wrong.

But no matter what shape your walls are in, keep the mud bed absolutely straight. A wall can be a little out of plumb and not show it, but if it is bowed either in or out, it will be noticeable. And again, if a glass door is to be installed against a wall, that wall must be straight and plumb. In certain circumstances it might be necessary to forego the glass enclosure and settle on a shower curtain.

Keep your hands and your tools clean as you go. Don't allow mortar to continually rub against your hands as you work. It takes no time at all for the sand in the mud to wear through your wet skin. Try to stay clean and dry. Cement is an irritant that causes rashes and sores.

Don't use your fingertips to work the mud. This can cause a condition known in the trade as "strawberries." All the layers of skin are worn from your fingertips before you know it, and your hands become useless. You can't even stand touching your clothing. It takes a number of days to recover from a good case of "strawberries." I don't wear gloves when I'm floating mortar on walls, but others do. It can't hurt.

On back walls of showers, that is on shower walls that abut other walls, you will need two float strips, one about six to eight inches from either corner. It is these float strips that will govern not only the thickness but the straightness of your mud wall. The float strips will also control whether the wall is plumb, as mentioned above. So pay a lot of attention to how you install the float strips. At this point they will make or break the job.

When both strips have been installed and checked for plumb and for straightness, you will fill in the area between one of the strips and the corner of the shower. Start applying mud at the top of the wall and work your way down. Allow the uppermost mud to extend up and over the line you made. It can be trimmed off later. Try to load enough mud on the wall so that it will protrude

Figure 121: The straightedge is riding on the 1/2 in. stop on the left and the float strip at right.

out a little beyond the float strip. At the same time, don't overload the wall. I know – ambiguity.

Wet the straightedge that fits this particular wall. It should be about 3 or 4 inches shorter than the width of the wall so that there's no chance of its continually dragging on the adjacent walls. This will become important when there is mud on the adjacent walls. Wet this board before using it so it won't suck moisture out of the mud.

Beginning near the top, and placing the straightedge gently against both float strips, rake the excess mud from the wall. Do not attempt to remove too much mud at one time; rather, make a series of short passes at it. Allowing too much mud to build up on the straightedge tends to pull the mud off the wall. (Figure 121)

Turn around and dump the mud off the straightedge and onto the mud board. Repeat the process until you've removed all excess mortar. If you find you've left depressions, which are referred to as "holidays," go ahead and fill them with additional mud. Rake the excess off with the straightedge. Don't use the straightedge any more than is necessary to remove the mud. Making repeated passes increases the odds of your pulling the mud from the wall. You are not doing finish work at the moment. The wall will be further straightened and smoothed after the mud has partially set, so don't strive for perfection at this time.

Repeat the entire mudding and raking process in the other corner. Try not to dig into the mud in the corner you've just completed. Accidents do happen, though, and at this point they are easily corrected with more mortar.

When you are satisfied with both corners, begin loading mortar at the top of the middle section of wall. You may want to stop halfway down this wall and rake the excess off before continuing on down to the lower wall. As you remove the mortar from this section of wall, keep the straightedge a little out of the horizontal. You can also move it back and forth endwise as you rake. These techniques will help preclude your pulling the mortar from the wall as you remove the excess. Rinsing the board periodically will help, also. (Figure 122)

You may be running out of mud at this time, and you'll need to mix another batch. Depending on how confident you are, you might want to mix a larger batch than you did the first time, but don't get over-confident. There is no great rush in this work unless you mix too much mud and need to get rid of it before it sets in your buckets.

Remember to keep everything washed off. Cement has a way of sticking to surfaces, and it's very hard to clean off after is has partially set. Leave it overnight and you won't get it off at all.

Figure 122: Mortar is raked from the wall.

Remember you can stop after completing only one wall, but you must complete the wall. It could well be that you only complete one wall in a day, and that is much better than doing more than you can handle and ending up with walls that are not workmanlike. A pro can completely mud a shower in an hour or two, depending on the complexity of the shower, but it might take you a day or two. Don't expect to become a mud pro in the course of building one shower. It takes much longer than that. I remember (barely) when I was learning to handle the hawk and trowel. I won't take the time and the space to describe the process to you, but it was not pretty. There was mud everywhere except where I wanted it to be – on the wall. I never wore Wing Tips after that.

End Walls: On the open walls of the shower you can use the 1/2 inch stop as one of your screeds, and this will eliminate the need for a float strip at that edge of the wall. Nail the stop to the wallboard with three or four slender nails. Drywall nails or finish nails work well. Don't use long nails that might penetrate deeply enough into the framing to make it difficult to remove the stop.

If it's to be used as a guide for floating mortar, the stop must be plumbed. I like to use bits of cardboard behind the stop to get it plumb and straight. Use your level frequently during the process. Errors made at this time will be difficult to correct later.

When you are satisfied with the stop, install a float strip near the corner of the shower. Load the wall area between the strip and the corner before you float the main section of wall. Doing the corner first allows you to concentrate on it so you don't gouge the adjacent wall

Figure 123: Float strip is removed from back wall and installed in mortar at end wall.

that has already been mudded. Having completed the corner, it's out of the way when you go on to float the larger portion of the wall. (Figure 123)

Remember to begin at the tops of the walls as you are floating them. This precludes the possibility of your dropping mud on a completed portion of wall and ruining it. You will find that starting at the top is a good idea in other aspects of tile setting, but let's not get ahead of ourselves.

To remove float strips and stops, you should first run your tool down one side of them. Then reach behind them with the tool and pry outward. In removing the stop, try to keep it away from the edge of the mortar, and in removing the strips, pry one edge out and twist the stick out of the wall. Scrape the sticks off.

In the case of float strips, you can remove them and place them right into the next wall to be floated. If you are finished with them, however, they must be washed off with the sponge and laid on the floor. Standing them in the corner will ensure they will be bent out of shape when you need to use them again. The stop should be washed, also.

After you've removed the float strips you must fill the depressions they leave. This is done by getting a small amount of mud on the hawk and flattening it with the flat trowel. This arrangement of mud will cling to the hawk quite well, and you'll be able to tilt the hawk and get a bit at a time off the front edge. Fill the depression, but don't try to smooth it with the trowel. Allow the mortar to protrude a little beyond the surface of the mud wall. You will scrape this off with a straightedge held against the mud surface. The short block of wood I called a "beating block" earlier will do the job or you can use a longer straightedge. Don't scrape any more than necessary. Each pass of a straightedge over the surface increases the chance of pulling the mortar from the wall. (Figure 124)

Figure 124: Use the little wood block to remove excess mud from the float strip groove.

Blocking: When the mud has partially set, the walls will need to be trued up and made perfect. How long it takes for the mud to reach this stage depends on room temperature and the amount of water you mixed into the mud. Taking a guess, I'll say an hour, but there have been times in new houses and in chilly weather when I've waited for hours to be able to smooth off the mortar. It's a one-shot operation. Do it too soon and you chance pulling down the mortar, and do it too late and... well, don't do it too late.

The first thing you need to do is check the walls once again with a straightedge. Hold the straightedge horizontally and then vertically and move it across the wall. You will notice that at the top of the wall and at the bottom the mud tends to flare out toward the inside of the shower. I won't go into the science of this, but the wet mortar tends to slump a bit at the top as it sets, and at the bottom it's usually a case of not getting quite enough off to begin with.

Holding your longest straightedge against the wall, scrape off the excess at the top and bottom, making the wall perfectly straight from top to bottom. You can scrape repeatedly if the mud is in the right stage of hydration. If water comes to the surface, or if the straightedge tends to create suction or dig into the mud, stop and wait a while longer.

Scrape horizontally with a shorter straightedge, so that the wall will be perfect in that direction, also. It's important that the final product be perfectly flat or "on plane."

Now pick up that little block of wood again, that's right, the "beating block," and laying it flat against the wall, start moving it around in circular motions. As you move the block you'll notice it cuts off any mud that might have been missed by the straightedge, and at the same time is smoothes the surface. You can run the block into the corners and square them up. Use the block on the entire floated area, but if it creates suction, hold off a while longer. There should be no water coming to the surface at this time. The mud should be fairly solid but not totally hard. (Figure 125)

Figure 125: "Blocking" a wall. Don't make repeated passes. Once or twice over is usually enough.

You can also use the flat trowel to cut into the corners and square them up. Be very careful when working down toward the shower pan, though. The sharp corner of the trowel can easily tear or puncture the liner material.

When you are confident that you have made your walls as perfect as possible, take a break, clean your tools and relax. Do a little standing around. You've earned it. While you are resting I'm going to explain a few of the finer points of mud work in showers.

Door Jambs: Having a helper in mud work is an advantage at any time, but it is especially important when doing some of the smaller, more intricate areas of the shower such as the curb, knee walls or wing walls and door jambs. All of these facets can be completed without help, but it'll take you twice, three times as long. Get yourself a helper and treat him or her with respect. You may be the head mud guru, but your appreciation of your helper will grow as your experience in this work increases.

When floating shower walls that are adjacent to door jambs, it is helpful to nail a straightedge into the jamb. The straightedge will act as a stop as you float the wall. It can also act as a screed if you install it plumb and use it (instead of a second float strip) to guide your straight-edge. Float the wall and then pull the nails and remove the straightedge.

When you wish to continue around the corner into the door jamb itself, you can't nail the straightedge into the wall you've just completed without destroying your mud work. But you can have your helper hold the board in place while you float the jamb.

If you tack another straightedge to the

Figure 126: Mudding a door jamb.

outside of the jamb, and have your helper hold another one on the inside of the shower, you will have both hands free for the very important work of slopping mud all over the place, hoping most of it ends up on the jamb. (Figure 126)

I should note that you can't do a lot of banging on the wall without causing damage to the mud already floated. So you "tack" the straightedge to the outside of the jamb; you don't drive heavy-duty framing nails into it. You can also screw straightedges on if you have a drill-driver.

It is critical that you get the jambs plumb and parallel to one another. First, plumb the straightedge that you are nailing to the outside of the jamb. Get it exactly vertical and then nail it or screw it. Check it with the level after it's fastened. Then have your helper hold the other straightedge against the mud wall on the inside of the shower. Use the level to get it

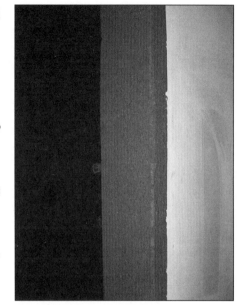

Figure 127: Mud jamb completed.

plumb, but at the same time, it must be square with the straightedge you nailed to the outside. A carpenter's framing square or a tri-square, if you have one, will aid you in this. The framing square is best, as you can line up one leg of it with the wall and use the other leg to get your two straightedges in line.

When you get the jamb floated, scrape the excess mortar off by holding the little block of wood against both straightedges and scraping upward. Don't let your helper pull the straightedge from the wall, or mud will come with it. A great deal of suction will have developed while you were floating the jamb. Have the helper slide the board toward the corner of the wall it's on, moving it away from the jamb. As the straightedge slides over the surface of the wall it can be lifted off without causing damage. To remove the straightedge that has been nailed to the outside of the jamb, first run your tool between the board and the mud. Then pull the nails and remove the board. (Figure 127)

When the jambs have partially set, they are checked and smoothed with a long straightedge. The sharp corners are reduced so that bull nose tiles can later be installed over them. It doesn't hurt to remove a little excess mortar from the corners themselves. It's better than having it in the way of the bull nose pieces after it hardens.

An alternative, of course, is to let the walls firm up before you float the jambs. Then there will be no chance of destroying work already completed. Prudence is sometimes better than

Figure 128: "Picture frame" return on outside of jamb.

bravado. Not often, but sometimes.

Picture Frame Returns: In many cases the door jambs will turn out onto the outside wall of the shower where bull nose tiles will later be installed to form what we call a "picture frame." You can float the picture frame returns by first tacking up a 1/2 in. stop and then having your helper hold the long straightedge on the inside of the jamb (after the jamb has been floated). This will create a very narrow mud wall (about an inch and a quarter wide) on the outside of the doorway. This "return" will go all the way to the bathroom floor on both sides of the doorway and across the top of the opening as well. (Figure 128)

Curbs and Bulkheads: Low walls that will catch shower spray are treated like curbs (dams) inasmuch as their tops are tilted slightly in toward the shower. As I mentioned earlier, nothing inside the shower is level, at least not where spray is likely to hit it. These low walls are called "knee walls," "wing walls," "half walls," "stub walls" and a variety of other names. For the sake of clarity, I'm going to refer to them as "bulkheads." Naval veterans will argue that all walls are bulkheads, but I'm an army veteran. And when I was a kid we had low retaining walls around the yard that were called bulkheads.

So a bulkhead is simply a high curb, and often a segment of a glass shower enclosure will be mounted on it. If that glass panel is designed to mount near the outside edge, the bulkhead can be used as a shampoo shelf. The top of the bulkhead will be waterproofed either before or after the mortar is applied. Waterproofing can be a scrap of shower pan liner or a commercial tile waterproofing product that is applied to the surface of the hardened mortar.

As with the curb, the waterproof membrane on the top of the bulkhead can be nailed only at the outside edge where nail or staple penetrations will be outside the glass enclosure. The same is true of nailing the lath. It can be stapled to the vertical inside portion of the wall but not to the horizontal surface, except at the extreme outside edge. We are going to do all we can to prevent water from ever penetrating the top of the wall, but should it happen, we'll be prepared for it.

I usually float the tops and ends of bulkheads in the same manner as door jambs. That is, I have my helper hold a straightedge to one side while I hold one to the other side. We get both the straightedges level with the outer one being about an eighth-inch (2.5 mm) higher than the inner one. If the outward side of the wall is to be tiled, you can nail a straightedge into it, thus freeing up a pair of hands. (Figure 129)

Curbs, because they are so low, can be handled a little differently than bulkheads. You can lay a bed of mud along the curb top and mash a straightedge into it. You can then use the straightedge as a guide to float the inside and outside faces of the curb. The top of the curb can be floated along with the sides, but I usually do that later, after the tiles have been installed to the curb sides. If the tiles are installed exactly level (as they should be), they

Figure 129: Top of bulkhead or "knee wall" is floated.

can be used as guides in floating the curb top. (Figure 130)

Niches (Shampoo Recesses): In mud showers, shampoo recesses are treated as separate projects, and I usually save them for last. By then the mortar on the wall surrounding the recess or "niche" has had a chance to partially harden, and holding straightedges against it will not harm it. I float the side walls and sill of the niche. The top, or ceiling, I make out of a piece of cement backer board. The back of the niche is made from the same material as the top. You might want to search for a scrap of backer board. Scout around where new homes are being built. You'll probably be able to pull a piece out of a scrap pile, or you can ask a tile installer for a piece. As a last resort you can buy a sheet of the material. (Figure 131)

Figure 130: Using the edge of the flat trowel to scrape mud from the side of the curb.

Niches, of course, can be quite elaborate with crowned or radius ceilings and more than one compartment, or they can be simple rectangular recesses. The photos in this section have been taken on several different projects. I hope that this jumping around from job to job will give you an idea of the possibilities available to you. Keep in mind that you can have more than one niche in the shower if you choose.

Many of the niches my helper and I build contain shelves crafted from pieces of marble tiles. If you don't want to go to the trouble of making a marble shelf, an option would be to have a stone fabricator make one for you. You could then build your recess to accommodate the pre-made shelf.

If you are very good at arithmetic and measuring, you can build the recess in the wall so that the wall tiles will hit it evenly. If you succeed at this, you won't have to make any cuts around the opening. If you are not sure of your abilities, just build the niche where you want it and cut the wall tiles to accommodate it. It will look fine so long as your cuts are neat and even with one another.

A trick I often employ is to not float the

Figure 131: Floated niche.

106

inside of the recess until I've run the tile up the wall containing it. This allows me some minor adjustment in the thickness of the side walls and in the height of the bottom shelf. In many cases I am able to make full tiles work where they would need cutting had I pre-floated the niche. It's worth a shot, and it gives you an excellent reason to procrastinate that portion of the work.

In tiling the niche, you should generally complete the face of it in conjunction with tiling the wall in which it is built. Install the bull nose or other trims around the open-ing, and then mud and tile the inside walls and the shelf or shelves. Since your ceiling is a solid piece of backer board, you will want to make very sure you hit the mark with the trims in that area.

As is the case with every other horizontal surface inside the shower, the shelves of the recess must be tilted ever so slightly in toward the shower drain. In the case of mar-ble shelves, I usually insert very small shims of cardboard near the back edges to keep them tilted until the grout is installed. The hardened grout will hold things permanently in place and at the right kilter. If your shelf is going to be tile, simply float the mortar under it at a slight inward tilt.

Let me give you a bit of warning. Building and tiling even a simple shampoo recess seems to take an inordinate amount of time. It is not a task to be entered into lightly. Be prepared to spend hours working in one small area.

But should you take the time to build the niche? Oh, most certainly. It is one of the features that can turn a rather ordinary shower into a custom installation. A well-crafted niche definitely adds "style" to a shower.

Building a Niche

"Niche" is another of those fancy words we like to use in the tile business. It impresses people much more than saying something like "hole in the wall to keep your stuff in." Actually, the niche can also be called a sham-poo recess or even a "shadow box." The depression or alcove, whatever you choose to call it, can be simple or ornate. My helper, Albert Nelson, and I have collaborated on the building of quite a few niches which contain shelves made from marble tiles. Here are a few words and pictures that will explain the process. Please don't limit yourself to what you see here, though. There are all sorts of possibilities. I have yet to build one with an arched top, for instance.

Figure 131-1: Install wood blocks between studs.

To "rough in" the niche, all you need to do is install a couple horizontal wood blocks between two studs. It's best to pick a spot that is not cluttered by piping or wiring, but I've been known to re-route pipes and wires if they happen to be in the spot my customer has set her heart on for the location of the niche. (Figure 131-1)

If you should decide the space is too wide for the niche you want to build, you can install a vertical piece of wood between the two horizontal blocks. Just remember that the opening will be reduced by the thickness of the mortar or CBU that you install, as well as by the thickness of the tiles themselves.

Cut a piece of CBU for the back of the niche. You can simply insert it against the drywall and hold it in place with the side pieces you will install, but it doesn't hurt to place a few small dabs of thin set on the back side of the CBU before you place it. Finish up by installing the top piece of CBU and another for the bottom shelf. The bottom piece of CBU should be tilted inward slightly. You can butter a bit of thin set on the under side of the piece for it to rest upon. Screw or nail everything securely, and you're ready for tile — almost.

If your niche is in an area of the shower that will receive spray, it should be waterproofed. You can install Schluter Kerdi inside the entire niche, allowing it to come out onto the shower walls a few inches, or you can use one of the various paint-on membranes that are available. I usually manage to locate my niches in areas that will not receive significant spray. I can then forego the waterproofing.

Figure 131-2: Niche being tiled from outside in.

I often tile the niche from the outside in. It's easier to install the trims around the recess and then tile the inside. Just make sure you provide enough overhang on the trim pieces to accommodate the tiles that will make up the inside walls. (Figure 131-2)

But before you fit the tiles for the sides, the ceiling and the bottom, tile the back of the recess. You can set the tiles so they will line up with the side pieces, or you can turn them on the diagonal and center them. I do that a lot. It looks very tricky, and it alleviates the need to keep things lined up. Occasionally, I tile the back of the niche before beginning the front or the sides. (Figure 131-3)

Figure 131-3: Tiling the back of a niche first.

If your niche will contain a shelf made from marble or some other solid material, it will be supported by the tiles at the sides of the recess. Generally you tile up to the height where you want the shelf, lay the shelf onto the tiles on either side and then continue tiling the sides. When you've finished, the shelf will be permanently locked into the structure. I insert small spacers (miniature wads of paper, wood, even grains of sand) under the rear of the shelf to tilt it ever so slightly toward the inside of the shower. These minute props become embedded in, and covered by, the grout.

Figure 131-4: Shelf is supported by tiles inside the niche.

Remember, nothing is quite level inside a shower. (Figure 131-4)

There are no hard fast rules on how to build a shampoo niche for your shower. Let your imagination guide you. You can have any number of shelves in your niche, and you can have more than one niche in your shower. It's just a matter of how many bottles and other containers you'll be stowing in there. Some folks only need space for a bottle or two, maybe a razor and a bar of soap; and other people can't seem to find enough horizontal space in the shower no matter how it's built and how many horizontal surfaces it contains. I won't mention any names, but... well, I won't mention any names. (Figure 131-5)

Figure 131-5: This niche belongs to a low maintenance person.

Benches and Foot Rests

There are several ways in which a seat or "bench" can be built into a mud shower, and we'll discuss two of them here. I will also include a sidebar that was developed on John Bridge.com which depicts the building of a mud "monument" style seat.

Wood Frame Bench: First of all, you can frame in a seat when you frame the shower. It must be built sturdily from 2 x 4s which are well braced. The surfaces of the framed bench are covered with plywood which is then waterproofed with a commercial waterproofing. The waterproofing must cover the entire seat and all wall areas that are adjacent to the top and sides of the seat. Allow the waterproofing to extend to a distance of six inches from the seat in all directions.

Lath can then be nailed on with roofing nails that are embedded in the same waterproofing. Special care must be taken to ensure that all nail penetrations have been sealed after the lath has been installed. In my opinion this is the least desirable method of building a shower bench.

The Official John Bridge "Monument" Shower Bench: If there's any way of doing a tile job with cement mortar and masonry units as a foundation, that's the way I'm going to do it. You can build a very serviceable bench using the same mortar used to float the shower walls. Bricks or concrete blocks (cinder blocks) will complete your material list and provide bulk to the structure. The monument type bench does not have to be waterproofed because none of its ingredients is adversely affected by water. If the bench leaks a bit, the water has nowhere to go but across the shower pan liner and into the drain weep holes. In my opinion this is the best possible way to create a bench in a tile shower. I suggest you give it a try.

The Monument Shower Bench
(copied from http://johnbridge.com)

I'm a mud man. I build showers out of cement mortar, which is reinforced with metal lath (expanded metal mesh). It's logical, then, that brick and mortar (or cement block and mortar) are the materials that go into the shower seats (benches) I build. I call them "monuments" because they are built up inside the shower pan liner and simply reside there. Gravity and friction hold them in place. They can leak, but any water that gets through one of my seats is contained by the shower pan and ultimately finds its way to the drain "weep holes" and down the drain pipe.

The mud-built shower seat will work in any shower installation, including those employing the cement backer board method, as well as the new Kerdi method by Schluter Systems.

Dave Misevich, who is the systems engineer for the John Bridge web sites and a moderator of the JB Forums, completed a seat in the shower he built for his family. Dave took a series of very good photos of his progress and offered them for use here. Muchas Gracias, amigo.

You can review Dave's shower project, as well as other ongoing tile and stone installations, at the John Bridge Forums. Check into the Advice Board.

It is important to note that, unlike seats built by other means, our masonry seat must be built entirely inside the shower pan. Do not build the seat and then install the shower pan in front of it. If you do that, I can guarantee it will leak profusely and cause you much misery.

Here's what you need in the way of materials:

— Brick mortar. This can be bagged mortar which contains sand and cement, or you can make your own from clean sand and masonry cement. I won't go into the finer points of making mortar here, so if you're not sure of the process, use the pre-packaged stuff available at such places as Home Depot and Lowes. I'll say a little more on the subject further on.

Figure 132: Bench materials.

— Bricks or concrete blocks. You have to accumulate enough of these in volume to completely "fill" the seat you intend to construct. The mortar will hold them together and provide a means of "fairing" the surface of the seat so it can be tiled.

— Mason's trowel, gauging trowel or pointer. A flat plastering trowel is helpful but not essential.

— You will also need a short level and your various tile tools. A hammer will come in handy for breaking up the blocks or bricks.

— Straight-edges. These can be short pieces of wood boards, anything that is straight and that will help you plane the surfaces of the seat/bench structure.

— Buckets, one for clean water and at least one in which to carry the mortar. Tile setters scrounge buckets any way they can, from painters, from drywall finishers — from anyone who might value the bucket less than the tile setter does. The last thing in the world a tile setter wants to do is actually purchase a bucket. It's just not good form.

Figure 133: Spread mortar on shower pan.

You might have to buy plastic buckets, though. Grin and bear it. Try not to end up with the ones that sport the orange label of a prominent big box store. That's really bad form. (Figure 132)

Making the Mortar

Brick/stucco mortar is made by mixing sand, portland cement and construction lime with water. An easier way is to buy a sack of masonry cement (Type S, N, or M) and mix it with sand and water — about 16 shovels of sand to the sack. Add water until the mix is pliable with a consistency similar to butter. An easier way yet is to buy the materiel shown in Dave's picture above and add water to it.

Mix the mortar in a wheel barrow, a wood box constructed for the purpose or on top of a piece of plywood or hardboard. You can use a shovel or a garden hoe to do the mixing. Allow the "mud" to stand for five minutes and then re-mix it. You will have about 45 minutes to an hour of open time.

Linda Preston

Todd Sherman

Building the Bench

Begin by spreading a bed of mortar on the shower pan material in the area in which you wish to build the seat. (Figure 133)

Set a block (or brick) in the mortar. Align and level it. Concrete blocks are thirsty and will suck moisture out of the mortar, so don't dilly-dally in getting the block level and straight. If the mortar gets hard before you have a chance to adjust the block to your liking, remove it and start out with fresh mortar. (Figure 134)

You can now begin filling in behind the block with broken fragments of block or brick, or you can continue the front by filling the voids at each end of the block you've set. Let's fill in behind the block and then move on to the ends. (Figure 135)

You can see that the areas on each end of the block will require pieces smaller than the first block set. Making these pieces will entail breaking a block with a hammer. It is not important how the block is broken, so long as you end up with a piece, or pieces, that will fill the voids at the ends. The pieces of block (or more bricks) are cemented to the first block with mud. The structure is also locked into the walls with mortar as it is erected. You should dampen the walls with a sponge before applying the mortar. This will keep the backer board from drawing moisture from the mortar prematurely. We don't want anything really wet, just damp.

The mortar will not stick to the backer board well. It will, however, lock into the tiny pits and crags of the surface and harden. That's all it takes. (Figure 136)

When the lower portion of the bench has been "roughed in," you can continue on to the next layer or "course" of blocks. We are using blocks that are eight inches tall, so two courses will do the job. You can make the seat a little higher by adding fragments of block to the top. (Figure 137)

Figure 134: Dave levels and plumbs the block.

Figure 135: Broken blocks are used to fill in.

The second course of block or brick is completed in the same manner as the first. Fill in the ends as best you can with fragments, and toss the remainder of the rubble into the block "cells" or behind the larger pieces. Use plenty of mortar to tie everything together. (Figures 138, 139)

Now, unless you are highly skilled, or have been extremely lucky, the front of your bench will not be perfectly plumb and straight. You can rectify this by "floating" additional mortar onto the front of the block structure and striking it smooth and straight with a straight-edge.

It is essential that the front of the bench be flat or "on plane," and it is also important to keep it plumb or vertical. It may take a little experimentation to get the mud onto the front and to get it raked off properly, but it can be done, and it must be done. This is no time to cop an attitude. Stay with it.

Turn the straight-edge in different directions to get things on plane, and check the seat front with the level to get it plumb. When you are satisfied with the front, you can begin finishing the top of the bench.

Nothing in a shower is built level. All horizontal surfaces are tilted slightly toward the shower drain. This is so that none of the surfaces will collect and trap water. The shower seat should be tilted or sloped about a half inch from back to front. As you finish the top, use your level in conjunction with a short straight-edge to accomplish the slope. At the same time, though, the bench top must finish up flat. You're not building a ski chute here.

A shower bench should finish out at about the same height as a chair, which is 16 to 18 inches high. You will be adding the shower floor, so you might want to add mortar or a combination of mortar and block remnants to the top before you smooth it off.

Figure 136: Using a straightedge.

Figure 137: A second course is added.

Figure 138: Bench is filled in with mortar.

When all the mortar has been applied, the bench should be allowed to set an hour or two. You can then go back and fine tune both the front and the top by scraping with a straight-edge or by slicing with the edge of a flat plastering trowel. Do not get the "it's-good-enough-attitude" at this time. Stick with it until the seat is as perfect as you can make it. If you don't, you'll most

certainly have the "wish-I-had-done-it-better-attitude" in the morning. This seat is going to become rock hard. (Figure 140)

Many showers are too small to contain a bench, and a number of people simply don't want a bench in their shower, but nearly everyone enjoys having a horizontal surface on which to prop one's foot. With this in mind, I've taken to offering miniature benches in the showers I build. I've come up with an original name for them, too. I call them "footrests." I'll see if I can have some color photos of some of the footrests I've built inserted somewhere hereabouts.

Figure 139: Dave uses a straightedge to true the mortar.

Figure 140: Two benches are built in the same shower.

The Better Bench™: There is another very good way to provide a tiled bench in your shower. It's called the "Better Bench," and it's made by the Innovis Corporation in California. Constructed of sturdy aluminum, it mounts on the shower walls and does not affect the floor.

Rough in your shower as you normally would. You can then install cement backer board and bolt the Better Bench to the walls. For a mud shower you could either mount the bench before floating the walls or wait until the floated mortar hardens.

Pack the Better Bench full of deck mortar, strike it off, and you're ready for ceramic tile or stone. You tile the top and the front face of the bench. The bottom is normally left unfinished.

What about a shower that's already built? Oh, you bet. Simply drill a few holes into the tiled walls, and off you go. Mud, tile and grout your Better Bench as you would if it were in a new installation. Finish it off with silicone caulking to make it watertight.

The Better Bench comes in three triangular-shaped sizes and an adjustable wall-to-wall rectangular model. The smallest corner model is used as a shelf or as a foot rest. Better

Figure B1: There are four Better Bench models.

Benches are sold at many tile stores through-out the U.S. and Canada and are available online as well. Visit Innovis Corporation at http://www.innoviscorp.com (Figure B1)

Flash! Hold it! I've just learned that my friends at Innovis have come out with a shampoo recess that is tile-ready and easily installed. Dubbed the "Recess-it™," it comes in two sizes, a 14-inch square model and a rectangle that is 6 by 14 inches. The two can be used individually or in conjunction with one another. (Figure B2)

When the mud work has been completed you must check and re-check every element of the shower to make sure all surfaces are smooth, straight and true. I use the block of wood to "block" the shower walls. A wood float, if you have one, works well also. Cut the inside corners clean with the edge of the flat trowel, but remember to be very careful when working down in the area of the shower pan. It's best to use a rounded trowel in that area.

Figure B2: Fitting the Recess-it.

Use your straightedges to check the surfaces, and scrape additional mortar off if necessary. Now is the time. Making adjustments after the mortar has completely set is difficult to say the least. Pay special attention to door jambs (if any) to ensure they are straight and plumb. Re-check the curb while you're at it. Round off all outside corners so they will accept radius bullnose when the time comes to install the trims. Check the inside of the niche, and clean out the corners at its back wall.

Okay, that's it for a while. Clean all the tools, including the straightedges and especially the buckets. Wash out the wheelbarrow and scrub off the hoe and shovel. You'll be doing more mud work but not for a while. Shove all the mixing tools off to the side, and begin organizing your tile setting tools.

You can stand around, but I wouldn't do a lot of it at this time. I know it's hard for you to keep your eyes off your handiwork, but you must make an effort to do so. Getting caught admiring one's work defines one as a "newbie," and you are certainly not that. No, you are an accomplished mud man or mud woman, and you must live up to the tradition. Go have a brewskie. Or a Coke.

Tiling the Walls

There seems to be some controversy in the modern tile trade as to which comes first, the walls or the floor, when it comes to shower building. This controversy did not exist in the days when all showers were built from cement mortar. No, siree, in the good old days the walls were always done first. That way there was no chance of dropping anything on the completed shower floor — you didn't have to stand on the nice new floor to work on the walls and ceiling. I don't see any good reason why that philosophy should have changed, and the "floor-first" folks have yet to convince me that I'm wrong.

My usual habit is to tile the wall furthest from the shower opening first, and I recommend you pick up the habit, too. You can then tile the walls in succession as you work your way out of the shower, saving the jambs and jamb returns, if any, for last. If there is to be some sort of decoration, it will probably be set on the "back" wall of the shower where it can be easily seen from the shower entrance.

Begin by using very stiff wall mud to make a "screed" at the bottom of the wall. The screed will be leveled, and the first course of tiles will be set upon it. An alternative is to lay a straightedge down and prop it up level with stacks of tiles and bits of cardboard. If you will want your shower floor tiles to eventually go under the wall tiles, you must gauge the height of the screed or straightedge accordingly. Depending on the size of the shower the height of the walls will be set at about 3/4 inches above the height of the drain. Having an adjustable drain is a boon in this situation.

I am usually not concerned whether the floor tiles go under the wall tiles or not. I just make sure the bottom course of tiles is low enough so the floor tiles will abut them. It doesn't matter to me if a half inch of wall tile ends up embedded in the floor. The exception would be in the case of a tile with a decorative border or some other feature that should be seen after the shower floor is built. In any case, get the bottom row level and supported by one means or another. You'll be loading considerable weight on these bottom tiles before the thin set attaching them has a chance to set up. (Figure 141)

Figure 141: Courses of tile supported by board.

There was a time when tiled shower walls in many parts of the country began with a row of "shoe base" tiles at the bottom. These tiles were rounded into a cove which met the shower floor. It was crucial, then, that the walls be started in such a way as to afford an easy transition from wall to floor. Getting the walls started at the right height was mandatory. If, by chance, you plan to use a cove at the bottom of your walls, pay particular attention to getting your screed or starter board at the correct height above the top of the drain, especially if you happen to have used a drain that doesn't adjust.

Centering: Remember there are two ways to center a field of tile. You can have a full tile on either side of the center line, or you can have a full tile straddling the center line with half of it falling on either side. Generally, you should use the arrangement that allows you the largest cuts in the corners.

If you have planned a geometric inlay or some other feature that must be centered in the tile field, it may not be possible to use the larger cuts at the corners of the field. Much depends on the layout of your insert and how many tiles it measures across. If there are an even number of tiles across, you will arrange for a tile to fall on either side of the centerline of the wall in question. An odd number of tiles would dictate centering a tile *over* the centerline. Experiment until you are certain you have arranged the layout so that no unsightly cuts will be necessary in the field or in the inlay itself. This is one of the areas in which artistry enters the equation, and it's a bit subjective. (Figure 142)

Mixing Thin Set: The thin set we'll be using to attach the tiles will depend upon the makeup of the tiles themselves. Relatively soft ceramic tiles can be attached with a good quality un-modified thin set mortar or "bonding mortar." If the tiles are of porcelain or if they are granite or another stone, I recommend you use a modified thin set that has been formulated for wet areas. Really dense tiles such as porcelains can benefit from the extra grip a modified thin set mortar provides.

Mix only enough thin set to last about an hour. Since you won't be tiling very fast, at least not until you get the hang of it, a quarter bucket of mortar will probably do it. Pour about two inches of water into the bottom of the bucket and begin adding the powder. Make sure you wear your dust mask when pouring and mixing.

Figure 142: Tile inlay is pre-assembled on floor.

Stir the mix with a flat stick or a long margin trowel as you add the powder, being careful not to over-pour. You'll want the mix to have some substance, but you won't want it to be too stiff, either. Creamy might be a good word, and of course "buttery" is another. You will want the thin set to be easily troweled onto the wall, and you will want the ridges to support themselves after the application.

Notched Trowel: The size of the notched trowel you use will again be determined by the condition of the backs of the tiles. For standard wall tiles and other tiles whose backs are fairly flat I use a 1/4 by 5/16 V-notch trowel. A 1/8 by 1/8 square notch might also be used. For tiles that have a distinct raised grid pattern on their backs you might have to use a 1/4 by 1/4 inch square or U-notch trowel. I don't go beyond that size trowel as it is difficult to get larger ridges to keep their shape when tiling walls – the thin set tends to sag. For tiles that require a more than usual amount of thin set, I back-butter them with my tool after spreading the wall with a 1/4 by 1/4 trowel. Very large ceramic tiles and all stone tiles are back-buttered in a special way I call five-spotting. Gobs of thin set are placed near all four corners and directly in the middle of the piece. The piece is then pushed against the wall and adjusted with the aid of a level. I am not concerned about getting total support behind the tiles. No one is going to be walking on them.

Four-and-a-quarter Wall Tiles: Standard wall tiles that measure four and a quarter inches square have been used extensively for nearly a hundred years in the U.S. and Canada. The tiles have spacer lugs built into them which make them fairly easy to set. There are numerous trims available for four-and-a-quarter tiles. Standard wall tiles also come in a six by six inch size for which the same trims are used. There are currently about a dozen manufacturers in the U.S. producing this type of tile, and other countries produce it as well.

Four-and-a-quarter tiles are "stacked" on the wall. You support the bottom course by one of the methods mentioned above and stack succeeding courses upon it. The spacer lugs keep the tiles properly spaced. Once you have determined the horizontal layout of the wall, you can set the courses from either left to right or right to left, depending on whether you are right or left handed. I happen to be a southpaw, so I generally set from right to left unless there is some compelling reason to do otherwise.

Even though the tiles are self-spacing, they are not perfect – no tile is. As you lay the wall up you will find it necessary to insert wedges or shims from time to time to keep the rows running straight and level.

Vertical alignment can be attained by holding the level against a vertical row of tiles. When you have this "starter row" plumb you can then set all the remaining tiles off of it. As with the horizontal alignment, you will find it occasionally necessary to move individual tiles from side to side to compensate for imperfections. You can do this by prying lightly with your tool as the courses go up. (Figure 143)

If four-and-a-quarter tiles are set to wet mud, they are beat in with the little block of wood (there it is again). When setting them on hard mud, tap them very lightly with the beating block. Very lightly. Hitting them harder will crack them.

Wall Tile Trims: The trims most often used in shower construction are bull-nose pieces, either radius style (A-4200) mud caps or surface style caps (S-4269). Which piece you use will depend upon whether your substrate is flush with the wall or whether it protrudes in front of the wall. In a mud shower the trims will most times be of the radius type.

Figure 143: Level is used to plumb vertical rows.

You can center the trims at the top of the back wall of the shower the same way you centered the field tiles, but if the wall has an open end, the trims will start full at that end and run into the corner, where the cut will be made. It just looks better to have full pieces at the edge. On vertical runs you should begin at the top with a full piece of trim and work your way down. You can support these pieces while they set with bits of masking tape. The cut will be made at the bottom of the run. (Figure 144)

An alternative to bull-nose is quarter-round (A-106). Quarter-round does not consume the space that bull-nose consumes, so it isn't as noticeable as the larger bull-nose pieces. The

Figure 144: AN-4200 corner is installed above A-4200 bullnose.

down side to using quarter-round is that it is much more tedious to install, since there is not much gluing surface. Additionally, the mud work has to be nearly perfect, or you'll be doing a lot of rubbing and chopping of the hardened mud in order to get the quarter-round pieces installed. Bull-nose affords more latitude.

You should install the trims for each wall as soon as you've installed the field tiles and cuts. There is no advantage to waiting until all the shower tiles are installed before installing the trims. Get it out of the way as you go. This will also rule out the possibility of discovering there isn't enough room for the trims after the tile adhesive has firmly set. I know you would never allow that to happen, but just in case... (Figure 145)

117

Other Tiles: Virtually any tile can be used in a shower. That doesn't mean, however, that I would use certain tiles in showers, because I would not. My philosophy entails using something in the shower that is easily cleaned and that sheds water readily. The problem with my philosophy is that it is overruled more often than not by the customer, that being the person paying my fee. I do encourage you to exercise a bit of common sense when it comes to choosing tiles for your shower, though. There are a million possibilities out there. Don't make life more difficult for the maid.

Figure 145: A-106 quarter-round trims taped in place at edge of bench.

Large format floor tiles have become very popular in showers as I write. I wholeheartedly subscribe to this trend, since large tiles are easily cleaned, and they shed water at least as well and maybe better than smaller ones. I also subscribe to it because, once again, I do what I'm told.

The main difference in installing large tiles, as opposed to the smaller wall tiles, in your showers is that the joints will be wider, and you'll have to use some sort of spacers to hold the tiles apart as they set up. Special vinyl spacers are available at tile stores and at home centers, and I recommend you get them. You can, however, use bits of wadded up cardboard to do the spacing. Vinyl wedges or shims are also very accommodating to this task.

In most cases you won't find matching trim pieces for your large bodied floor tiles. I often use wall tile trims that will coordinate with the floor tiles. (Figure 146)

Figure 146: A-4200 wall tile trims are used to compliment large floor tiles used in shower.

Stone Tiles: Marble, granite, slate, limestone and other stone tiles require a bit more time to set than ceramic tiles do. Being man made, ceramic tiles are relatively uniform in both girth and thickness and can generally be placed against the setting material and tapped into position. Stone tiles, on the other hand, are often irregular in size and thickness. You can install stone tiles by smearing thin set onto the setting bed and then placing the tiles, but I've found I can end up with a nicer job if I "spot" the tiles up the wall.

Spotting, as I mentioned earlier, is merely the act of gobbing thin set onto the back of a tile and pushing it into the wall or other setting bed. A level is used to keep the tiles even or "on plane" and to keep all the tiles in a plane running plumb and square. The stone tiles I set are not beaten upon with the little wood block. I keep my rubber mallet handy for tapping a piece now and again. Most stone tiles are somewhat fragile. This is particularly true of marble and limestone tiles, to include travertine. (Figure 147)

I spend approximately twice as much time setting stone tiles as I do ceramic tiles. Much of this time is consumed by cutting, as all stone tiles must be cut with a wet saw rather than with a tile cutter. Additionally, whereas ceramic tiles are often accompanied by matching or coordinated trims, there are usually none available for stone tiles. You will either have to mill your own or take some tiles to a pre-fabricating shop to have them milled.

On the stone showers I do (always in upscale homes), the trim issue is solved by using slab stone of the same specie as the tiles to finish off the jambs, the curb and the tops of seats. The slab pieces, of course, have to be cut and milled on their edges, so there is no gain in cost savings. In fact, locating and having the pieces

Figure 147: Large body tiles are "spotted" onto the wall.

milled or "fabricated" is often more expensive than simply having some of your stock of tiles bullnosed at a fabricating shop.

Stone Tile Showers

Mud work for stone tile showers is no different than for ceramic tile showers inasmuch as the walls must be straight, plumb and on plane. Smaller stone tiles are laid up with thin set in the manner that ceramic tiles are set; thin set is spread on the wall with a notched trowel and the tiles are applied directly to it. This would also be the case with showers built by other means, which would include the backer board method.

But larger stone tiles, those measuring a foot or more square, can be installed as individual slabs, which is in fact what they are. Thin set can be "spotted" onto the back of each piece as it is set. The tile is pushed against the wall and adjusted for plumb, level and plane with the aid of a level. The distance between the backs of the tiles and the substrate should be an eighth to a quarter of an inch (3 to 6 mm) to begin with. This will allow for the inclusion of thicker tiles as you lay up the walls. Do not be fooled into thinking that all your tiles have been sawn and milled to the same thickness.

Figure 148: Granite tiles laid up in shower.

A three- or four-foot level works well for keeping things running straight and true because it will span several tiles at once, but a shorter level can be used, say a two-footer. Applying a strip of masking tape to the edges of the level will prevent it from scratching the surface of your tiles. This is important when highly polished tiles are to be laid up. (Figure 148)

It is best to work all walls more or less simultaneously by setting one or two courses of tiles completely around the base of the shower. This allows setting time for the lower courses before the considerable weight of the succeeding courses is placed upon them. The number of tiles it takes to cover an average size wall in a shower can easily weigh in at 150 to 200 lbs. Without a solid base your wall tiles could begin to settle or sag. Ever heard mention of "that sinking feeling"?

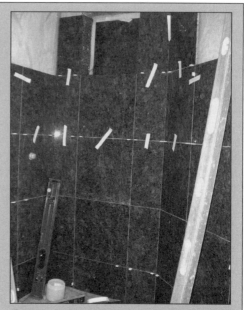

Figure 149: Stone tiles held in place with masking tape.

The main advantage to spotting individual tiles up as opposed to installing them directly against the wall is that you are able to control the "plumb" factor to a very high degree. All cuts for a particular wall, for example, can be pre-made, and as the walls are laid up and the cuts installed there will be no question as to whether your corners are plumb and straight. The identical cuts will dictate it.

Tiles can be spaced with store-bought plastic spacers or wedges or with other spacers of your own creation. I prefer the plastic wedges as they allow for the minor adjustments that are always necessary when laying up stone tiles. Stone tiles, like ceramic tiles, are not perfectly calibrated. It is customary to space stone tiles at gaps ranging from a thirty-second of an inch upwards to three-sixteenths. The calibration range of the tiles will dic-

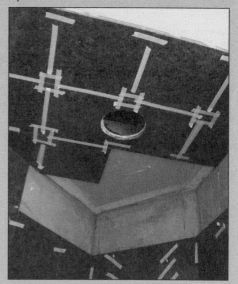

Figure 150: Installing a ceiling.

tate your spacing regimen to a large degree. Do not consider "bumping" the tiles directly together. Some grout is always needed, both for waterproofing and to allow a cushion for the microscopic expansion and contraction that occurs in all matter.

You can tape your tiles in place with masking tape. Have a couple rolls on hand because you will use a lot of it. Regular painter's tape can be used if you will remove it within a day or so, but if you might leave the tape in place for a longer period, use the blue, easy-release tape that costs a bit more. There is nothing worse than having to remove masking tape that has been allowed to stay on the tiles too long. Mineral spirits will ease the job, however, should you

become careless. (Figure 149)

Tiling the shower ceiling can be done before the final wall cuts are placed, or it can be done after the walls have been completed. The advantage to tiling the ceiling first is that the cuts at the edges of the ceiling will be hidden by the upper-most wall cuts, which are easier to make than ceiling cuts. So, when you have all the walls up save the final cuts at the ceiling, you can use your level to locate where the joints will occur in the ceiling tiles, make the necessary cuts and install the ceiling. The ceiling tiles can be cemented directly to the drywall or plaster. There will never be enough water up there to cause any problems. (Figure 150)

In most cases it will be necessary to make holes in individual tiles in order to accommodate shower valves and the shower head. It might be possible to arrange the tiles on the plumbing wall so that the holes fall along the vertical joints of the tile field, and then you would be able to get around the obstructions by sawing into the edges of tiles. Unfortunately, this arrangement will sometimes cause the cuts at the corners to be small and unsightly, and holes will have to be bored through the bodies of certain tiles. It is best that you use a diamond hole saw for this purpose. The tools are a bit expensive but well worth the investment. (Figure 151)

There will be occasions when it is desirable to polish the edges of certain

Figure 151: Large hole was sawn through from back side of tile. Small hole drilled with diamond core drill.

Figure 152: Edge of marble shelf is finished.

tiles. For instance, the edges of tiles framing a shampoo recess could be finished. This would eliminate the need for other trims. A grinder equipped with sanding and polishing discs will do the job, and so will a belt sander if you're good at controlling the monster. On the other hand, regular sandpaper and emery cloth will do an excellent job. Wet/dry sanding cloth is what I look for. You may have to search around for the necessary fine grits.

Start with something fairly coarse, say 150 grit sandpaper, and work your way down to about 800 grit wet/dry paper or cloth. With patience you'll come up with a fairly acceptable edge. Using auto buffing compound on a cloth wheel will enhance the finish. (Figure 152)

Setting stone tiles is slow and painstaking work. This is no time to get in a rush. I am a fairly efficient tile setter, and it will usually take me two days to lay up the walls of a stone tile shower, with maybe another half-day for the ceiling. If it takes you two or three times that long you'll be doing well. Keep in mind, also, that there are many experienced ceramic tile shower builders who have never attempted a stone tile shower. It is not an endeavor to be taken lightly. Maintain your composure at all costs.

Decorative Tiles: Decorative tiles or "decos" can be inserted into a tile field if they are the same size as the field tiles or if they are "modular" to the field tiles. Modular means that tiles of varying sizes can be placed together without having to cut them, so a group of four two-inch tiles could be inserted into a field of four-inch tiles and they would be "modular."

You can also cut the field tiles in order to insert decos. This is a less desirable option but one that will be needed from time to time. You may, for example, discover a decorative tile that you simply can't live without that is not modular to the field tiles you are using. In a case like this you would do whatever it takes to get the piece installed, but you would still want it somehow centered in the field or centered in the group of tiles it is adjacent to. (Figure 153)

You can also make decorative inserts from scrap pieces of listellos and other trims. Just about anything can be inserted into a tiled wall. Remember I said "just about" anything. (Figure 153A)

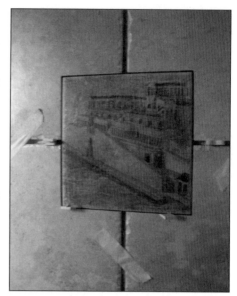

Figure 153: Decorative tile let into larger tiles on shower wall.

Listellos and Other Border Tiles: *Listello* is an Italian word for a piece that is composed of smaller segments. The listello might be made from pieces of tiles glued to a backing material, or it might be a solid piece that is composed of various design elements. I give you this word because it is commonly used in the tile business, and you'll need to deal with it when shopping for tiles. An easier, and much more practical word for a listello, however, is "border." That's all it is. It can be inlaid in the tile field or it can occur at the edge of a field – right before the bullnose piece, for example. (Figure 154)

There are other narrower decorative tiles that are referred to as "liners." Liners are usually two inches wide or less, but there is no hard and fast rule. Liners can be as narrow as about a quarter-inch (6 mm).

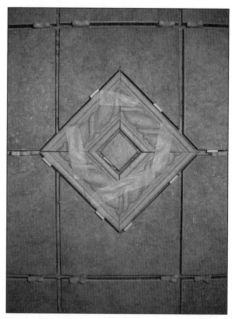

Figure 153A: Deco insert made from scrap listello pieces.

Multiple Tile Inserts: I do custom tile work for a living, and the work you'll be doing for yourself and friends will be custom work, too. There are no production schedules to maintain here, and of course your budget is limitless, so why not make your shower exciting? I mean, why not really let it all hang out? I don't know of a better way to do that than to create a large work of art on one of the walls, usually the back wall of the shower, since it is the first that is seen when entering. My art work is most often geometric, but it wouldn't have to be. If you're the artsy type you might want to design and create a mosaic to install inside your shower. Fish and birds are popular, especially parrots. I'll leave that to the true artists, though.

One of the things I do quite frequently is center a border in the middle of the back wall and use various tiles to create a sort of tapestry inside the border. All of this is carefully laid out on the floor before the wall goes up. Any cutting that needs to be done can be done at that time. It doesn't pay to wait until the wall is smeared with thin set to do your creating and cutting. In some cases you may wish to design your "tapestry" to fit modularly in the tiled field, and at other times you may want the insert to be complete and modular within itself, whereupon you would cut the field tiles to accommodate the insert. In any case, do all of the calculating and cutting beforehand.

Figure 154: Broken tile listello.

Making Cut Tile Listellos

As you may have already found, pre-assembled cut tile listellos and borders are pricey little devils, and broken tile mosaic sheets are often even more expensive. A way around this expense, or a portion of it at least, is to make your own borders and other mosaic sheets.

An excellent backing for cut tile mosaics can be made from a piece of waterproofing or anti-fracture membrane such as the Kerdi product made by my friends at Schluter Systems. Other membranes will of course work. The process is simple. You glue your pieces of tile to the matting with dabs of thin set mortar and then glue the mat to the substrate with additional thin set. With just a little practice (trial and error) you'll soon have things going your way. (Figure 155)

Figure 155: Cut tile listellos mounted on Kerdi matting from Schluter Systems.

Maintaining the proper spacing between pieces is a particular problem when doing a piece composed of uneven sized pieces. You may want to use a combination of spacers, tile wedges and cardboard to support the pieces as they go up. You might also find it useful to drive small nails (sheetrock nails, maybe) into the hardened mortar to help support individual tiles. (Figure 156)

Masking tape is nearly indispensable in this process. I go through roll after roll of it. If I'll be able to remove it within a day or so I use the less expensive

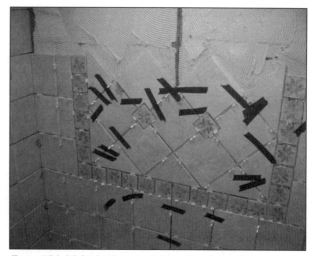

Figure 156: Multiple tile inserts held in place by masking tape.

white or yellowish masking tape. If I know it's going to remain stuck to the tiles for a longer period I use the more expensive tape that is blue in color. It will release better when the time comes. Don't attempt to use any tape that costs forty-nine cents a roll. It won't work. Being a conservative fellow, I've tried every cheapo product I've come across. I have now resigned myself to spending at least two or three dollars on a roll.

Tiling Jambs and Bulkheads

When tiling door jambs and small walls it's often advantageous to install the bull-nose tiles first and then the field tiles. That way you can ensure that the corners of your jamb go up straight and true. You can then install the field tiles, if any, and finally the cuts. Inside the jamb it's common to have all cuts. In general, I try to keep everything going at once.

In the case of a shower doorway that did not get floated absolutely plumb (I know you meant it to be plumb), it is possible to install the bull-nose tiles in such a manner that the jamb will be plumb when you've finished. This is done by determining which way the jamb is leaning and starting there with the bull-nose tiles. It doesn't matter how much space is left for the tiles or cut tiles in the jamb as long as there is enough room for them to go in. You can use increasing amounts of thin set on the backs of the tiles to build them out even with the trims you've already installed. When you've finished, your door opening will be slightly smaller than you planned, but it will be plumb and the sides of the opening will be parallel with each other. Imagine the complements you'll get when the shower door person comes to measure the opening. (Figure 157)

Figure 157: Trims fitted to mudded door jamb.

Tiling Curbs (Dams)

As I mentioned earlier, the tops of curbs, bulkheads and other horizontal planes in a shower are never level. They are tilted slightly toward the shower drain so that no water becomes trapped on them. For this reason I like to tile the inside and outside faces of the curb and then install the trims on top. I can set the outside face of the curb an eighth of an inch higher than the inside face and then use the tops of the tiles as a guide to finish off the curb. The system is nearly fool proof. There is no chance of ending up with a curb that is level on top or, worse yet, one that is tilted outward toward the bathroom floor. (Figure 158)

Figure 158: Sides of curb are tiled first.

Tiling Ceilings

In the old days everything that was intended to receive ceramic tile was floated with mortar, including shower ceilings. It takes two days to float a ceiling, a day to apply a scratch coat and another day to apply the flush coat of mortar. There is no good reason to do this nowadays. We have adhesives, including thin set, that will hold tiles tight to sheetrock, and it is sheetrock that forms every shower ceiling I tile. Yes, even an old mud man can bend the rules once in a while, and a shower ceiling is a good place to do it.

Whether you tile your ceiling is optional, and whether you tile it before you tile your walls or afterwards is also optional. If the ceiling tiles are to line up with the wall tiles, I usually tile the walls first and make the ceiling match. If, however, the ceiling will not line up with the walls, I often run the ceiling on the diagonal and then bring the walls up to it. The diagonally set ceiling lends interest to the installation, and it's much easier than having to make things line up.

In any case, I recommend you use the same thin set on the drywall ceiling that you use on the mud walls. You might also consider using mastic. It hurts me to say the word. I don't use m- m- mastic for anything, but I know other tile setters do. It's up to you. I just won't speak to you anymore if I find you've used it.

Grouting the Shower

Grouts come in sanded and unsanded versions. If the tile joints are narrow, say a sixteenth of an inch, you should use unsanded grout. You would grout standard wall tiles with unsanded grout, for example. The basic rule of thumb is to use unsanded grout in joints narrower than one-eighth of an inch and sanded grout in joints wider than an eighth of an inch. I have found, however, that sanded grouts work well in some joints that are narrower than an eighth. Square porcelain mosaic tiles come to mind. I almost always use sanded grout for them no matter the joint width.

Mix the grout to a "creamy" consistency. You don't want it so hard that you can't work it, and you don't want it "runny," either. Too much water is your enemy when it comes to grouting. This applies to both mixing and placing of the product as well as during cleanup.

If you are using unsanded grout on joints that are fairly narrow, a couple of quarts of grout might do the entire shower. If you used floor tiles spaced at a quarter-inch or so, you might use a couple gallons of grout, depending on how much you drop on the floor. Since you are a "newbie," though, you should start out with a very small amount of grout and work your way up to bigger and better things. If using unsanded grout, place about a pint of water in your bucket and begin slowly adding powder to it, stirring it constantly with a stick or your margin trowel. For sanded grout, start with a quart of water and work from there. Keep track of your recipe so you'll be able to make successive batches the same way.

Unsanded grout will cling to the grout float quite readily, but sanded grout will not. I use my hawk to hold the grout when I grout walls with

Figure 159: Tiles set with wide joints are grouted with sanded grout.

sanded grout. I've gotten quite good at catching the grout before it hits the floor. Sanded grout doesn't like to stick to walls any better than it likes to stick to the float.

Allow the grout to partially set in the joints. This may take ten minutes, or it might only take a minute or two in the case of very soft, absorbent tiles. I would not wait much longer than ten minutes, though, no matter how porous the tiles are. You cannot afford to allow the grout to set on the surfaces of the tiles. You must get it off. I would rather wash the tiled surface too soon than wait too long. Grout is cement, remember, and cement can become quite permanent in a short time. (Figure 159)

Stories abound in which people have been called away during the grouting process for other "important" business. I will tell you that short of a family emergency, there are no more important things for you to be doing than cleaning up the mess you've made by smearing cement all over your new tiles. You'll only have one chance to make things beautiful again. Don't waste it. And even in the case of an emergency, you should try to get someone to wash the grout from the surface of the tiles.

In washing the grout, wring the water completely out of the sponge. As I have said, water is your enemy. Too much of it can wash the grout out of the joints, for one thing. Excess water can also affect the final shade and coloring of the grout. Wipe the sponge across the joints but not along them. I use a circular motion when washing a grouted surface. Rinse the sponge frequently, and pay close attention to the joints themselves. Concentrate on the joints, and the tiles become nearly invisible. When the joints are straight and eye-pleasing, stop. Get a bucket of clean water and give the surface a final pass, making sure to wring the sponge completely and frequently. I wring it after each pass.

Allow the surface to "haze over," meaning as it dries you'll see it cloud up. Wipe (dust) the surface with a dry cloth. If you notice grout smearing at the edges of the joints, stop and wait a while longer. If when you try again you notice smearing on the surface, abandon the wiping, and rinse once again with clean water. The grout residue, if any, can be cleaned off with white vinegar and water after the grout has set a couple days.

The Shower Floor

Don't commence the shower floor until everything else has been done inside the shower. This will include installing the plumbing trim to the shower valve, as well as the shower arm and head. That way, if a bit of brackish water drains out of the piping, it won't have a chance to stain your new shower floor.

The same mortar you used for the pre-slope under the shower pan is used for the floor itself. Keep the mortar on the dry side – just enough water to hold the mud together and activate the cement. You remember, don't you?

I usually begin by leveling the perimeter of the floor, packing down the mortar with a level. Packing the perimeter forms a screed that I can work to when shaping the floor. This level screed should be about 3/4 inches higher than the top of the drain in the average size shower, one that is three to three-and-a-half feet square or thereabouts. This will give you a final slope or "pitch" of about 3/8 inches per running foot. I do like to see the water heading for the drain and not lingering near the shower walls. Larger showers will of course require higher perimeter screeds.

When you get the mud leveled all the way around the perimeter of the shower, fill in the area between the perimeter and the drain and pack the mortar down with your flat trowel or with a wood float. You can then begin scraping the excess mortar off the surface with a short straightedge. That little wood block (the beating block) might become a straightedge at this time. Do the scraping carefully. Don't get in a rush.. Scoop excess mortar off the surface by pushing it onto the edge of your flat trowel with the little wood block. Although I don't want you to get in a hurry, you should complete the floor within about half an hour to forty-five minutes. The mortar won't be usable for much longer than that. So this is not the time to stand around. (Figure 160)

Remember to allow for the thickness of the tiles at the drain. The mortar there must be scraped down below the top of the hair strainer. You can do this by eye, or you can make a little "trick stick" that will allow you to

Figure 160: Floor mud is screeded between the drain and the perimeter of the floor.

easily gauge the depth. The stick can be made from a scrap of lattice or any small thin piece of wood. Make a notch in one end that will correspond with the thickness of the tiles. The notch will ride on the rim of the drain as you scrape the mud away.

When you are satisfied with the shape of the floor, smooth the surface of the mortar with the flat trowel. It's not necessary to push hard. Just get the mortar smoothed to the point that all the grains of sand have been imbedded.

A mud man would lay the floor tile immediately into the fresh mortar, and you can certainly do that if you wish. You might decide, however, to wait until another day to set the tiles. Just make doubly sure your floor is smooth and well shaped and that you have sufficient depth for the tiles to be set flush with the drain. I'll show you how to set the tiles in wet mortar. If you allow the mortar to harden, you will use mixed thin set just as you did on the walls.

I do recommend you wait at least a day to grout the shower floor no matter which method you choose to set the tiles. This will allow most of the moisture to evaporate from the setting bed. Once again, water is your enemy when doing grout work. Excess moisture in the shower floor can cause your grout to discolor.

Wet-setting the Shower Floor

There are measurable advantages to setting shower floors as soon as they have been floated. For pros it may mean the elimination of another trip to the job site, and each trip costs time and money. This would not be a consideration for the amateur, however, who has nothing but time on his or her hands.

Setting the floor in the wet state allows all the tiles to be tapped into the mortar, and this is an advantage over the dry set method for pros and amateurs alike. This is particularly true when using square mosaics for the

Figure 161: Dry thin set is dusted onto shower floor and sprinkled with water.

shower floor. You can ensure that everything is level and smooth by running your hands over the set tile. If a piece protrudes, it can be pushed or tapped into the fresh mortar.

Although it is possible to spread mixed thin set onto a freshly mudded floor, it's not the best approach. The thin set has to be very runny in order to flow over the mortar, and extreme care must be taken to not lift up on the notched trowel, as sections of deck mud can be lifted up with it.

A better way is referred to as "dust and dash." Dry thin set is dusted over the surface of the floor and then water is sprinkled over the thin set. The tiles are then laid over the wet thin set and tapped in. Set all your field tiles as quickly as possible, leaving the edge cuts and those around the drain for last. This will ensure that most of the floor tiles have been installed before the wetted thin set has a chance to skin over and prevent full adhesion. (Figure 161)

When all the full tiles have been set, tap them down with the little wooden block and the handle of your tool. I say tap. Don't "beat" the tiles down, or you may get them too low. It doesn't take a lot of tapping to get things smoothed out. (Figure 162)

Now make the cuts for the edge and finish up around the drain. I like to fashion the drain cuts with the biters, but a wet saw will do the job as well. Butter a dab of thin set on the back of each cut as you install it, and push it into place. If a piece ends up a little low, you can remove it and add a bit more thin set to its back. (Figure 163)

When everything is in place, run your hands over the entire surface of the floor once again. Make sure there are no corners sticking up and that all cuts are flush with the field tiles. When you have satisfied yourself that everything is up to snuff, take a break. Just remember to not stand around admiring your handiwork if others are watching. You are a mud man/mud woman. Walk away with the nonchalance that is typical of all good mud men. Maintain your composure and do it with "style."

Figure 162: *Tiles are tapped in with the little wood block.*

Figure 163: *Cuts are made around edges and finally around the drain.*

And now it is time to engage in the most enjoyable experience a mud man or mud woman can contemplate – standing around and gazing upon a completed project. It doesn't matter if anyone sees you doing it at this point. You've earned the privilege. In fact, why don't you get a brewskie and stand around an hour or so.

And don't forget to take a picture and send it in to the John Bridge Forums. We'll be happy to display it to the world for you. I just know the job is going to be spectacular and beautiful.

Oh, I can't wait to see it.

Backer Board Showers

Not everyone wants to be a mud man, and everyone is not capable of being one. It doesn't make you a bad person if you choose to build your shower by some other means. In fact, many good tile setters are not mud men. They instead build very serviceable ceramic and stone tile showers using cement backer board as their substrate. A properly built CBU shower can last a lifetime if correctly maintained.

As you have learned, the mud method allows a bit of flexibility. Studs don't have to be perfectly straight, and walls don't have to be perfectly plumb. The mortar allows you to correct these minor inconsistencies. You will not have this luxury when using the backer board method to build your shower. Inconsistencies in the framing will telegraph right through to the backer board and ultimately to the tiled surface. It is crucial that you have a straight and true framework to begin with.

Additionally, you will not have the continuity a reinforced mud job provides. You will not be creating a monolith. Even though you will reinforce the joints and corners of the backer board installation, you won't be able to depend on these reinforcements. Each time the framing shifts or "breathes" the backer board will move with it. The idea is to create a structure that will move as little as possible. Extra bracing in the corners is certainly worthwhile, and screwing the members together instead of nailing them will go a long way toward overall rigidity. Take particular pains to ensure that all studs that form inside corners are screwed to one another and not simply standing free.

Installing the Pan: Since you won't have the mud and drywall to accommodate the thickness of the folded shower pan liner, you will have to handle it with the framing. Otherwise, the bulk of the material gathered at the walls will cause your CBUs to bend inward near the bottom of the shower. This is not a desirable effect.

The best way to handle the situation is to notch out the studs in the area the shower pan will cover and set the backing blocks back appropriately. Existing studs can be notched with a large wood chisel, while new studs can be notched with a saw before they are installed. A quarter inch is ample room for the shower pan in the corners, and along the intermediate studs an eighth of an inch will do the trick. The CBUs can then overlap the pan material and remain straight and plumb. As you might suppose, you cannot drive any fasteners in the portion of the CBUs that overlaps the liner. Other than having to make room for the shower pan material, the liner and pre-slope are done exactly the same way as for a mud shower.

The curb is also done with mortar exactly as it is done for a mud shower.

CBU to Drywall Joint: Cement backer board can be taped and finished with regular drywall compound if it is going to be painted or papered, so outside the wet area that's all you need to do. Inside the shower, though, all taping is done with the special fiberglass mesh tape that is especially made to be used with CBUs. You will find this tape where backer boards are sold. It is bedded in thin set at all joints inside the shower. It is important to skim the thin set into the tape and not create a build-up which might interfere with setting the tiles.

So on that connection that usually appears at the point where the shower door will be, you'll have backer board taped with thin set on the inside of the shower and drywall compound finished sheetrock outside the shower. You can use the drywall compound over the mesh tape. You can also extend the backer board out beyond the curb of the shower and tape and finish the entire joint with drywall compound.

Moisture Barrier: A moisture barrier is installed directly to the studs. Although it could be 15 lb. roofing felt (tar paper), I recommend that you use clear poly (plastic sheeting) in this instance as it will allow you to see the studs when installing the backer board. Overlap the pieces of poly, and allow the material to extend down over the shower pan liner by two to three inches.

Installing CBUs: The backer boards themselves can be either screwed to the studs over the moisture barrier or nailed to the studs with hot dipped galvanized roofing nails that are an inch and a half long. Do not use the "electro-galvanized" roofing nails that are often sold in home centers and chain hardware stores. These nails have negligible holding power and tend to rust in no time at all. Nail according to manufacturer's directions. However, as a general rule, I would place the nails about six inches apart with a few extra nails at the joints. Remember, no nails or screws in the shower pan area.

The shower floor mortar will hold the bottoms of the boards in place. Before you place them, butter a bead of thin set on the backs of the boards where they go against the shower pan liner. Push the boards against the liner material until they are straight. This bit of thin set, when hardened, will prevent the boards from bending back into the space you've created for the liner material.

Edge Backing: It is a good idea to provide solid backing blocks between the studs where the backer boards come together. The blocks will ensure that these joints will not flex or otherwise become deformed after the boards are installed. It doesn't take a lot of time or material.

With all the CBUs in place, the shower is now ready for tile. Tiling is accomplished as it would be for a mud shower, except that flat trims are often used in place of the radius trims that would normally be used in a mud shower. Some backer boards have a tendency to draw moisture from the thin set as it is applied. It is recommended that the boards be dampened with a sponge prior to spreading thin set on them. With all styles of backer board it's a good idea to begin by spreading only small areas until you get the feel of the material.

United States Gypsum Company, maker of Durock brand cement backer board, has contributed an article on CBU installation. Find it in Appendix VI at the back of the book.

Installing Backer Board Over Sheetrock: As an alternative to installing backer board directly to the studs you might consider first installing a layer of water resistant sheetrock (greenboard) beneath it. This system alleviates the problems associated with matching CBUs to adjacent drywall outside the shower. The sheetrock inside the shower matches perfectly with the outside walls. Joints that are going to be exposed can be finished with drywall tape and compound. It is not necessary to tape the joints that will be covered by CBUs and tile. In fact, I recommend that you not tape them, as the tape and compound might get in the way of the CBUs and cause them to bulge.

It is important to note that the sheetrock acts only as a spacer in this instance. The CBUs could be extended out by using anything that is a half-inch thick — strips of 1/2 in. plywood nailed to the studs, for example. By installing the CBUs over the wall board, radius (mud) trims can be used at the edges of the tiled area.

A poly (plastic sheeting) moisture barrier is tacked to the sheetrock, and the CBUs are installed in the normal manner using longer screws or nails. As mentioned, the outer edges of the CBUs will eventually be finished off with radius mud trims, and the final look will be exactly that of a mud shower installation.

Steam Showers: We will not have enough space here to go into detail on building steam showers, but I must mention waterproofing. You can obtain complete technical standards on steam showers from the Tile Council of America and from manufacturers of waterproofing materials.

The point I wish to make is that instead of using a moisture barrier behind the CBUs or mortar when building a steam shower, you would apply a waterproofing coat to the surface prior to setting the tiles. These waterproofers are tile friendly. Thin set will stick to them.

The Kerdi Shower

The premise that governs the building of showers from mortar and from CBUs is not new. Few changes have been made to the basic system in decades. A shortcoming of the method is that it allows water into the substrate to be captured and repelled by a waterproof membrane or moisture barrier after the fact. This is particularly true in the area of the shower floor. Water gets through the tiles and grout and enters the mortar bed. The moisture is collected on the surface of the shower pan liner and channeled into the drain weep holes. While the system works efficiently for disposing of water, it provides an opportunity for bacteria and fungus to grow within the shower floor and lower shower walls. Additionally, it is possible for drain weep holes to eventually close or become constricted, causing the mortar bed to retain water. In turn, water can leach or "wick" from the mortar bed into the lower portions of shower wall substrates.

How much better it would be if a system were devised that would prevent the waste water from entering the mortar bed to begin with. Well, this is exactly what my friends at Schluter Systems have accomplished. The Kerdi shower positively prevents any moisture at all from getting into floor mortar beds and into wall substrates as well. Prevented from entering the substrate, the small amount of moisture that does get into the tiles and grout has more than ample time to evaporate between shower uses. This is especially true if you employ the John Bridge method of shower maintenance, i.e., hand drying the shower after each use.

An important component of the Kerdi shower is the Kerdi-drain. Conventional floor/shower drains do not provide a positive watertight connection between the bonded waterproof membrane and the topmost portion of the drain. The Kerdi-drain, by comparison, is equipped with an extra wide, thin set compatible bonding flange to which the membrane is attached. When installed, this flange resides on the surface of the mud bed. As of now, no one but Schluter markets such a drain. The Kerdi shower is unique in this regard.

When it comes to installation, a distinct advantage of the Kerdi shower is that the materials used in its construction are commonplace and well within the ken of the advanced weekend warrior. You are an advanced weekend warrior, aren't you?

The shower is framed like any other shower from straight wood framing members. No extra bracing or backing is needed. When you are satisfied that the framing is strong and true, you cover the entire structure, including the curb, with sheetrock. You do not even have to use water resistant sheetrock, as no moisture will be allowed near it with the Kerdi matting in place.

Taping the Sheetrock: The sheetrock has to be flat and straight as well as plumb because sheetrock, along with the Kerdi matting, forms the actual substrate upon which the tiles will be set. It's important to not build up the joints with drywall compound because that buildup will telegraph through to the tiled surface. Corner joints (angles) should not be taped at all. The Kerdi matting will provide more than enough strength to hold the corner together and much more than could be afforded by drywall tape and joint compound. The long edge joints of the sheetrock, which are known as "recesses," should be taped and filled only to the surface level of the board. "Butt joints," those joints occurring where the narrower ends of boards meet, should not be taped at all. Taping the butt joints would cause a bulge in the surface of the drywall. In fact, I would go so far as to suggest that you incorporate no butt joints at all in your Kerdi shower. It might cost you another board, but sheetrock is cheap.

The drywall can be either nailed or screwed to the studs. I recommend screwing the boards if you have the means. Screws are always better than nails, although as I said, nails will work. Use good quality drywall nails if you don't use drywall screws.

I do not recommend taping the curb area for the same reasons I stated above. The tape and compound are not needed and will only hinder you in getting the Kerdi to lay flat. And so you won't use corner beads on the curb, either. It is essential to keep your drywall installation smooth and on plane, as this will directly determine the final shape of your shower.

The sheetrock on all the walls and on the inside of the curb must extend to within an inch of the sub-floor, and the drywall on the outer face of the curb must extend all the way to the floor, or at least to within a quarter-inch of it. Remember that the Kerdi-covered drywall will be the only substance behind the tiles.

When you are satisfied with the sheetrock shower enclosure, it'll be time to begin building the mortar bed floor. I can hardly wait to get started. This is so exciting. (Figure S1)

Kerdi Shower Drain: As I've mentioned, the Kerdi shower drain by Schluter Systems is unique to the tile and plumbing industries. None other like it exists anywhere. It incorporates a bonding flange to which the Kerdi matting can be directly bonded – no upper flange assembly is needed. There are, however, lateral and vertical adjustment devices and, of course, the grate, which happens to be stainless steel. The grate is square instead of round, which makes cutting around it fairly simple. I've recently learned that a new brass finish grate is in the works and will be available by the time this book is published.

I would be hard pressed to say too much about the importance of mounting the drain flange absolutely level. It is not unusual to find drain risers (the drain pipe which rises vertically from the trap) badly out of plumb. Since the Kerdi-drain is glued or otherwise attached to the riser, either the riser will have to be plumbed, or the trap will have to be disconnected and re-installed. Much depends on the age of the plumbing system and the type of pipe that was used.

Figure S1: It's important to build the shower straight, plumb and level.

PVC and ABS systems are easily adjusted, while cast iron and lead pipes will require a bit more plumbing expertise. When I've exhausted all other methods in my bag of plumbing tricks, I resort to the Fernco connector to rectify the wrongs of my plumbing predecessors. The Fernco, discussed earlier, is somewhat flexible – it can bend.

Traps and Risers

In a bathroom, as well as in other areas of the house, all waste plumbing is led into a waste/vent system where the waste water goes down and where sewer gas is vented up and out the roof.

Water traps are built into, or under, each plumbing fixture in the room, including the shower. The water traps, commonly referred to as "P" traps due to their shape, prevent sewer gases from backing out of the drain and into the room. How these traps are installed determines what happens above them. If the shower trap is not level and straight, for example, it is difficult to get the riser and thus the drain on straight and level. (Figure 163A)

A common occurrence is a drain line that has too much pitch. If the line running from the trap to the vent stack has more than about a quarter-inch per foot pitch, it's difficult to get the riser to come straight up out of the trap, and this, of course, affects the position of the drain. New plastic plumbing can be "tweaked" a little as it is installed. Pressure can be applied to the various connections to straighten them a little as the glue dries. I think you can see why having

Figure 163A: Drain line through wood trusses.

excessive pitch in the drain line would make this difficult, if not impossible, to do. (Figures 164, 165)

With the cast iron traps and steel risers of old, the problem could be easily handled by simply holding the riser vertical as the molten lead was poured into the bell housing of the trap. But certain plumbers of old were no more careful than certain modern-day plumbers, and it's not unusual to find steel and lead risers that are out of plumb. The easiest method for correcting them entails the use of Fernco (or similar) connectors.

Figure 164: Coupling is added to cut-down riser.

Figure 165: New drain installed and held level until glue has set.

Installing the Drain: On wood sub-floors the Kerdi-drain should be installed with its bonding flange a minimum of 1-1/4 inches above the sub-floor. This will allow for a mud bed that is two or more inches thick at the shower's perimeter. I state this as a minimum, and another inch of mortar won't hurt a thing. Too much, though, and you'll be stepping high to get into the shower. One layer of metal lath or chicken wire reinforcing is nailed to the sub-floor over a vapor barrier of tar paper or sheet plastic.

On concrete floors the height of the mortar bed is not important, since it is bonded to the concrete and derives its strength therefrom. Modified thin set makes an excellent bonder. Spread the thin set and immediately dump the deck mud on top of it. I would set the Kerdi-drain at least a half inch off the floor, though, just to facilitate getting enough mud under the drain to provide complete support. The drain, of course, can be set higher. No lath or other reinforcing is used when mortar is bonded to a concrete floor. The mortar derives all its stability from the concrete below.

It is essential that the bonding flange of the drain be totally supported by mortar.

In new construction where there is access to the drain plumbing, Schluter recommends setting the unconnected drain in mortar and then connecting the drain line from underneath after the mortar has set. This allows for the drain to be pushed down onto the wet mortar without the force of the drain riser pushing against it. In remodeling this will seldom be possible. It will often be necessary to glue or otherwise attach the drain to the riser and then pack mud under it all the way around from the drain perimeter. If the drain is not completely supported it can crack and cause a leak. I've never done it, but I instinctively know that having to replace a cracked Kerdi-drain would not be a pleasant operation. It helps to loosen (add a little water to) the mortar that is packed under the drain flange. (Figures S2, S3)

Figure S2: "Loose" mortar is placed around the drain hole. Don't be skimpy.

Figure S3: Kerdi-drain bonding flange is pushed into mortar and leveled.

Mortar Bed Floor: Our next step will be to build a mud screed all the way around the perimeter of the floor. We'll use deck mud for this, the same material used in showers built by other methods. The screed must be higher than the bonding flange of the drain to ensure that water will flow out of the shower. Current recommendations stipulate a slope of one-quarter inch per running foot of floor. This means that in a shower floor where the walls are two feet from the drain, the screed should be one-half inch higher than the drain flange.

In showers that are long rectangles, the slope should be figured from the furthest walls at about a quarter-inch per foot. This will cause the slopes from the nearer walls to be more severe, but that's how it has to be. Don't be tempted to flatten or nearly flatten the slope from the furthest wall to arrive at a quarter-inch pitch on the nearer walls. You could very well end up with a floor that doesn't drain properly, and that can cause extreme consternation after the shower has been built. Please don't go there. When I'm in the shower I like to see the water fairly rushing away from the walls and toward the drain.

Place mud around the perimeter of the shower and pack it down with the flat trowel or with a wood float. Then, using a straightedge and a level, gauge the height of the screed from the drain flange. This is exactly the same process we discussed earlier when building the floor for the mud shower. (Figure S4)

From your reference point begin leveling the screed in both directions until you have worked your way completely around the perimeter. If you scrape down a bit too far, pull all the mortar out of that segment and pack it back in. Trying to add a bit of mortar over the top of the previously packed mortar will not work due to the fact that the mortar has probably already begun to air dry on its surface.

With the level, check several locations around the perimeter of the floor to ensure you have a proper slope to the drain. Do not try to rush this process. Having a perfectly level floor perimeter not only ensures proper drainage: it also facilitates the wall tile setting process, since the floor itself will be used as your starting point. (Figure S5)

When you are satisfied with your perimeter screed, fill in the area between the drain and the perimeter with mortar and pack it down. Now, with straightedges that will fit between the drain and the perimeter, carefully rake the excess from the packed mortar bed. Take your time in doing this. You can allow the drain end of the straightedge to ride on the

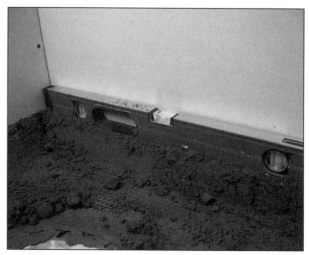

Figure S4: Mud screeds are formed and leveled around perimeter of shower.

Figure S5: Check the slope of the floor all around.

bonding flange of the drain, but you must be very careful not to dig into the screed at the perimeter of the floor.

As you work your way around, you will begin to see the final shape of the floor develop. If this is your first time, you will derive something akin to a sense of joy in the simplicity of what heretofore seemed to be a very complex project. The floor will almost shape itself, but not quite.

As an alternative to the straightedge, you can use a wood float or a flat wood block to fair the mortar between the drain and the perimeter. Try both methods and use the one that suits you best. (Figure S6)

When the shape has been attained, move a straightedge around the floor and check for low spots under its edge. These low spots (bird baths) could cause water to pool in the completed shower floor. When you are satisfied that the floor will drain from all directions, smooth out the surface of the mortar with your flat trowel. Don't push overly hard, but get the surface smooth so that it will accommodate the Kerdi matting.

Make sure all the particles of sand are embedded. (Figure S7)

Stand back and have a look. The drain is level, and the smoothed deck mud slopes upward from the drain toward the walls. The floor is level around its entire perimeter. There are no "bird baths" in the floor, and the mud surface is smooth. Life is good. (Figure S8)

Clean your tools and grab a beer or a glass of wine. You won't be able to attack your project again until morning when the mortar has become hard enough to walk on. If you don't like beer or wine, grab yourself a Coke, a coffee or a cup of tea. You have earned a break. You are well on your way to becoming a Kerdi shower builder. I'm telling you, I can't wait to welcome you into the club.

Fine Wines: Tile setters/fixers are wine and beer connoisseurs, and I'm one of the best, I don't mind saying. I've traveled the world, and I've had my share of bad and good. I must confess I've run into very few beers that I haven't relished, but wine is a different commodity altogether. Through years of trial and error I've developed a system for never having to experience an inferior vintage.

Never be fooled into buying the lack-luster wines that are sold in exclusive liquor stores and wine shops in those skimpy slender-necked bottles with cork stoppers in them. A quality wine will come in one of only two types of containers. It will either arrive in a gallon jug with a handle on its neck and a genuine metal screw-on cap or in a plastic lined cardboard box with a spigot at its bottom. Enough said, I think.

Figure S6: A wood block can be used to smooth the mortar.

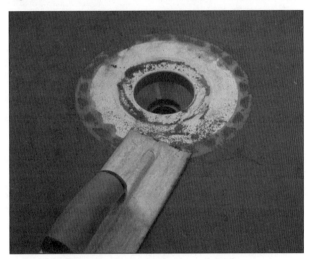
Figure S7: Smooth the floor with a steel trowel. Make sure you imbed the grains of sand on the surface.

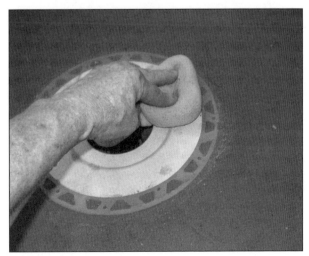
Figure S8: Keep things cleaned up.

Applying the Kerdi: It's morning. Wake up and smell the coffee. Let's get moving.

Oh no, don't tell me you drained that entire box of fine wine. I hope you didn't do that. It contained a whole gallon, nearly four liters!

We will begin by preparing a piece of Kerdi for the shower floor. It will be necessary to cut a round hole in the piece of mat that will accommodate the Kerdi-drain. Kerdi comes in a convenient one meter width (approximately 39 inches). Cut a piece that stretches almost to the walls, let's say to within about an inch. Now measure the distance from one shower wall to the approximate center of the drain, and make a corresponding pencil mark on the Kerdi. Measure from the other direction and make another mark. By measuring from two adjacent walls you should be able to locate the center of the drain on your piece of Kerdi. But measure also from the other two walls just to check your work. Since you left about an inch all the way around your piece of Kerdi when you cut it, it will only be necessary to arrive at a point within an inch of the exact center

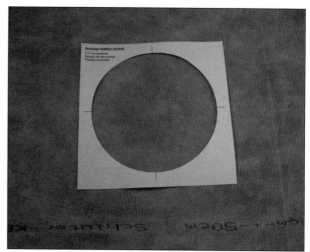

Figure S9: A template for the drain hole is packed with the Kerdi-drain.

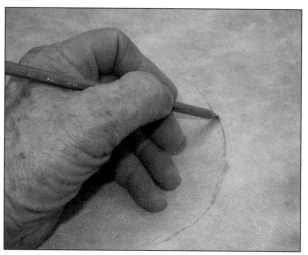

Figure S10: You can feel the edge of the adjustment flange depression and mark the hole accordingly.

of the drain, but do try to get it as close as you can.

Use a small compass or a makeshift trammel and pencil to trace a circle on the Kerdi that is exactly 6-1/2 inches (16.4 cm) in diameter, or trace around the paper template that is packed with the Kerdi-drain. Cut the material out of the hole with a sharp razor knife or with scissors. (Figures S9, S10)

An alternate method of determining where the drain hole should be entails laying the piece of Kerdi over the shower floor. By pushing down on the matting in the area of the drain, you should be able to see the outline of the lateral adjustment ring depression and mark the cutout with a pencil. Remove the matting and cut out the hole.

Since the substrate in this case will be mud, the Kerdi can be bonded with dry set mortar, which is another name for thin set that contains no polymers. Modified thin set mortars (those containing polymers) will also work, of course. But if your thin set is modified, make sure it is rated for wet areas, since some modified mortars are not. You can determine the suitability of the mortar by reading the back panel of the bag it comes in. Whichever product you use, it must be appropriate for cement mortar substrates.

I like to use white thin set, but gray works just as well and is a bit cheaper to buy. You will mix the thin set rather loose – almost runny but not watery. The semi-fluid consistency will facilitate getting the matting flat as you apply it. The thin set should be applied with a 1/4 by 3/16 in. "V" notched spreading trowel.

Spread the thin set liberally on the shower floor with the flat side of the trowel (all the way to the walls) and comb it with the notched side of the trowel to ensure a consistent application. The mortar is spread onto the bonding surface of the drain, right up to the depression for the adjustment collar. It doesn't matter if a bit of mortar goes beyond that point, as long as it doesn't go down the drain. The excess can be wiped away with a damp sponge after the matting has been installed. (Figure S11)

It helps to loosely fold the mat in half as you place it over the shower floor. When you have it properly oriented with the walls and over the drain, unfold it, position it accurately over the drain and begin flattening the material with the straight side of the trowel, pushing it in all direc-

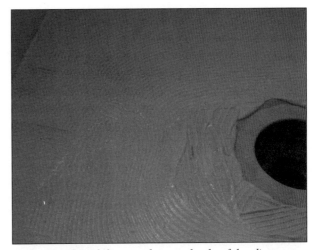

Figure S11: Spread thin set right up to the edge of the adjustment flange depression.

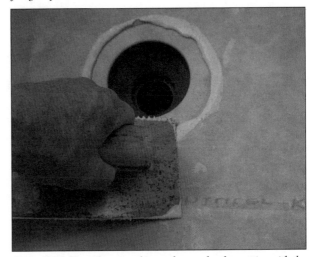

Figure S12: Force the excess thin set from under the matting with the flat side of the notched trowel.

tions away from the drain. Many pros prefer using a five- or six-inch drywall knife for this operation, for the process is much like pressing drywall tape against plaster board. (Figures S12, S13)

Work the material thoroughly to ensure that it's embedded in the thin set over every square inch of the floor. Push the air bubbles out from under the material at the edges and at the drain opening. The material must lie perfectly flat against the thin set-coated mud floor. Pay particular attention to the bonding surface of the drain. Make sure the material is pushed down flat all the way around.

As I mentioned above, a number of pros have found it convenient to use a drywall taping knife. I'm one of those pros. It seems I'm able to apply a bit more pressure with the drywall tool than with the trowel. Give it a try. If you don't have the drywall knife, you should buy one. You'll be needing it to finish the walls outside the shower and possibly for other chores.

For extra large showers you will have to use more than one piece of Kerdi, but this presents no problem at all since Kerdi is easily joined by simply lapping the material two inches or more and bonding the pieces together with thin set mortar. I would recommend you arrange for the seam to occur someplace other than through the drain area. Off to either side would be fine.

To cover the remaining inch or so at the edge of the floor and to start up the wall you can either cut strips of Kerdi in widths of about six inches (15 cm), or you can use pre-cut Kerdi-band. The advantage of using the Kerdi-band is that it is thinner than Kerdi matting and will create less of a build-up at the lapped joints. Kerdi matting will do the job, however.

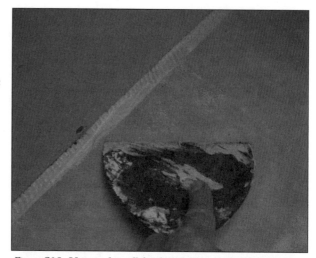
Figure S13: Using a drywall finishing knife to work the matting.

One of the secrets to a successful Kerdi shower is accurate measuring. Take your time at this and get it right. Measure out a piece of band that will reach from corner to corner on one of the walls and then add 4 inches (10 cm) to your measurement. The extra inches will allow the material to extend around and onto the adjacent walls. Thus, if your wall is 37 inches across, you would want your strip of band to measure 41 inches in length. Mark off one side of the band to correspond with the exact dis-

Figure S14: Cut notches into the ends of the Kerdi-band or strips of Kerdi.

tance between the corners of the wall, exactly 37 inches in this case. Cut corner notches into the ends of the band to create tabs that will wrap onto the adjacent walls when the band is installed. (Figure S14)

Carefully install the length of band with thin set. Crease it into the corners with the edge of your trowel or drywall knife and push all the excess thin set from behind it. Make sure you leave no voids or air bubbles under the band. Now, repeat the procedure on the remaining walls (including the curb), measuring accurately and allowing the "tabs to overlap the other pieces of band. The band will go up the walls about two inches all around. Two inches (10 cm), you'll recall, is the minimum. It doesn't hurt to increase the fabric overlap. (Figures S15, S16 S16-1)

The "Vortex": When I attended the Schluter course at the Tile School (CTEF) in South Carolina, I was concerned that at all the inside corners there were no preformed waterproof corner pieces. When you fold and install the flat inside corner pieces provided with the drain or the lengths of band you prepare for starting up the walls, you will notice there are lapped thicknesses of Kerdi everywhere... except right in the corner

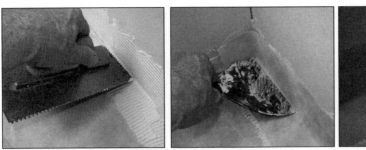

Figure S15: Apply thin set to the floor-wall juncture.

Figure S16: Install Kerdi-band and force it into the juncture. Note the overlap on the end.

Figure S16-1: Completed corner connection.

itself. No matter how tightly you fold the corner, it seems you'll have at least a pinhole remaining, and there will be no lap of material behind it. I began calling this pinhole a "vortex." I repeated the word and the concern so many times that I'm sure there were at least a couple Schluter people who would have liked to have slapped me before the course was over, and a couple of the guys are pretty big and strong.

I also think I might have instilled skepticism in the remainder of the class because a demonstration was staged to dispel my "vortex" theory. If you take one of the corners that comes with the drain and fold it around into a cone, you can fill the cone with water and it will not leak through. You have to twirl the materiel fairly tightly and hold the overlap closed, but if you do, it won't leak through the "vortex." I saw it with my own eyes, and I've since done it at my own bathroom sink. The water does not come through because Kerdi is hydrophobic. It doesn't like water at all and repels it at every encounter. It's amazing. You can see the little pinpoint of light indicating a hole, but the water just seems to back away from it. (Figures S17, S18, S19)

Figure S17: I'm folding the corner piece into a cone, trying very hard to close the "Vortex."

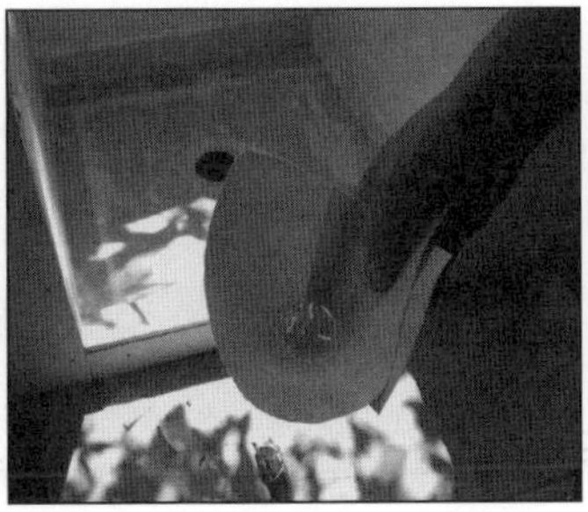

Figure S18: I've added water to the cone. Note how the Kerdi seems to repel the water.

Figure S19: The water does not come through the pinhole.

As I write, there is a cardboard box in the tool room at the Tile School that was lined with Kerdi nearly a year ago. The box has been kept full of water ever since and has not lost a drop through any of its four "votexes."

Lap Joints: You've learned that the general method of using Kerdi as a waterproof membrane is to overlap all its sections by two inches or more. The only "glue" used is thin set mortar which is squeezed tightly between the folds. In initially testing the material, the Schluter folks rigged an experiment wherein they were able to contain a 15-foot-tall column of water within a Kerdi-clad container. After a couple weeks, water migration was checked at the lap joints. There was no leakage at all, and at no point had the water infiltrated more than a quarter-inch (6 mm) into the laps. I think that is quite remarkable. Under no circumstance will your shower ever have to measure up to that sort of standard.

And so I've finally put the "vortex" theory to bed.

To sum up, Kerdi won't leak if it is installed correctly. Now, let's get on with it.

The Curb: Two sets of corners are provided along with the Kerdi-drain. One set is for above the curb, and the other for the lower inside corners where the curb meets the floor and the walls of the shower. Make sure the "vortex" is twisted tight on both of the inside corners. Smooth the corner pieces firmly into the thin set. There will be some minor build-up caused by the various layers of matting, and that can't be avoided. Just don't add to the build-up by failing to work the material thoroughly. (Figures S20, S21, S22, S23, S24, S25)

I don't know about you, but I'm ready for another break. Sponge off any remaining excess thin set, and make sure all your lap joints are flat and smooth. Guess I'll have to have a brew, seeing as how you gulped down the whole box of fine wine.

The Walls: With the floor and the first two inches or more of the walls completed, it's an easy matter to continue up the walls. Just make sure you provide for a two-inch overlap at every joint. Although it is possible to fold the larger pieces of Kerdi around the inside corners, I've found it easier to use Kerdi-band or cut strips of Kerdi in the corners as a prelude to gluing up the larger sheets. (Figure S26)

Sections of Kerdi are installed from the floor upward with the joints overlapped in a roof shingle fashion. The upper pieces of fabric overlap the lower pieces. It's a good idea to cover the floor with cardboard or a tarp to protect it. (Figures S27, S28)

The Kerdi should be installed up the walls to the height of the shower head. The thinking is that there is no possibility of water getting behind it at that point. The tops of knee walls (bulkheads) are covered with custom-cut pieces of Kerdi which overlap the walls below them by the required two inches.

Figure S20: Install the corner piece. Push the split portion tight to the top corner of the curb.

Figure S21: Smooth down the corner piece. Make sure the corner is closed with thin set.

Figure S22: Install the second corner piece over the first.

142

Recess-It™

Karen Jay

Wrapping the Curb: I wait until last to finish wrapping the curb with Kerdi. I suppose I'm used to backing my way out of showers, and the curb is the last portion encountered on the way out. You could wrap the curb as soon as you've installed the corner pieces, though. The sequence is not important.

Cut a piece of Kerdi large enough to cover the inside, top and front of the curb. I always cover the front, even though it's technically outside the wet area of the shower. It can still get wet. Smear the entire curb with thin set and apply the matting. (Figures S29, S30, S31)

Outside Corners: I like to apply Kerdi to outside corners, even though they might not be tiled on one side. Wrapping the corners will ensure there is no chance of water getting through to the sheetrock, and the matting is easily finished over with drywall compound. You can tile right out to the edge of the shower and then finish around the corners with drywall mud. (Figure S32)

Tiling in the Drain

The Kerdi-drain is adjustable both vertically and horizontally. You slip the height adjustment collar into the lateral adjustment ring and cement the latter to the drain flange with thin set. Then mount the stainless steel grate to the top of the height adjustment collar. (Figures S33, S34, S35)

You can move the lateral adjustment ring about a half inch in any direction from center, and the height adjustment ranges from 1/4 inches to 1-1/4 inches. The square shape of the drain makes it easy to install the tiles with minimal cutting. Just make sure you get it all worked out before the thin set takes hold. (Figures S36, S37, S38, S39, S40, S41)

Grouting and Caulking: As is the case with a backer board shower, all the changes in plane in a Kerdi shower are caulked and not grouted. This includes all wall corner junctures as well as wall to floor connections. Outside corners can be grouted.

I know. Caulking is messy, and sometimes it traps moisture behind it, which in turn can cause mildew to grow. Well, Schluter has thought of this and has provided a system

Figure S23: Force the piece into the thin set with either the notched trowel or the drywall knife.

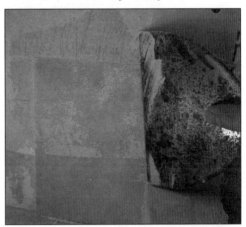

Figure S24: Flatten the piece into the corner, forcing the excess thin set from behind it.

Figure S25: Completed top and bottom corner detail.

Figure S26: Install kerdi-band or strip of Kerdi at wall intersection.

Figure S27: Install sheet of Kerdi over corner band.

Figure S28: Work from the center of the sheet in all directions.

Figure S29: Cover the curb with thin set, inside and out. Allow for an overlap at the floor.

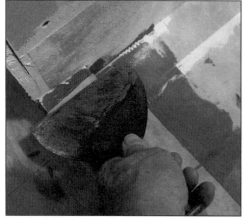

Figure S30: Applying Kerdi to curb.

Figure S31: My curb piece was a bit short, so I made a patch.

Figure S32: Wrapping the outside edge of the shower.

Figure S33: l. to r., horizontal adjustment flange, grate, hair strainer, vertical adjustment flange.

Figure S34: Insert the vertical adjustment flange into the horizontal adjustment flange.

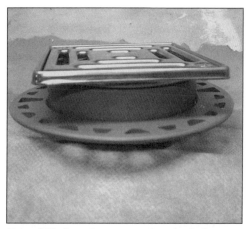

Figure S35: Snap the grate into the vertical adjustment flange.

Figure S36: Push the assembly into the thin set. Make sure it goes all the way down against the bonding flange of the drain.

Figure S37: Spread thin set over the entire floor right up to the grate.

Figure S38: Tile set around grate.

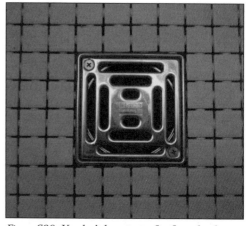

Figure S39: You don't have to use 2 x 2s or 1 x 1s on your shower floor, but notice that if you do, you won't have to do any cutting around the drain.

Figure S40: You could also turn the drain and the floor tiles on the diagonal.

Figure S41: To install the hair strainer simply remove the two screws from the grate. (Don't drop the screws down the drain. It happens.)

whereby caulking does not have to be used at inside corners. It is called Dilex. Dilex is a complete line of corner profiles and other movement joint accommodations. If you still have the video CD-ROM that came with your Kerdi-drain, you'll notice that Dilex HKW was used on the wall/floor junctures, and Dilex EKE was used in the corners going up the walls.

Tiles can be cut to go behind the Dilex profiles so that neither grout nor caulking is needed at the shower corners. End caps and inside corner pieces are available which will ensure a well-thought-out and professional looking job. You will find Dilex and many other Schluter trim profiles displayed at better tile stores. You can also log onto the Schluter web site for a complete list of Schluter products, along with complete descriptions of each. You will find the friendly folks of Schluter waiting to welcome you at: http://www.schluter.com

Outside corners of the shower can be completed with bull nose tiles, of course, but there are also Schluter trims that can be used in these areas. Schluter Rondec comes in a number of styles and forms a very nice outside corner treatment. As I said, in many cases you will want to use matching bull nose pieces to finish off the shower, but sometimes those trims are not available, especially when using floor tiles for the walls of your shower. It is in situations such as these that your appreciation of Schluter trims, including Rondec, will grow.

Top off your Kerdi shower with an application or two of a good quality sealer, and you will be set to enjoy your handiwork for many years. Employ the official John Bridge method of maintaining the shower interior, and your Kerdi shower could last forever.

Okay, almost forever.

Tub Surrounds

Anyone who can build a shower can easily tile a tub surround (tub/shower), but maybe, just maybe, you've never tiled anything and only want to tile a tub surround, which is also called a tub "splash" in our business, and in some quarters it's known as a tub "back."

If you are installing the tub yourself, the most important thing is to get it level all the way around. As any tile setter can tell you, having to work on a tub that is out of level is not fun. Often the entire bottom course of tiles will have to be trimmed off in order to get the field of tile plumb and level. Don't do this to yourself.

Figure 167: A plumb line is made at center of wall.

Since I'm a mud man, I'll be showing you pictures of mud installations, but the procedures for tiling CBU tub surrounds and those formed with Schluter Kerdi over drywall are precisely the same once the substrate has been prepared. For the mud shower, the moisture barrier and lath are installed as they were in our earlier shower application. Float strips are used to get the walls plumb and flat, and the little wood block is used to smooth things out.

Figure 168: Thin set is spread on one side of centerline.

The long (back) wall of the tub area is tiled first. We'll center the field of tile on that wall. Remember, now, there are two ways of centering, and it will depend on the size of your tiles as to whether you'll have a piece on either side of the centerline or whether you'll have a piece of tile astride the centerline. Measure from the corners and mark the centerline on the back wall, using your level as a guide. (Figure 167)

It turns out my tiles will be set on either side of the centerline. This arrangement will allow for the largest possible cuts in the corners. I'll spread thin set on one side of the line high enough to accommodate three to four rows of tile. (Figure 168)

Set the tiles beginning at the centerline and work your way to the corner, spacing the tiles as you go. Make the cuts in the corners as you lay up the courses. Then shift over to the other side of the line and repeat the process. Use your level frequently to make sure your courses are running true. It doesn't take long to get out of level, especially if your tiles are not well calibrated.

If there is to be a border, a good place for it is at about eye-level. Please do arrange it so that it doesn't encounter any obstacles, i.e., soap dish, shower valve, etc. I sometimes set the border and allow it to firm up before proceeding with the courses of tile above it. At other times you might want to let the field tiles set up a bit before installing the border. Much depends on the make-up of the border and how well it supports itself. It seems I have river rocks to deal with here. They'll have to set before I can load the weight of the field tiles onto them. I will, therefore, tile the end walls up to the level of the border, install the river rock border and let it firm up. (Figures 169, 170)

Figure 169: Tiling up to the border level.

Figure 170: River rock border has been set.

There is a niche in the end wall opposite the shower head, and that will have to be tiled in and allowed to set before the border and upper wall tiles can be set. Generally, I'll work my way around the shower, doing all three walls more or less simultaneously. (Figure 171)

You might also have decorative tiles to insert into your field of tile. This is best done as the courses go up. Don't wait until later. Your decos might not fit. Liberal amounts of masking tape and spacers are used to hold everything in place while the thin set firms up. (Figures 172, 173)

Grout the installation, but caulk the joint between the tile and the tub. It is recommended by the Tile Council of America that the corner joints where the walls meet be caulked as well, but I grout them. If there is enough movement down the road to cause the grout to crack out, you can always go back and caulk. (Figures 174, 175)

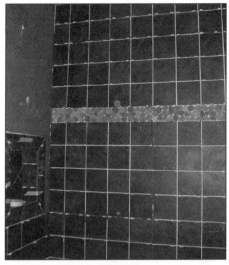

Figure 172: River rock border must set firmly before wall tiles can be loaded above it.

Figure 171: Niche is tiled. Border will be set above it.

Figure 173: Small decos are inserted into a field of larger tiles.

Figure 174: Grouted and washed.

Figure 175: Anyone for a shower?

149

CHAPTER 4

COUNTERTOPS AND BACK-SPLASHES

Gravity is a Mixed Bag

Here we are back in the kitchen. I told you that's where the gathering usually ends up. This trip we're going to have a look at your countertops with the idea of converting the working surfaces to ceramic or stone tile. By now I'm sure you feel you've learned most of the basics and that this job is going to be a breeze. But not so fast, amigo. Tiling counters and back-splashes presents new challenges. Try to control your excitement while I give you a few pointers. You can then have at the project in the sure knowledge it will be completed with competence and with "style."

I'm going to present two methods of tiling a kitchen or bathroom countertop, one employing cement backer board and the other employing Schluter Ditra. That's right, Ditra, the matting we talked about back in the flooring section of the book. Ditra makes for an excellent countertop installation, one that is solid and waterproof. I will also demonstrate how to do a mud countertop. For that project we'll move into the bathroom. But let's begin in the kitchen area.

Before we get too far into the actual tile installation, please allow me to explain a few general characteristics of kitchen counters. First of all, countertops get wet, so having an installation that is waterproof is a definite boon, and although it is not absolutely necessary, waterproofing will be addressed in this section as we go along.

Second, countertops take a real beating; at least in my kitchen they do. We are not particularly careful people when it comes to cooking and general kitchen duty. But whether you are careful of your countertops or not, it makes sense to use a quality tile, one that will not be easily scratched or marred.

And one more thing. You might not think of your countertops as structures, but that's exactly what they are. The structural aspects of counters really come into play when parties or other social gatherings take place in your home. It's a given that a large portion of the crowd will end up in the kitchen. Don't ask me why, but that's how it is. Maybe it's because the kitchen is the root source of food and drink. In any case, you know from experience that what I'm saying is true.

Some gatherings can become quite boisterous and lively, and before you know it, someone might decide to jump up and sit on the countertop. I know it's not polite to do that, but again, it happens. This might not represent a huge concern if the person doing the jumping and sitting is trim and lightweight. But guess what. Just as the party always ends up in the kitchen, it seems it's always the largest and heaviest person present who decides to jump up and sit on the counter. Again, don't ask me why that is.

Where am I going here? I'm about to tell you that your countertop may not currently be strong enough for a truly bullet-proof tile installation and that you may want to beef it up a bit before you get into the actual business of setting tile upon it. But you might take other precautions instead. You could not allow party guests in the kitchen, or you could restrict your list of invitees to trim and slender people. Of course, you wouldn't be able to invite me to your party. (There are some who wouldn't consider that a sacrifice.)

Countertop Carpentry

Many modern countertops are made from either plywood or particle board which has been covered with plastic laminate. The plywood or particle board is almost always 3/4 inches thick (about 18 to 20 mm). Other than at the very front and the very back, the board is usually only supported where cabinet sections join together, and this is fine for a plastic laminate top. It might be fine for a tile top, but let's not assume it is. If you can push down from above and cause your top to deflect downward, it's not strong enough for tile.

You can shore the structure up by removing drawers and installing stringers directly to the bottom of the plywood or particle board. If you can get a power screw driver in there, great. If not, you can simply glue the stringers in with carpenter's glue, the yellow professional type.

The stringers can be made from pieces of solid wood that are thin enough to fit in the space above the drawers without interfering with drawer operation. 1 by 4s make excellent stringers. Perhaps you'll need one about every two feet where there are not cabinet walls already supporting the top. Now, you may elect not to install the stringers, but I'm telling you it's an easy thing to do. It doesn't take a lot of time, and it doesn't cost a lot of money. Good idea, I think.

Whether you can use your existing countertop as a base for tile will depend on the type of top it is. Many tops are square at the edges with low back-splashes that are simply glued to the wall. By removing the splash sections and cutting back the overhangs, these counters can be considered a fine base from which to begin your installation. But your counters may be of the molded and rounded edge type with low integral splashes at the back. The front edges are often contoured slightly upward to keep liquids from dripping over onto the floor. If you have this type of countertop, the best thing to do is remove it and start over, using good quality 3/4 in. plywood as your base.

For a tile top, I usually start out with a base or "rough top" that is flush with the cabinet face frames at the front. The tile itself will create an overhang, or a finished wood edging can be used to both trim the tiled surface and to create an extention over the drawer and door fronts. So whether you are using your existing top or whether you are installing new plywood, I would suggest you hold the front of it flush with the cabinet face frames. An existing overhang can be sawn off with a circular saw.

Whether using the existing top or new plywood, you should nail the top into the face frames, the cabinet back, partitions and stringers. 6d box nails (six penny nails) will do the job. Do not use common nails as they are larger in diameter and may cause the wood to split. Nail about 8 inches on center along the face frame and along the back of the cabinets. A couple of nails in each stringer will do the trick. Nailing the tops in solid will help eliminate unnecessary "bounce."

Sink Cabinets: Kitchen sinks are most often fitted into a cabinet with a couple doors on it's front, a cabinet that is not too much wider than the sink itself. What this means is that the sink is well supported all the way around – by the two side walls of the cabinet and by its face frame at the front and its rear panel. If you do not have this common arrangement at the sink area, and if your sink is not well supported at the sides, I would suggest you do some shoring up in that area. A couple of stringers, perhaps. Everything under a tile top must be rigid and solid, and the sink receives a great deal of use.

Bar Overhangs: It is not unusual to have an eating bar incorporated into the kitchen cabinet scheme, and bar tops require special consideration when it comes to installing tile on them. Being open on the underside (overhang), it's difficult to provide the support needed to ensure a lasting tile installation. Support can be provided with angled brackets installed under the overhang, with legs or wing walls going down to the floor or by providing reinforcing within the top itself. You can double the thickness of a plywood top that will be used as a bar, for instance. Whatever the case, the bar top cannot move when the weight of a person (that heavy guy at the party?) is placed upon it. If it moves, fix it, or content yourself with non-tile surface treatment for that area.

Plumbing and Appliances

Sinks, cook tops and other fixtures mounted in or on the counters must be removed. Do not consider tiling up to and around them. Do not be afraid of the plumbing (and possibly the electrical) work this will entail. It is not hard. It is only time-consuming, and time you have. You are not getting paid for this project, so there's no need to get in a rush.

Sinks are disconnected from below and removed. Stainless steel and enameled steel sinks are held down with special brackets around their perimeter. These can be unfastened from below. Enameled cast iron sinks are usually caulked to the countertop. You can use a razor blade or a utility knife to cut through the caulking.

Cook tops are most often simply resting in the cut-out. Gravity holds them down. Occasionally, though, I've found a bracket or two holding the cook top down. These can be loosened from underneath. Turn off the circuit breaker that controls the range. It should be clearly marked in your electrical service panel. In the U.S. and Canada the breaker will usually be of the "double pole" variety, meaning it will have two toggles side-by-side which are clipped together. The breaker will most often be a 40 amp fixture.

Then disconnect the cook top from underneath. The wires will often be sheathed in a flexible conduit, but not always. If you are not familiar with electricity, you might want to hire an electrician to disconnect and reconnect your cook top for you, but it is really not a complex operation. Just remember to never work on an electrical circuit while that circuit is on.

Cement Backer Board

Can you install tiles directly to your plywood or laminate top? Yes, you can, but I don't recommend it. There are certainly glues and thin sets available that will do the job of adhering tiles to almost everything, but that doesn't mean it's a good idea to do so. I recommend that you add a little something to the surface before installing the tiles, something that is more in tune with the expansion and contraction cycles of a tile installation than is either plywood or particle board covered with laminate.

And don't for a minute consider installing tiles directly to particle board. Particle board, when it gets damp, can swell to nearly twice its thickness, cracking and breaking ceramic tiles or stone as it does so.

Installing cement backer board to a countertop is no different than installing it over a wood sub-floor. You cut the pieces to fit and nail them down with galvanized roofing nails. The CBUs are bedded in thin set mortar which is spread over the rough top with a notched trowel. Usually, one-quarter inch backer board is used on countertops, so the nails you use should be about an inch to an inch-and–a-quarter long. Any longer and they might come through and hinder the operation of your drawers.

You can thin set and nail narrow strips to the front of the cabinets and top to act as an overhang. By the time you add tile to the front you'll be out about even with the drawer fronts and doors, and that's where you want to be.

CBUs on counters must be taped just like the ones that are installed on sub-floors. Remember to use the special acid resistant tape that is specially made for the purpose. Apply the tape with thin set mortar.

And I'll remind you that different backer board manufacturers have different ideas about how their materials should be installed. Make sure you pick up a copy of the manufacturer's directions when you buy the product.

Waterproofing

It is not essential that you waterproof your countertops, but having waterproof tops is certainly a nice idea. There are a number of ways waterproofing can be done. There are semi-liquid membranes that can be brushed onto

Figure 176: Slate counter with wood edge treatment. (Barb Freda)

the backer board, and thin set will adhere to them. This might be your easiest approach, but it can be a bit messy. There are also numerous waterproof mats on the market that will do the job. Schluter-Kerdi, of course, is one, and Ditra is another. All of these materials will accept a direct thin set application when it's time to set the tiles.

Wood Edge Treatment

Wood and tile go together. There's something about it. Maybe it's the softness of the wood contrasting with the hardness of the tiles. If I were a decorator, I'd be able to tell you all about it. In any case, consider the wood edge treatment. I know I like it. (Figure 176)

Back-splashes

In most cases, the back-splash can be installed directly to the wall board. I would not bother installing cement backer board in the back-splash area. It's not necessary, and it might even get in the way of your trim pieces and cause them to stick out from the wall. If you are using radius or mud type bull-nose as trims, you might consider adding a second layer of 1/2 in. drywall to the back-splash area. The new sheetrock is simply nailed over the original. Make precise cuts around electrical outlets and switches so the tiles will be well supported in that area.

Face plates are removed from switches and outlets, and the fixtures themselves are unscrewed from their junction boxes and left dangling on their wires. They will be re-installed after the tile work has been completed. You will need longer screws than the ones you removed in order to accommodate the thickness of the new tiles.

Turn off the circuit breakers that control the outlets and switches before you attempt to remove them. Tape over all the connecting screws and wires with electrical tape and then turn the circuits back on so that you'll have light when you need it.

Layout

As it is with every other tile project, layout is crucial to the satisfactory completion of the project, and we won't rush the process. In fact, in most cases, countertop and back-splash layout is even more critical than floor layout and wall layout. There really isn't a lot of room for slop when you're dealing with an area only a couple feet wide.

For one thing, most kitchen counters are not simply long straight rectangles. They will often have at least one "L" turn and possibly two. "U" shaped countertops are not uncommon.

Figure 177: Granite tile countertop in shape of "L." (Monica and David McDonald)

"L" Shaped Counters: If your countertop has only one turn in it, your tile layout will most probably begin in that "L." To do otherwise would mean not having full pieces of tile along the front of both legs of the cabinet, and that would be undesirable from a design standpoint. The tiles along the front of the counter should always be full pieces. So it is best to start right in the corner and work from there in both directions. (Figure 177)

That does not mean, however, that you must necessarily continue in both directions with full pieces of tile. There are times when placing a row of cuts from front to rear on one or both legs of the counter is desirable in order to prevent a design foul-up further down the line. But if you are installing your tiles square to the edge of the counter, and the tiles on the back-splash will be installed in the same manner, everything is going to have to line up. So any cutting you do in the counters will have to follow up the wall. You'll have to be careful, then, when planning cuts in the countertop. Always keep an eye to the back-splash area.

There is a way around this, usually. If you start your layout exactly in the "L" and run full tiles out of there in both directions, it usually won't be long before you run into the sink on one leg. And equalizing the cuts on both sides of the sink is a desirable thing to do. So you end up with a certain size cut on the side of the sink that is closest to the "L." You then go to the other side of the sink and install the same size cuts over there, and then continue on up the length of the counter with full pieces of tile until you reach the end, where, unless you are incredibly lucky, you'll have to make another set of cuts.

You might be thinking that going from both sides of the sink with the layout will cause misery when trying to tile the back-splash, but it won't because we (you and I) are going to employ a design trick in that area behind the sink. There is often a window there and not much wall at all. It's not hard to come up with some sort of balanced arrangement that will end up matching the countertop tiles on both sides of the sink.

We might, for example, turn those wall tiles behind the sink on the diagonal and balance a panel of them under the window. That way nothing has to line up. It only has to be balanced, either on the window or on the sink and hopefully on both. (Figure 177A)

Diagonals: Another option that has been employed for ages is turning the countertop tiles on the diagonal but running the back-splash tiles straight and square with the countertop. Nothing has to line up in this situation. The only concern is to create a balanced layout in the area behind the sink and under the window, if there is a window and even if there is not. If there is nothing but wall behind the sink (and that's unusual), we would merely come up with a balanced layout on that wall. We would then continue from that area with full tiles until reaching the ends of the counter or running into a wall.

We would then layout the countertop on the diagonal, starting in the "L" and working in both directions from there. The same thing applies to the range or cook top. Achieve balance on the back wall and let the countertop (running on the diagonal) take care of itself.

You could also run the tiles square to the counter edge and use a band of diagonals on the splash, say one full diagonal tile alternating with half diagonals. Above this arrangement you might return to the square layout. The diagonal break would disguise the fact that the tiles on the counter and those on the splash are

Figure 177A: Full tiles on both sides of window opening. (Monica and David McDonald)

not perfectly aligned. It just doesn't matter if no one is likely to notice.

And this brings me to a philosophical point that has followed me through my tile setting career. When it comes to design and layout, if a tile job looks good, it is. If it doesn't look good, it's not. It doesn't matter whether everything has been done correctly from a technical standpoint if the job turns out looking less than perfect. And, of course, the reverse is true. You can make little design mistakes as long as the overall job looks good. None of this means we should not strive for perfection. We should, but none of us is perfect.

Different Size Tiles: Yet a third option would be using tiles of one size on the back splash and tiles of another size on the counter. This is often done when stone tiles are used. A very popular combination is 12 in. by 12 in. granite tiles for the countertops and tumbled marble in a smaller size for the back-splash. Or, granite slab counters and tile splash.

Designing With Decos: Decorative tiles, called "decos," can be used on the splash to rectify the problems that might occur because of necessary cutting that has been done on the counters. With decorative pieces, one is often able to cover up problem areas and make them look like design features. And then, of course, design features including decorative tiles are in many cases planned from the onset.

Decos can be tiles of the same size and type as the field

Figure 177B: Plain tiles of a different color can be used as decos.

tiles, or they can be tiles made from different stock altogether. In some cases the field tiles will have to be cut in order to accommodate the decos. The decos themselves should never be cut in my opinion. Tiles which are a different color from the main tile can be considered decos, also. (Figure 177B)

Liners and Listellos Add Style: Listellos (an Italian word that is popular in the tile industry) are border pieces that are made up of several components. They may be composed of numerous pieces of tile mounted on a backing material, or they may be solid pieces with painted-on or bas-relief features. They can also be sculpted. They are often very complimentary to a countertop tile job when used on the splash.

You could use the English term *listel*, which is nothing more than a normal border, or you could simply say border, but how much fun would that be. I mean, here is another opportunity to favorably impress someone, a friend, for example, with your unique knowledge of matters pertaining to tile and to decorating. Let me give you an idea of how a really impressive dialog might go:

"Uh, what's that?"

"Oh, why that's a multi-faceted *listello*, listello deriving from Old Italian and meaning border, narrow molding or fillet. Don't you think it adds a unique flavor, well I mean it provides a rather stunning counterbalance to those somewhat droll bas-relief insets I'm using on the wing walls? I'm concerned with ambience here more than anything else, of course."

"Uh, what's a fillet?"

"Well, of course, I should have simply said *listel* which is closer to English but derives from Old French, and means..."

When you see your friend's eyes roll back and glaze over, you'll know you've carried it off. Remember what I've been saying about style? (Figure 177C)

Liners are borders or inlays that are narrower than listellos, generally two inches or less in width. Liners might be of a solid color, or they might be multi-colored. They might also have a texture to them, or they might be sculpted or carved in bas-relief. Very thin liners of one-half inch or less are referred to as "pencil liners." These were very popular in bygone decades, and they are still used occasionally.

Mosaic Tiles: Mosaics tiles, as you will recall, are those tiles which are about two inches or less in both surface dimensions. That doesn't mean the tiles necessarily have to be square, but in most cases they are. The best mosaic tiles from a durability standpoint are those which are not glazed. The pigment arrangement of the clay dictates the color and style, and it goes all the way through the tiles.

There are many styles of glazed mosaic tiles, most of them porcelains, but some made from softer clays. There are not many tiles in this category that I would consider adequate for kitchen counters. The glazes are often much too soft and too easily scratched or marred. And tiles made from the softer ceramic

Figure 177C: Carved slate listello set into tumbled stone back splash.

157

clays are not a good choice since their resistance to impact is somewhat limited.

Mosaic tiles are often accompanied with matching trims, but other trims might be used as well. For example, you might consider using unglazed mosaic tiles for the countertop field but then using something else for the back-splash and the edge trim of the counters. An arrangement such as this provides a very durable work surface and also affords a variety of choices for areas that will not be subject to the severity of use the countertop itself will receive. Tough tiles on

Figure 177D: Tumbled stone splash with tiny marble inserts over granite counters.

the deck but softer more elegant tiles on the splash, in other words.

Standard Wall Tiles: For many years it was common to use standard four-and-a-quarter inch wall tiles on kitchen counters. I don't know who started the trend (some things began even before my time), but it was not a good idea at all. Wall tiles are soft-bodied and the glazes used on them are not designed to bear up under the rigors a kitchen counter can be expected to undergo. Wall tiles are fine for back splashes, though. It is not unusual to find a situation where floor tiles are used for the counters and wall tiles have been used for the splash. In fact, that is the precise arrangement I chose for my own kitchen when I wrote *Ceramic Tile Setting.* Those tiles are still in place. The grout joints have acquired a sort of "patina" through the years, but the tiles are still in good condition.

Solid Tops: In recent years I've come to the conclusion that ceramic tile counter-tops are not always the best possible choice for the kitchen. I know it's blasphemy to anyone in the tile business, but it's my opinion that some of the newer solid surface choices are more easily maintained. And some people simply don't want tile.

There are dozens of products on the market, including Corian ™ by Du Pont, Wilsonart ™ (made in Texas), Avanza ™ and Silestone ™, which are granite-like products, and then, of course, there is real granite. Unfortunately, none of these products is available to do-it-yourselfers. All are restricted to licensed installers. But it is still a consideration for your project. You could have the tops professionally installed and then complete your own tile splash. It's an option. (Figure 177D)

Granite Tile Countertops: If you cannot afford professionally installed granite tops, you might want to consider granite tiles that you can install yourself. Granite tiles are available in various sizes, with the bulk of them measuring 12 inches (30 cm) square. 12-inch squares work well for kitchen counters whose depth is usually in the area of two feet. Specially milled granite edging is available, or you can have bull nose pieces fabricated for your tiles at local stone fabrication shops. There are many varieties of granite tiles available, all of them costing more than ceramic tiles, but some of them quite within reason. Almost all granite is porous and must be sealed, but it is otherwise very durable.

Quarry Tiles: As you'll recall, quarry tiles are in the "burnt clay" family as are bricks and brick-like tiles. To be a quarry tile the clay that goes into its makeup is extruded rather than cast in a mold. Most quarry tiles are very hard and durable – the color, of course, goes all the way through the body of the tile, so they are not likely to wear out – ever. Using quarry on a residential kitchen counter might be considered unconventional by some, but there are hardly any conventions anymore when it comes to designing with tile, and quarry could lend to your kitchen's country or rustic appeal if that happens to be the direction in which your creative juices flow.

Figure 177E: Cut-away of Ditra countertop installation.

An advantage to quarry over other floor tiles is that there are usually accompanying bull-nose trims available. There are also molded base pieces and outside corners. It's a thought.

Slate, Soapstone and Other Sedimentary Rocks: Slate has an appeal to it, no question. So if you're inclined toward it, I probably won't be able to talk you out of putting it on your kitchen counters, but I'll try. Most slate is extremely difficult to maintain. It is soft and fragile. It flakes, it chips and sometimes rubs away. It is a very poor choice for kitchen counters from a maintenance and durability standpoint. It would, however, look very nice on your back-splash over a countertop tile that is a little smoother and more durable. Soapstone is similar to slate, and maybe even softer.

Marble, Limestone and Travertine: Limestone is highly susceptible to acid, and acid is present in many food items, to include orange juice, tomato paste and dozens of others. Acid is also present in many cleaning substances. Marble and travertine are composed of limestone to a large degree and are therefore at peril of acidic foods also. For this reason, and for the fact that these stone species are also soft and easily marred, I do not recommend marble, travertine or limestone as suitable paving for your counters. In the bath, okay, but not in the kitchen. I realize that this goes against certain traditions in Europe and other areas, but that doesn't change my opinion. As mentioned, tumbled marble or tumbled travertine works well on the back-splash.

Schluter Ditra

You remember Ditra. We discussed it a while back when we were figuring ways to cover kitchen floors and other areas. It's the product (one of the products) made by my friends at Schluter Systems. It "uncouples" the tile installation from the substrate, remember? Uncoupling is a very good thing to do to a tile installation. You can install Ditra directly to the countertop and tile right over it. Besides uncoupling and protecting the installation, Ditra will render it watertight, and depending on how messy you are in the kitchen, that can be a godsend. (Figure 177E)

Making Ditra waterproof is simple, and it doesn't require any special products. You simply cover any seams in the material with Schluter Kerdi or Kerdi-band and cement it into place with thinset, the same thin set you'll use to set your tiles. It is even possible to waterproof the joint between the countertop and the back-splash by using Kerdi on the splash behind the tiles. You install the Ditra right up to the back wall and then lap Kerdi down over it. Remember, the lap is two inches.

Glue strips of Ditra on the countertop edges and tape over them with Kerdi or Kerdi-band. The thin set used to attach the Ditra and Kerdi to the counter itself must be rated by its manufacturer to cling to plywood or plastic laminate if that is the case. At the same time, make sure you use a product that will withstand the dousing it will receive. I'm getting the feeling you could very possibly be a kitchen abuser like I am. But even if you are not, Ditra represents an excellent installation method for you to consider. The cost is not great because the area, relatively speaking, is not large.

Figure 177F: Ditra countertop installation with Schluter trims.

Whether you are using Ditra on your countertop or not, you can take advantage of the edge trims made by Schluter Systems.

Tiling Around Sinks

So we've figured out (you and I) how to lay out the tiles for the counter in the best manner possible and we're hard at it. We've started in the corner and are working our way toward the sink. We are not apprehensive. We know exactly what's going to happen when we run into that obstruction. Or at least I hope we do.

We can simply make the cuts that naturally fall alongside the sink, or we can run a row of full tiles by the sink and make the cuts against them, keeping in mind that whatever occurs on one side of the sink has to be mirrored on the other. We need balance in this area. We are certain, also, that there will be some cutting to be done one way or the other.

How close we need to cut the tiles to the sink hole will depend on the type of sink we are using. Self-rimming sinks made from enameled cast iron and other materials are the easiest. Self-rimming sinks usually allow a variance of at least one-half inch (12 mm), and some of them will allow more. Generally speaking, as long as the sink covers all the cuts, life will be pleasant. New self-rimming sinks usually come with a paper template packed in the box. Follow the template accurately, and you're home free.[14]

Stainless steel sinks are a different matter. I don't quite know why, but stainless sinks have always been a bit skimpy when it comes to their rims. The variance is often only a quarter-inch. Leave the tile hanging over the edge of the hole slightly and the sink won't go all the way in. Cut it back a little too far and the cut edge will show. Careful marking and careful cutting will ensure a minimal amount of waste and frustration.

---

[14]*"Home free" – Doing all right.*

Trims and Edging

Whether to put the trims on first or the field tiles on first is a question that often arises and one that has answers that are conditional. If I am using "V" Cap (A-8262) or Mud Caps (A-4200), I like to put them on before I run the field. I can get them straight and level without the field tiles getting in the way.

Figure 178: Double row of A-4200 bullnose pieces used to trim countertop edge.

Then when the edge is straight and perfect it's just a matter of bumping the field tiles up against the trims, as the trims don't have to line up with the tiles (unless you are using 6 inch standard wall tiles). (Figure 178)

If, on the other hand, you are using trims that are meant to line up with your field tiles, it is probably best to run the tiles and trims at more or less the same time. Working out of a corner or other starting point, you would set a few pieces of trim and then catch up with the field before the thin set holding the trims has completely set. Working quickly but carefully, you can make adjustments as you go. Often the trims are not quite calibrated to go with the tiles even though that was the intention of the man-ufacturer. Trims are always made at a different time than the field tiles, and sometimes a little tweaking is necessary in order to get things lined up. I know, it shouldn't be, but it often is.

I would try to work a section of counter that is about two lineal feet in length (about four square feet or so – maybe a third of a square meter). Don't get in a rush, but don't rest until you are sure everything is in place. Check it a couple times from dif-ferent perspectives, and then take a breather. I do not recommend stopping mid-length in a span of countertop and resuming the next day. It is to your benefit to finish the run in one session, checking it and then making small repairs or adjustments before the thin set has a chance to begin the curing process in earnest. Coming back the next day or the day after and discovering that your layout was off a little can be very disheartening. It can cause you to develop the "attitude," and you know what that means. Not a pretty picture.

Getting around the range top, if you have one in the counter, is the same as tiling around the sink. There will be an area of wall directly behind the cook top that stretches up to the vent hood. This is an area in which design features, including murals and bor-ders are often installed, and this entails achieving balance from one side to the other. This balance, of course, has to be carried up from the counter to the splash area if the areas are supposed to line up. You must keep this in mind as you tile the counter. One way to do things is to lay a row of tiles out on the counter and use a steel framing square to transfer their positions back to the wall. You can make vertical lines on the wall using a short level. Adjust things until a layout is achieved that balances everything out.

When you reach the end of a counter it is usually best to simply end the layout with whatever cuts are necessary. Set the trims on the end and then cut to them. Special care is needed to make the cuts as perfect as you can get them. Cuts that are made in places other than a corner or back wall receive particular scrutiny from every-one who might wander by. And the ones who will comment on your indiscretions are the ones you would least want to hear from, so do not get the "it's-good-enough atti-tude" in this area.

Tiling the Splash

If the tiles on the splash are meant to line up with the tiles on the counter, you can start anywhere you choose. It really makes no difference. If, however, the splash is not intended to lined up with the counter, or if you are tiling a splash over a solid surface counter, the splash is treated as a separate project with its own layout scheme. Balance in the window area behind the sink and in the area behind the stove will most likely be your chief concerns. What happens everywhere else, simply happens. That is unless you make special cuts in the field to adjust the layout.

Figure 179: Balance is important in the range/stove area.

I like to start in the sink area. I can fiddle around and get everything equalized on both sides of the window if it is centered and then work off in both directions from there. The tiles on one side often end in a corner, and on the other they just end where the upper cabinets stop. I can then return to the window area, fill in under it and tile the sill. The tiles and trims in the window area are simply "fit in." I may start in the center of the sill and work outward, making cuts at both ends, or I might start with full pieces at both ends and work toward the middle, making a "Dutchman" or a double "Dutchman" there. It just depends on what will look the best. Remember, the key is balance. A "Dutchman" is a cut tile that occurs in the middle of a tiled field. (Figure 179)

The same is true on the wall where the stove resides. Start in the area under the hood and get everything in balance, incorporating whatever design features have been planned. Then continue off in both directions. What happens in corners where wall sections meet is of little consequence. No one notices the cuts there, and if someone does, he or she should be run out of the kitchen and back into the den. (Figure 179)

Bathroom Counters

In most homes bathroom counters receive much less abuse than kitchen counters do, so I've relaxed my standards for tile durability a bit when working in the bath area. You're not going to be placing skillets and sauce pans on the bathroom counters and sliding them around causing abrasion, and you are not going to be conducting your parties in the bath area either. Wait a minute.

Figure 180: Bath vanity top tile with standard wall tiles.

No, you're not going to be doing that, are you?

Softer tiles might be considered for bathroom counters or "vanity tops." Still, it's good practice to use the best and most resilient material that will fit into your decorating scheme. While slate and marble will often be considered, it is prudent to select those species which are the easiest to maintain, not that any marble is truly easy to take care of.

Wall tiles can be used on bath vanity tops without a great deal of concern. In fact, in years gone by it was the norm to use one wall tile throughout the bath area – in the shower, on the wall wainscots, on the counter and on the floor, too. I would not however, consider using wall tiles on the floor nowadays. There are much better options. (Figure 180)

Other than the size of the sink (lavatory) and the height of the splash, tiling bathroom vanities is no different than tiling kitchen counters. Use a good plywood base with cement backer board or Ditra over the top. As in the kitchen, waterproofing is not required, but it is a blessing in certain households. If you live in one of these, do the waterproofing before you do the tiling.

Mudding a Countertop

While doing mud work on kitchen countertops may seem a bit much for the average home craftsman or craftswoman, mudding a vanity in the bath is certainly within reason. Dave Misevich, the fellow who did the monument shower seat, also floated his vanity top, and I've borrowed the pictures he took of the project.

Since he is a woodworker, Dave built his own cabinet, but a pre-built vanity cabinet will work the same way. Set the top level, and make sure it's well supported. Dave used 3/4 in. plywood, and

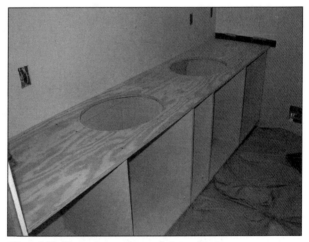

Figure M1: Plywood screwed securely into cabinet.

that's what I recommend you use. Nail or screw it securely to the cabinet.

Locate and cut a hole for the sink or sinks. New sinks are often packed with paper templates that can be used to mark the holes to be cut, but a sure-fire way is to use the

sink itself. Turn the sink upside down and trace a pencil line around its rim. Remove the sink and trace another line about an inch in from the first. Cut to this second line Try the sink in the hole before you go any further. (Figure M1)

Having considered the various ways the vanity top could be trimmed at its edge, Dave chose to use a double mud cap (A-4200).

Figure M2: Double bullnose edge treatment.

The method affords a clean looking, rounded edge overhang. (Figure M2)

You might also consider a wood edge treatment which would be attached and finished prior to mudding the top and setting the tiles. You could also use one of the various Schluter trims at the edge of your counter.

Lay a moisture barrier of either tar paper or sheet plastic over the countertop, and then install the metal lath. Cut the lath so that it bends over the front edge of the cabinet and extends downward 1 in. (25 mm). Fasten the lath securely with staples or nails. If using nails, drive them in only a half inch and then bend them over. Don't let them poke through the bottom of the plywood. As an alternative to metal lath, you can use chicken wire (poultry netting).

In order to install the bullnose pieces at the edge of the top, the mortar must protrude past the edge by a distance of 1/2 in. (12 mm). Dave has nailed a strip of 1/2 in. plywood just below where the mud will stop. The plywood strip has a two-fold purpose: it stops the mortar from falling down the front of the cabinet; and it acts as a spacer, limiting the mud overhang to 1/2 in. (Figure M3)

Over the plywood strip, Dave will install a second strip of plywood which will extend above the countertop to the height desired for the mud. This strip must be installed straight and level, as it will determine the final shape of the mud bed. It will also act as a form for the mortar that will become the overhang.

You will need to create a level

Figure M3: Lath is bent over edge. First plywood strip in place.

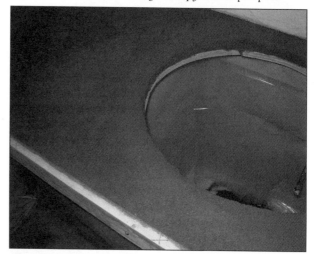

Figure M4: Counter is mudded.

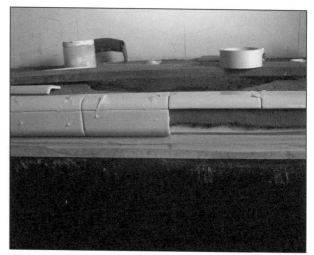

Figure M5: Installing the bullnose. Masking tape helps.

screed from deck mud along the wall at the back of the counter. Make it the same height as the final wood strip at the front. Pay particular attention to keeping the screed straight and level.

I like to use stiff fat mud around the sink hole and at the edge of the counter. It holds together much better than deck mud. Pack it an inch or two wide around the hole and down the front of the cabinet. Push it all the way down into the slot created by the two strips of ply-wood. Then finish off the deck with dry pack (deck mud). The deck mud will blend into the fat mud and become as one with it. Just beautiful, isn't it? (Figure M4)

When all the mud has been packed and raked off, smooth it with your steel trowel to embed the particles of sand at the sur-face. Don't push too hard. You wouldn't want to create a "bird bath."

A mud man or mud woman would remove the plywood strips

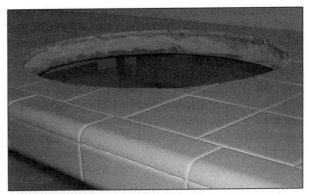

Figure M6: Cutting around sink hole.

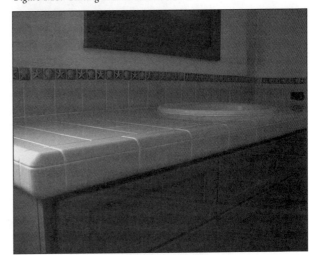

Figure M7: Decorative trims at splash.

and tile the top while the mortar is wet, but you can wait for it to set-up. Do remove the outer plywood strip and round over the edge of the mortar so that the bullnose will fit snuggly over it.

I like to tile the edge first. Center the bullnose or start at the outside corner if you have one. Install first an upper piece of bullnose and then its lower counterpart. Use tape to hold everything together while it sets. Check often with a straightedge to ensure the edge is straight and true. (Figure M5)

When you are satisfied with the edge, begin setting the field tiles, starting at the front center if you are balancing the installation. Start at the outside corner, otherwise. Ideally, all cuts are made against the walls. This isn't always possible, though.

The cuts around the sink hole do not have to be exact. In fact, I often chop around the sink hole with the biters. The rim of the sink will cover the cuts. Make sure each cut is well supported with thin set. (Figure M6)

Complete your countertop by putting on a splash. You don't need to mud it. You can either glue your tiles and trims to the wall, or you can add a layer of sheetrock or backer board to bump the splash out to accommodate mud trims. You might also con-sider some sort of decorative trim for the splash. (Figures M7, M8, M9)

Remember to keep your composure during all of this. It's a tile project, after all. You can joke around a little, but don't allow anyone to think this work is anything but dead serious – it's right up there with national defense and football. You are a tile setter/tile fixer. You represent a breed that roosts on a higher rung than the ordinary chicken. You owe it to your contemporaries and predecessors to carry out your duties with composure, competence and *style*.

Figure M8: How about a tumbled stone vanity?

Figure M9: Dave's vanity.

CHAPTER 5

FINISHING UP

The Final Details

Thought you were finished, eh? Not quite, my friend. Seems as though there are always minor details to be attended to. A tile man's (tile woman's) job is never done, but then who would want it to be? What else could one possibly want to do?

Sealers

Sealing your handiwork is one of the things that, while it might not seem significant, can make a world of difference in how your project holds up to the rigors it will be subjected to. A good protective sealer can prevent spills from becoming disasters. It can also prevent mold from taking root in the shower area. It would be wonderful if there were one product that would do it all, but there isn't. My friend Tim Thomas, restoration specialist and chemist, will acquaint you with a number of tile and stone care products.

Tile and Stone Maintenance
by Tim Thomas

Congratulations! You've just completed a quality tile job, but now what do you do to protect and maintain this beautiful surface? With proper maintenance, tile and stone can look as good as the day you installed it, virtually forever.

Preventative Maintenance

Preventative maintenance covers the initial deep cleaning and protection of your surface. It is of utmost importance to remove all grout haze from the tiles. Not only will grout haze make the job look unprofessional; it will also trap dirt and other contaminants on the tiled surface. A little pH neutral cleaner added to your grout clean-up water will make haze removal much easier. Always follow manufacturers' instructions when using any tile care product.

If the grout haze has had some time to set-up, you will have to move on to heavy-duty products, those designed specifically for grout haze removal. A solution of one part white vinegar and one part water has been used with much success on tile that is not acid sensitive, such as ceramic, quarry and porcelain.

If you have no luck with the vinegar and water solution, move up to a stronger acid. Phosphoric or sulfamic acid should be your next step. Both are readily available at most home centers and professional tile stores. These two acids have been used by tile restoration contractors for a number of years, but they are corrosive materials. Follow manufacturers' instructions carefully.

A new acid has entered the market within the past couple of years. Marketed as a "low pH cleaner" or as an "acid alternative" because it really does not have a name, it is composed of a low pH organic salt, usually the salt of hydrochloric acid. This acid is more efficient at dissolving portland cement based products than is phosphoric or sulfamic.

Almost all grouts used today are modified grouts. This means they have been mixed with an additive, usually an acrylic, to enhance performance. The additive can inhibit an acid's ability to dissolve the cement in the grout haze. In many cases an alkaline cleaner should be used before acid is tried. Alkaline products are usually sold as heavy-duty tile cleaners. They have the ability of dissolving the additive in the grout haze, allowing the acid to come into contact with the cement. It can easily take more than one application, accompanied by vigorous scrubbing, to remove the haze.

When dealing with grout haze on an acid sensitive natural material such as marble, travertine, limestone and even some slates and granites, do not use vinegar or any other acidic cleaner, as it will etch the stone. Haze removal on these surfaces will require the use of a good neutral cleaner, razor blades and a lot of elbow grease. When all the grout haze has been thus removed, do a final damp mopping with clean water and a pH neutral cleaner.

Once your new tiled surface is clean, you must seal it to protect it from the effects of daily use. Sealing has become a controversial issue when it comes to natural stone. Some professionals maintain that all stone needs to be sealed — sort of a general safety net if you will. Others claim only certain stones need to be sealed and that it is a waste of time and money (or it is harmful to the stone) to seal it when it is not required.

Truth is, not every stone tile needs to be sealed, and, conversely, not all man-made tiles are impervious to staining. There is a simple test you can conduct at home to determine whether your particular tile needs to be sealed. The test should be done while deciding on a tile at the very beginning of the installation process. Not only will it determine if the material in question needs to be protected, but it will also tell you if and where it should be installed. Many professionals are against the use of marble in the kitchen due to its sensitivity to acidic materials such as lemon juice and vinegar, but with proper prevention and the full understanding by you (the one who will have to live with it), it can be used.

The Test

You will have to obtain a sample piece of tile. Place a few drops each of lemon juice and olive oil and let dwell for 15 minutes. Wipe the tile clean and let it dry for another 15 minutes. Closely study the tile. You are looking for dark (or light) spots and a change in texture. If the lemon juice etches the tile, you may want to think long and hard about where you will be placing this material. Acidic products are abundant in a kitchen, but again, if you have your heart set on an acid sensitive tile and you are willing to deal with future etching, don't worry about it. Just remember there is not a sealer available that will prevent acid from etching these surfaces, not yet at least.

Now let's say the olive oil produces a visible stain. You can still use the tile anywhere you like, but it will have to be treated with a high-end penetrating sealer, also known as an impregnator. As far as impregnators go, fluorochemical type products exhibit the best oil resistance. This is due to the low surface tension of the sealer. Surface tension is basically the energy, or staining and cleaning ability, of any liquid. Most water-based materials will have a surface tension in the neighborhood of 30 to 35 dynes/cm. Oil-based materials will measure much lower, usually around 20 to 25 dynes/cm. Fluorochemicals, when used in an impregnator formulation, will produce a surface that measures from the high teens to the low twenties. With the surface tension of the sealer being lower than that of most common staining materials, it will be difficult for these staining materials to penetrate into the surface.

The same rule applies for cleaners, mainly neutral cleaners or cleaners that do not clean the surface using alkaline or acidic chemicals. The surface tension of the cleaner must be lower than that of the contaminant being removed. This enables the cleaner to get between the contaminant and the surface and break the bond (the energy, between the two).

Fluorochemical impregnators are still somewhat new to the market, but impregnators have been around for many years. Older impregnators use resins such as silicones or epoxy. These sealers do not rely on surface tension technologies, it comes down to chemical resistance. Resin is deposited into the pores of the surface, rendering it water resistant, stain resistant or both.

Due to the general nature of fluorochemical treatments, you will see some darkening when water comes into contact with the surface, but this is just water vapor in the pores near the surface, not actual penetration. Fluorochemical treated surfaces will dry out much faster than untreated surfaces.

The stone's finish will also dictate whether or not it will benefit from a protective treatment. For example, a polished marble may not show any staining, but a piece of the same material that is honed instead of polished might stain easily. A polished surface is very dense at the top and will often not need to be protected. A stone surface that is not polished can be porous, on the other hand.

Impregnators are also used on cement-based grout. They are particularly useful in wet areas such as showers, because they allow for vapor transmission. In short, impregnators "breathe." This means that the drying process of the surface and subsurface is not hindered by the sealer.

Some stones, such as slate and sandstone, and tiles such as Saltillo, tend to perform better when a topical coating is applied. This topical sealer/finish not only seals the surface, but it also acts as a sacrificial coating that will absorb the brunt of daily use.

Ceramic, quarry and most porcelain tiles will not benefit significantly from the use of a sealer. If you are looking at a "through-bodied porcelain," meaning the color is the same all the way through, you need to run the stain test to determine if a sealer is needed or not.

Grout Stain

The popularity of grout staining products has grown over the last 5 years. Besides producing color consistency throughout the installation, something that grout alone seems to have a hard time doing, grout stains seal the grout. Inconsistent grout color is a major concern for contractors and homeowners alike. Many variables exist that will determine the color of your joints. A difference in joint depth or width, the amount of water used in mixing the grout from batch to batch, different people mixing different batches of grout and the humidity on the day the grouting is done are all factors that bear directly on grout color and shade. Grout stains are typically matched to the grout manufacturers' grout color charts, so you are not only applying a tenacious sealer; you're getting the color you chose to begin with.

Routine Maintenance

How you conduct day-to-day maintenance will determine how good your tile looks now and later. A proper maintenance regimen bears directly on the useful life of your tile installation. First and probably most important, you will need to sweep at least the heavy traffic areas daily. Dirt, sand and other grits are the number one cause of premature hard surface failure. You may not see the majority of these little culprits, but they are there. Use the softest, finest push type broom you can find. A fine broom will get down in the grout joints and remove most contaminates, and this type of broom will not damage the tile by applying excessive pressure on the hard surface as you drag the abrasive particles over it.

Push vacuums have been recommended for years to perform the sweeping task on tiled floors, but they do not pick up all of the abrasive particles. Furthermore, it is just not worth the risk of catching a sharp piece of sand or grit under a wheel and scratching the tile as you push. Dust mops are another option, but as soon as the mop acqires even a fine film of dust and dirt, it will scrape across the lip of one tile and deposit the dirt that was cleaned off the preceding tile into the grout joint. Grout joints can exhibit discoloration from this procedure in as little as a month after installation.

Preventing abrasive contaminants for entering the building is your best stra-tegy, and carpet mats are hands down the best tool at your disposal. It is a proven fact that it takes at least 7 steps to remove the majority of abrasive parti-cles from your shoes, so you will need more than just a welcome mat in the entryway. You will need to place a mat on both sides of your exterior door to achieve the distance needed. Not any old mat will do, either. Use a synthetic or natural fiber mat without a rubber backing. Rubber contains aggressive chemicals which keep it soft and flexible, and these chemicals can leach out and stain the surface of your floor. This is the reason garden hose manufacturers tell you not to drink water from their hoses. The only backing recommended for contact with a tiled surface is one made from PVC, but it needs to be ventilated to allow mois-ture to escape from under the mat. Otherwise, water staining can occur.

Having controlled all those pesky abrasive contaminants, you will need to address dirty water residue from shoes and other contaminants that can stain your floor. Damp mopping will be in order. Use a clean string mop, a mop bucket with a wringer and a small amount of neutral cleaner. A string mop will remove most contaminants from the grout joints, whereas a sponge mop acts just like the dust mop I mentioned above. It picks up dirt from the tile and deposits it into the nearest grout joint.

Do not mop with dirty, or even cloudy, water. Using dirty mop water accom-plishes nothing. You will merely be pushing dirty water around the surface, and once the water evaporates, you are left with dirt. This is one reason why grout joints turn gray and why a lot of folks in the industry will try to steer you away from using light colored grout. With proper
preventative and routine maintenance, you can use whatever grout color your heart desires.

Restoration

Restoring a tiled surface involves deep cleaning, stain removal and some-times resurfacing. Restoration is something that may need to be done every 3 months or every 3 years. It depends on how much the surface is used and how well it has been maintained.

Deep cleaning can mean using clean water and a neutral cleaner coupled with a good scrubbing. Nylon brushes and synthetic scrub pads work well for this. You may also have to purchase heavy-duty cleaning and stripping products designed specifically for tile and stone to handle problems that go beyond the capabilities of your daily neutral cleaner. Stains caused by dirty car oil tracked in from the driveway will require specialty products—a heavy-duty tile cleaner or a stain-removing poultice, perhaps.

The best approach to deep cleaning will entail flooding the area with an appropriate cleaning solution, agitating to suspend the contaminant in the solution, and then using a wet vacuum to finish up. The process might need to be repeated a number of times to achieve a clean surface.

Stain removal is typically best addressed with a poultice. A poultice is an absorbent material such as a clay powder or diatomaceous earth, but white paper towels and even cotton balls can do the trick. These would then be mixed with an appropriate chemical and applied to the surface. Cover the poultice with plastic wrap and tape it at the edges. Allow the poultice to dwell for 24 hours. Remove the plastic and carefully scrape the powder from the surface and then rinse. The chemical in the mixture will leach from the poultice into the surface and break up the staining material. It will then be sucked back into the poultice material as it dries.

The cause of the stain will dictate which chemical to mix the poultice material with. The most common staining materials tend to be oil-based. Oil-based stains are best addressed with solvents such as mineral spirits, acetone or methylene chloride. Some oil stains can be removed with water-based alkaline solutions such as a heavy-duty tile cleaner or ammonia. Use bleach, hydrogen peroxide, acetone or lacquer thinner on ink stains. For coffee, tea, food and plant stains use ammonia or hydrogen peroxide. Use bleach or ammonia for deep-set mold and mildew stains. Do not mix any of these chemicals together, they can emit toxic fumes when mixed, just use them one at a time with the poultice material of your choice. The chemicals mentioned here are usually safe to use on all surfaces, including natural stone, but you should nevertheless try your compound in an out-of-the-way spot.

Resurfacing is performed only on natural stone, and it should be done by a professional. Abrasive contaminants will eventually win the war, and traffic patterns will become visible. If the stone was honed to begin with, or if it was left in its natural state, it will take much longer for wear patterns to show. This is opposed to a surface that has been polished.

Showers

No matter what kind of tile surface you decide to use in a shower, you can bank on years of service as long as you wipe the shower dry after each use. This will prevent hard water deposits, soap scum and body oils from building up. Using a little neutral cleaner diluted with water in a spray bottle and dry towels are best for this. After use, liberally spray the neutral cleaner solution on all tiled surfaces in the shower area and wipe dry with a clean towel. You will also need to seal any porous natural stone used and all grout joints. By design, a shower needs to be able to breathe, so you should not use any topical coatings or even grout stains. These sealers do allow for some vapor transmission, but nowhere near the rate that is provided by a high quality impregnator. Silicone impregnators exhibit the best water resistance, but silicone will leach out of the surface eventually. It will also attract oils and other contaminates, which usually results in yellowing of the surface. Once again, fluoropolymer impregnators are the best for repelling oils and they will not leach out of the surface or attract other contaminants. They will however show slight surface wetting, especially in a wet environment, but this is just water vapor sitting in the pores of the surface and not actual water penetration. Any darkening that occurs on a fluoropolymer protected surface where water vapor is the culprit will dissipate quickly after the water is removed.

I will leave you with the following list of tips.

Use a soft, fine push type broom daily, especially in high traffic areas.
Use fiber walk-off mats to remove abrasives from shoes.
Use a clean string mop and bucket to mop with.
Change mop water as soon as it gets cloudy.
Use a neutral cleaner designed specifically for use on tile and stone.
Clean up spills right away. Blot them up; do not wipe them.
Always start off with the least aggressive products and techniques when
    faced with a cleaning task.
Use only products designed specifically for tile and natural stone.
Towel dry tiled showers and wet areas after each use.
Do not use standard household cleaners on tile. Most of these contain harsh
    chemicals.
Do not use a vacuum, dust mop, Swiffer or sponge mop.
Do not use rubber backed or unventilated walk-off mats.
Do not use water alone to clean with. Neutral cleaner acts on water to lower
    its surface tension, making it a better cleaner.
Do not use vinegar and water to clean with, even though the practice is often
    mistakenly recommended by tile suppliers. Vinegar is acidic, and it will
    slowly erode your surface. And besides that, acid is not a good cleaner
    due to its high surface tension.
Following these rules will ensure you many years of use and enjoyment from
your tile and stone. May your surfaces always glisten.

*Tim Thomas is the official chemist of the John Bridge Forums
and the producer of Tile Your World tile and stone care products.
He can be contacted via email: kemikalguru@aol.com*

Replacing Damaged Floor Tiles

When I install tile floors in people's homes I always make sure there are extra tiles at the end of the job. They will be kept in an out-of-the-way spot — the attic, a corner of the garage, the crawl space, etc. — in the hope that they will never be needed. But occasionally they are needed.

The tiles we install nowadays are ten times more durable than those installed only a decade ago, but still, they are ceramic tiles, and they can be damaged. The most usual place for a tile to suffer a blow is directly in front of the refrigerator. Someone opens the door, reaches for the water bottle or some other heavy container and drops it on the floor.

The tile that is struck, if it has been properly installed will not crack or break, but it will be pitted. In some cases the pit might be described as a crater. The severity of the chip and your tolerance for blemishes will determine whether you replace the tile or whether you repair it by some means — filling the pit with matching enamel paint, for example.

But let's say the blemish is so severe or your tolerance is so low that replacing the piece cannot be avoided. We'll start by removing the grout from around the tile.

The tool to use is called a "grout saw." It is a small hand tool that can be purchased at tile suppliers, at home centers and at some hardware stores. The grout saw consists of a handle to which a small blade is attached. The business edge of the blade is coated with carborundum particles. The tool is not expensive, and the blades are replaceable.

The grout saw works by rubbing the blade back and forth in the middle of the grout joint. As you work the tool, avoid contacting the edges of the tiles. Take your time and stay in the middle area of the joint. Eventually, you will cut (wear away) a line of grout all the way to the substrate, be it concrete slab, backer board, or some other flooring material.

In this manner, you must cut the grout all the way around the tile to be removed. This will relieve any pressure that might occur on adjacent tiles as you remove the damaged piece. I can't stress this enough. If you get in a hurry here, you will be replacing more tiles than you anticipated.

When the grout has been sawn all the way around, you can break or pulverize the tile with a hammer and remove the fragments with a cold chisel. You will also have to remove any setting material (thin set, dry set, etc.) that remains on the substrate. Make a smooth surface for the replacement tile to be set upon.

The next step is to remove the grout that remains attached to the sides of the adjacent tiles, and this is probably the most tedious part of the operation. I find it convenient to use a very small cold chisel and a hammer. The chisel is not hit hard but only tapped with the hammer, so as to avoid damaging the edges of the tiles as the grout is chipped away, bit by bit. The reason for removing all the grout is that the new grout will not match the old, and it is better to have the entire joint one color than to have half of it one color and the other half another.

If, however, the tiles you are working with are very soft, such as Saltillo, raw terracotta or very soft glazed tiles, then the chisel should not be used. You can attempt to somehow wear the remaining grout away, or you can simply leave it in place and live with it. In any case, using the chisel will almost certainly result in damaging the edges of the tiles.

Installing the new tile is fairly straightforward. Use the same type adhesive that was used in the original installation, whether this is a cement product or some sort of glue or mastic. Allow the repair to set at least 24 hours or the time recommended by the adhesive manufacturer.

If you know the original grout brand and color, use it, even though it will not match initially. It will blend in eventually. If you don't know the original color, you must try to make a match as best you can. You can make a sample of the grout you intend to use, let it dry and compare it to the existing grout. An inexact process? Yes.

Before applying the grout, dampen any existing grout that the new material will contact. Just dampen it; don't soak it. This will prevent the existing grout from immediately drawing the moisture from the new grout and weakening it.

Place the new grout, allow it to begin to firm up, and then wash the surface of the tiles and joints with a sponge or soft cloth, moving more or less diagonally across the joints. The sponge or cloth should be wet but not soaking. Make repeated passes, wringing the sponge or cloth thoroughly each time. When the joints are uniform and straight, stop.

You're finished, except for wiping the haze from the tiles after the surface dries. This is done with a dry, soft cloth. If there is still residue on the tiles, you can rinse them again with the sponge and clean water. Wring the sponge thoroughly, though. Not much water at all.

Protect the repair for at least 24 hours.

To preclude the necessity of making this repair in the future, stay out of the fridge.

Replacing Damaged Wall Tiles

Replacing wall tiles is quite a bit more difficult than replacing floor tiles. The wall tiles I'm talking about are the standard 4-1/4 in. tiles that are made from white "slip," the same material used in figurines. Standard wall tiles also come in a 6 in. by 6 in. size.

Joints are usually wide enough in a floor tile installation to allow the use of a grout saw to cut the grout down to the substrate. This is not possible with wall tiles, because the joints are narrow, and there are spacer lugs formed into the tiles themselves which are in the way. The spacer lugs actually cause the tiles to contact one another under the surface of the grout, making it extremely difficult to remove the tiles.

I have heard people mention using small rotor-type tools (Dremel and others) to remove the grout from between wall tiles, but if you slip just once with an electric tool, you can ruin tiles adjacent to the one you are trying to replace. The job could go on a long time at that rate.

I have found it convenient to use a utility knife to scratch the grout from between the tiles. You will certainly wear down a number of blades in the process. You can also use pieces of hacksaw blades gripped in locking pliers to wear the grout out of the joints. Be very careful not to harm the edges of the adjacent tiles.

To remove a tile, you must remove most of the grout from around it. This relieves pressure from adjacent tiles when you begin the removal process. You won't get all of the grout out, but you must at least get down to the spacer lugs.

You will not, of course, proceed unless you have a replacement tile on hand. Having a damaged tile in the wall is better than having something there that will look worse.

With a small chisel and a hammer, make a hole in the center of the tile to be removed, and then chip away small portions of the tile, working from the center out toward the edges. Don't get in a hurry. This is especially important when you approach the edges of the tile. You must be very careful not to damage the adjacent tiles.

Do not hit the chisel toward the adjacent tiles. Rather, strike the tool in a manner that directs the force of the blows away from the tiles which are to remain. Again, take your time.

Do not attempt to pry up on the tile. This will almost certainly cause damage to other tiles. Just keep knocking small pieces away one at a time. When the tile itself has been removed, you must remove the setting material that remains in the void. This will usually be thin set mortar, but it might be mastic or some other glue. You've got to get this out so that the new tile will go in flush with those around it.

Installing the new tile may entail removing some or all of its spacer lugs. Ceramic tiles may look all the same size, but I can assure you they are not. In many cases the replacement tile will not fit into the hole unless something is done to adjust the lugs. You can nip them off with biters, or you can break them off with common pliers. You can also file them down with course sandpaper. This would be the prudent thing to do if you only have one replacement tile.

Regardless of what type of adhesive was used in the original installation, you can use thin set mortar to attach the new tile to the substrate. Use the white thin set that is formulated for wall tiles. Allow the repair to set overnight before grouting. Grout with unsanded tile grout.

In some cases, people want to replace tiles because they have had holes drilled through them. I should point out that in certain situations it might be easier to cover or disguise the hole than to replace the tile. If you can find or mix an enamel paint to match the tile surface, you can fill the whole with thin set or grout and paint over it. The repair will not be perfect, but it may be all that is needed.

There are also available small decorative ceramic pieces that are made to be planted onto existing wall tiles. These are sometimes called "spotters," and they may be the answer to your repair needs.

In my opinion, wall tiles that have hairline cracks should not be replaced. If they

Recess-It™

Cementitious backer units classified by Underwriters as fire resistance directories, as shown in the label

Art and John

Cal, Dave, Michael and John

Eric Rattan and John Bridge

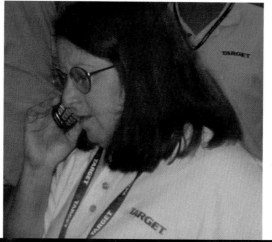

Joann

John, Andy and Sonja

Patti, John, Dave Misevich and Kelly Chaplin

are not unsightly, leave them alone. There is always a chance of damaging other tiles in the field. It is very possible to end up with a worse situation than the one you set out to rectify. I have been there. Don't go there. Aloha.

Shower Pan Replacement

We have, of course, already covered installation of PVC (or CPE) shower pan liners in new showers, but what about replacing a shower pan that has begun to leak, one composed of lead which has oxidized itself out of existence, for example? Before the actual installation can begin, a portion of the shower bottom will have to be removed. Plug the drain by taping over it with duct tape or by removing the grate and stuffing a rag tightly down the drain pipe.

What has to come out? The top and inside of the curb/dam must be removed to allow the new pan material to come up and over to a point outside the shower door or curtain. The tiles on all the walls must be taken out up to a height equal to two inches or more above the curb. Finally, the shower floor must be broken out. Actually , the floor should come out first, because in most cases it will have been installed last. You can break the floor into segments using a maul and a heavy chisel. A wrecking bar comes in handy for prying up the segments.

Removing tiles from the walls and the curb is a somewhat delicate operation, if you can consider demolition delicate at all. Saw or scratch out the horizontal grout joint where you intend to make the break. Get the grout worked down as far as possible. This will minimize the shock to the upper wall tiles that will remain in place.

I use a three-pound maul to break out the tiles. Start at the bottom near the floor and work your way up toward the sawn grout joint. When you are within one course (of tiles) of the saw cut, slow down. You may have to remove the final pieces of tile with a small chisel in order to avoid damaging the tiles above. The same delicacy is required when removing tiles from the curb. If you aren't careful, you could find yourself replacing the entire curb.

When the lower walls, along with the top and inside of the curb, have been removed and the debris has been cleared away, you're ready to begin the shower pan installation. The procedure is exactly the same as for a new shower. If no backing blocks were originally installed between the studs, install them. Create the pre-slope if none was provided in the original installation.

If you are working with a mud shower, you can tack pieces of lath right up under the last course of existing tile, the same place you fastened the new pan material. You can't, of course, nail the lath all the way down. Just let it dangle. You can pack some wall mud against the bottoms of the pieces when you begin floating the walls.

Floating the walls is a sort of free hand operation. I gauge the depth of the mud by running a new tile under the last course of existing tiles. Get the mud back so that the new tiles will be flush with the old. A short straightedge can be used to get the walls straight from side to side, and a torpedo level works well for keeping them plumb.

It's possible to bend an L-shaped piece of metal lath and nail it into the top of the curb outside where the shower door closes. Pack mud against the bottom of the piece inside the shower and then rough it in with mortar. Allow the mortar to set an hour or so and then use a straightedge to get it in line. You can smooth the mud with the little wooden block. Allow the mud to set a bit before you attempt to set tile to it.

I back-butter the individual tiles onto the mud, using masking tape to hold them up under the existing tiles. Work your way around all the walls of the shower, and then do the curb.

I like to grout the walls before putting in the shower floor. That way, when I'm finished with the floor I can walk away.

A shower pan replacement in a backer board shower is done in much the same fashion. The pieces of CBU are nailed at the top and allowed to drape downward. The joints are taped. In this case, I would put the mud floor in and allow it to harden before installing any tile. The mud floor will be the only thing holding the bottoms of the CBU portions in place.

It is seldom that a shower with a reconstructed floor and lower walls will look as good as it did when it was new. Replacing a shower pan must be considered radical surgery. There will be the cold joint between the old and new tiles — the new tiles won't match the old, even if you somehow manage to acquire the same tiles used originally. It's not unusual to crack some of the existing trims during the demolition process. Often these trims won't be available; they will be simply grouted over. The shower will be serviceable. It won't be a decorating focal point, and nobody from House and Garden magazine is going to come knocking on your door wanting to take pictures.

Grab Bar Installation

Showers can be treacherous places in which to spend one's time. Surfaces are wet; they are covered with soap, shampoo and all sorts of other concoctions people carry into the shower with them. And as if that weren't enough of a challenge, you're expected to stand on a shower floor that is not level; it's tilted. Make one false move — take one wrong turn — and you could be headed for the drain along with the water, the soap, the shampoo and other flotsam. As they say in Texas, Yee Haw!

Using a tub shower is even more hazardous than using a full shower, in my opinion. There is nothing worse than standing barefooted in a soapy, wet tub. And then there is the front side of the tub that must be negotiated when getting in and out. Extreme care must be taken to avoid accidents.

Yes, one can't be too careful when using the shower, especially when one begins to get older. I've noticed during the past few years that I sometimes experience dizziness when washing my hair (which I still have plenty of, by the way). I think a lot of folks do it the way I do it. I lean my head over under the spray with my eyes closed. The dizziness occurs when I straighten up and reach for the towel, eyes still tightly closed. At times I've almost lost my balance and done the "Yee Haw" thing. It's a bit scary, but I have to admit it's aerobic. Gets your heart rate right up there in a hurry. I somehow suspect the dizziness is not going to subside as I get older still.

I've thought about installing a grab bar or two in my shower. I've installed hundreds of them for other people, people who are usually older than I am but also for people young and old who have some sort of physical disability. The devices are a godsend for anyone who finds himself or herself in anything less than perfect condition. A strategically located grab bar is not a bad idea for anyone, for that matter.

Speaking of strategy, location is important. Most people face the spray head the majority of time they spend in the shower, so a grab bar on the plumbing wall makes a lot of sense. If the bar or a portion of it is located near the shower entrance, it will provide a handhold when entering or exiting the shower, the prime instance in which a person may be a bit off balance. Another bar should be located on the adjacent wall within easy reach of the showering person when he or she is facing in the opposite direction.

Height is also a factor that must be considered. The bars should be placed at about stomach level or just a bit lower. I "fit" grab bars to the people who will be most likely to use them. I stand the person in the shower and ask him or her to reach out toward the wall with eyes closed. I actually hold the bar at the appropriate height and have the person grab it. I then mark the location on the wall with a pencil.

Grab bars should be installed horizontally, in my opinion. Vertical bars are hard to hold onto, especially when your hands are wet and possibly soapy, and they are not easy to locate when your eyes are closed. Bars installed at angles are nearly as bad. The horizontal bar will provide more stability, and it provides the largest target when you are groping for something to help you regain your balance.

I don't like grab bars that have squared-off brackets at their ends, as these can cause cuts and bruises. The bars that are rounded on their ends are the way to go. Most of these are actually welded into a one-piece unit, which makes them exceptionally rigid and strong. Having knurling or some sort of texture tooled or molded into the bar is a plus.

If you are building a new shower from cement backer board or from Schluter Kerdi and drywall, you should pre-determine where your grab bars are going to be located. Install flat blocking between the studs wherever a bar will mount. Using wide material (2 x 10 or 2 x 12) ensures you'll have plenty of support. When the shower is complete, you can drill through tile and backer board and then install your grab bars with heavy wood screws.

In a mud shower the bars can be mounted anywhere. Drill through the tile and mortar and use either toggle bolts or plastic anchors and screws to hold the bars in place. I guarantee you won't be able to pull a properly mounted grab bar out of a mud and tile wall. I place all my weight on the bars I install before pronouncing them satisfactory. I weigh 230 pounds, and I've never budged a bar that I've installed.

If you are installing a bar in an existing shower, you won't have backing blocks to screw into. You may be able to locate a stud that will support one end of the bar, but the other end will probably be supported only by the tile and backer board. In this case you must use toggle bolts, as large as will fit into the mounting bracket. A bar that is supported by a stud at one end and securely fastened to the wall at the other will provide adequate support in most cases. I say "in most cases" because some showers are in such a state of dilapidation that they will not support grab bars adequately, and if that is the case, the shower should be torn out and re-done. Don't take a chance of contributing to the injury of someone by installing a grab bar that can't be depended upon. (Figures 181A, B, C, D, E, F)

Cleaning

Tiled surfaces are easily cleaned, but you must do it routinely. I've already imparted my secret method for maintaining ceramic and stone tile showers. You'll recall that I admonished you to completely dry the inside of the shower after each use. If you do this, your shower will remain clean and new-looking indefinitely. The same is true of tiled floors, but since they won't be routinely wet, you'll have to use water and an appropriate *neutral* cleaner on a regular basis. I emphasis "neutral" because both acidic and alkaline cleaners can have adverse effects on many ceramic tiles, all stone products and portland cement grout. Neutral cleaners work by thinning the cleaning water they are added to. And so they are safe for any surface that is not adversely affected by water.

Relying on acid to tidy up a new tile installation is a different matter. When using the dense and nearly impervious tiles that are common today, it is not unusual to end up with grout haze or cement scum on the tiled surface after the grout has dried in the joints. Although you would never want to use acidic products on a continuing basis, it is usually safe to use a mild acid to remove the haze. A number of acid cleaners were discussed near the end of Chapter Two. Use them cautiously.

Figure 181A: Grab bar is held in place while hole locations are marked.

Figure 181B: Small pits are made in the glaze of the tiles to keep the drill bit from wandering.

Figure 181C: Holes are drilled with carbide masonry bit.

Figure 181D: Plastic anchors are inserted.

Figure 181E: Grab bar is attached.

Figure 181F: Et voila!

One More Plug for Tile Your World

Exciting things are happening at Tile Your World.com and at the John Bridge Forums. We have recently opened our online store, and we are busy stocking it with new products to make your tiling experience easier and more fun. A complete line of tile and stone care products is on the way, for example, and we are scouring the globe for other tile related items to offer you. Stop in often.

Tile Your World.com and John Bridge.com are intertwined. You can use either Internet address to reach either site: *http://www.tileyourworld.com or http://www.johnbridge.com.* And, of course, both addresses lead to the store and to the John Bridge Forums. You will never find the place locked up because we never close. Your friends in the tile business are waiting there to welcome you.

Hope to see you there soon.

Farewell

And so it seems we have arrived at the time for parting. I've enjoyed immensely the hours I've spent with you, and I sincerely hope I haven't bored you with my ramblings. I know I haven't been able to answer all your questions, but I trust I have at least given you the knowledge you need to pose new ones.

If you will permit me to leave you with one final iteration, it is this. Take your time. Don't get in a hurry no matter what happens. Enjoy yourself, and find joy in your work. If you can do that, I'm confident your projects will end gloriously – your workmanship will exceed your expectations. If you *can't* have fun while you work, well, then I have taught you nothing.

Tile on, my friend.

APPENDIX I

UNCOUPLING REVISITED

William M. Carty, Ph.D.
New York State Center for Advanced Ceramic Technology –
Whiteware Research Center
New York State College of Ceramics
at Alfred University
Alfred, NY 14802, USA

Peter A. Nielsen
Schluter Systems, L.P.
Plattsburgh, NY 12901, USA

Centuries ago, European builders developed a reliable means of installing tile for high-traffic, high-use applications which relied on the laying of a sand strata between the structural substrate and the mortar-bed/tile composite top layer. Due to space (height) requirements and other concerns, the sand strata method for tile installation is, for all practical purposes, extinct. Modern theory, however, explains that the sand strata "uncouples" the tile from the structure, allowing structural movement without damage to the tile layer. Approximately fifteen years ago, a modern analog of the sand strata system was developed in which a thin, polyethylene sheet membrane with a grid structure of square, cutback cavities and an anchoring fleece laminated to its underside, functions as the uncoupling layer. This article will provide the basis for the claim that a configured membrane allows the normal loading forces exerted on the tile surface to be widely distributed through a forgiving shear plane, similar to that which would be expected in the sand strata. These results contradict other work and theories which suggest that extremely strong bonds are necessary between the tile and substrate to maintain a crack-free tile surface. In fact, it is proposed that a weak interface is more forgiving, allowing substantial movement in the substrate without any evidence of cracking in the tile or the grout joints. This system also allows differential expansion and contraction between the tile and the substrate and can be used on a wide range of substrates which have traditionally been viewed as problematic; including plywood, OSB, post-tension concrete slabs, green concrete, radiant heated floors, and gypsum underlayments. To understand how this system accommodates stress within a tile assembly, the stress-strain relationship for materials under load will be reviewed, followed by a ceramic matrix composite analogy that illustrates how stress buildup and stress reduction are possible within composite layers. The shortcomings of directly bonding tiles, or setting tiles in a force-conductive assembly, will be evaluated in the context of large-scale tests performed on tile directly bonded to concrete slabs. Finally, it will be demonstrated that an effective means of "uncoupling" the tile covering from the substrate, fundamental to successful tile installations, can be achieved in a contemporary thin-bed application.

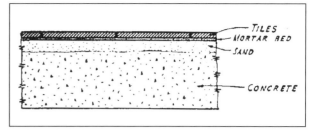

Figure 1. A schematic cross-section of the traditional method for uncoupling the tile from the substrate – the sand strata method.

The primary challenge the tile industry faces is successfully joining or *marrying* the various components that make up a tile assembly, components that are not only dissimilar in their physical properties, but in their function as well. Traditionally, each component or *layer* of the tile assembly could be divided into four distinct categories: 1) structural elements, 2) substrates or bases, 3) bonding materials and joint fillers, and 4) the ceramic tile layer.

Ceramic tiles are the veneer components of the assembly that function not only as decorative treatments, but as a working surface of the finished building environment. Because ceramic tiles are hard, brittle, and unforgiving materials, they are dependent upon the dimensional stability of the assembly to which they are bonded before they become a viable surface covering.

Movement forces are present in all tile installations due to the dimensional instability of construction elements that make up the assembly. Dimensional instability is largely a function of changes in moisture content, temperature, and loading (both dead and live loads) of the construction elements themselves. The resultant forces can be classified as compressive, tensile, and shear and manifest at the shear plane or material interfaces of the tile *sandwich*. It should be noted that these forces occur in combination.

Analysis of the physical properties of each material in the tile sandwich dictates that an intermediary component, one that will allow independent movement between the tile covering and the building structure without contributing a stress dynamic of its own, is necessary to achieve a crack-free tile surface.

Centuries ago, European builders developed a reliable means of installing tile for high-traffic, high-use applications which relied on the laying of a sand strata between the structural base and the mortar bed/tile composite top layer (Figure 1). The sand strata was the intermediary component that *uncoupled* the tile from the structure, allowing structural movement without damage to the tile layer. In addition, it allowed the normal live load forces exerted on the tile surface to be widely distributed throughout a forgiving shear plane.

A more recent analog of the sand strata method is a wire-reinforced mortar bed over a slip-sheet or *cleavage membrane*. As shown in Figure 2, the principle elements that make this type of installation viable are: 1) the mass of the mortar bed holds the floor section to the structural base; 2) the mortar bed provides

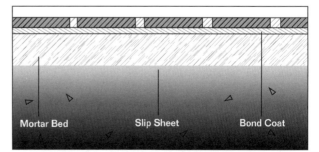

Figure 2. The more recent approach to the sand strata method—the wire-reinforced mortar bed over a slip-sheet (cleavage membrane). The wire has been omitted for clarity.

an effective load distribution plane, allowing normal live load forces exerted on the tile surface to be widely distributed throughout the assembly, and 3) the cleavage membrane isolates the entire floor section from the structural base, preventing stresses in the building structure from telegraphing through to the tile covering. However, the principle disadvantage of this system compared to the sand strata method of installation is that the mortar bed can contribute to the assembly its own dynamics (e.g. shrinkage during the hydration process, thermal expansion and contraction, curling, etc.), which can lead to damage of the tile covering.

Nonetheless, due to many factors (e.g. assembly height and weight, which, in most cases, affect the structural design requirements of today's building environment; economic viability; the shortage of skilled labor; and the demand for simplification of the installation process), the sand strata method for tile installation and its more recent analog are, for all practical purposes, extinct.

Today, the landscape has changed dramatically. The most fundamental change our industry has undergone in the last millennium has been the shift from the traditional mud-set installation to the thin-bed or direct-bond method of installation, as illustrated in Figure 3. The implications of this shift are profound and far-reaching.

Traditional wisdom has always maintained that an intermediary component that allows for independent movement between the tile covering and the building structure, without contributing a dynamic of its own, is necessary to achieve a crack-free tile surface. In light of this, contemporary wisdom states that an extremely strong bond between the tile and substrate is all that is needed in a directly bonded system to achieve a crack-free tile installation. The problem with this line of reasoning is that the contribution of each layer in a traditional system to the system's overall mechanical viability is either ignored or not addressed.

Approximately fifteen years ago, a modern analog of the sand strata system — one in which a thin, polyethylene sheet membrane with a grid structure of square, cutback cavities and an anchoring fleece laminated to its underside, functions as the

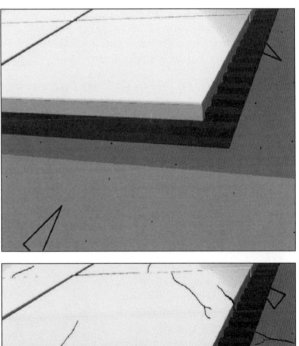

Figure 3. The direct bond method of tile installation, in which the tile is directly bonded to the substrate using a thin bond coat. No method of uncoupling is used in this case and, as illustrated on the right, cracks in the substrate become cracks in the tile.

uncoupling layer (commercially known as "DITRA") — was developed. The configured membrane, illustrated schematically in Figure 4, allows the normal loading forces exerted on the tile surface to be widely distributed through a forgiving shear plane, similar to that which would be expected in the sand strata. This system also allows differential expansion and contraction between the tile and the substrate and can be used on a wide range of substrates which have traditionally been viewed as problematic; inclu-ding plywood,

Figure 4. Membrane in a typical installation, serving to uncouple the tile layer from the substrate, allowing the tile assembly to act independently from the substrate.

OSB, post-tension concrete slabs, green concrete, radiant heated floors, and gypsum underlayments. To understand the mechanisms of this system, one must first evaluate the relationship between stress and strain.

Stress-strain relationship (a brief introduction)

To provide a basis for evaluating the various bonding systems, and the causes of installation failure, it is necessary to briefly review the importance of the stress-strain relationships for materials under load. Figure 5 is a typical stress-strain relationship for a ceramic (brittle) material. There are basically two ways of approaching the stress-strain problem: 1) from a perspective of the applied stress; and 2) from the viewpoint of the strain within the material.

The first approach is probably the most common, viewing the problem as dictated by the applied stress. Under an applied stress, a strain is developed, following an elastic behavior. This means that the strain is proportional to stress and that upon unloading of the specimen, the sample returns to its original dimensions. For brittle materials, the elastic behavior model reasonably describes the deformation behavior. In addition, defects or flaws within the material represent stress amplifiers; the magnitude of the amplification is dependent on the orientation and morphology of the flaw. The weakest link theory, as frequently used to describe the mechanical behavior of chains, appropriately states that the largest flaw dominates the strength of a brittle material. The presence of tensile stresses is often difficult to discern, as the

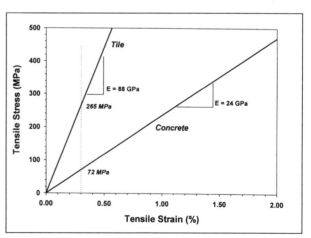

Figure 5. A stress-strain diagram illustrating the difference between typical concrete and a ceramic tile. Note the substantial difference in stress developed in the ceramic tile (264 MPa) and in the concrete substrate (72 MPa) at a similar strain level (0.3%). (Note that the typical failure strain levels for tile and concrete are 0.11%, so the strain level in this illustration exceeds typical failure strain levels by nearly a factor of two.)

stress state within the material is dictated by the geometry of the specimen and the loading conditions. This failure is usually catastrophic, as there are few toughening mechanisms available to absorb crack energy, so the crack is free to grow at a maximum rate of half the speed of sound in the material. From this perspective, we tend to evaluate performance based on the stresses imposed on the system.

For non-brittle materials, such as metals, instead of observing failure at a critical stress level, the system begins to deform plastically. The critical stress level is referred to as the yield point. Once the yield point has been exceeded, and the sample has plastically deformed, the sample exhibits permanent deformation upon unloading. Although plastic deformation is probably not a possibility in a tile system, it is useful to recognize that the mechanical behavior of metals provides the basis for the evaluation of most mechanical property problems.

The second approach views the problem as the amount of strain a material can sustain until failure occurs. In this case the amount of stress exhibited in a material is dictated by the amount of strain imposed. If the strain is sufficiently large, the critical stress is exceeded, resulting in failure. As before, the failure mechanisms are identical — the perspective is slightly different however. This perspective is ideal for interpreting tile installation failures (and successes).

Finally, the relationship between stress, σ, and strain, ε, is determined by the elastic modulus (or Young's modulus), E, following Hooke's law. The larger the elastic modulus, the larger the stress is developed (or necessary) for a given strain level. The elastic moduli for concrete and ceramic tile differ, as well as the elastic moduli for ceramic tile of different compositions. In more general terms, the greater the elastic modulus, the stiffer the material. These descriptions are generally used to describe tensile (or compressive) stresses but can also be used to describe shear behavior, in which the shear stress, τ, is related to the shear strain, γ, through the shear modulus, G. The equations for tensile and shear behavior are:

$$\sigma = E\varepsilon \qquad \tau = G\gamma \qquad (1)$$

In the case of tile installations, the strain level can be developed through a number of avenues, and as such, the strains are additive. As described above, these strains are proportional to stress levels, and when a critical amount of stress is developed, failure in the form of cracking or de-bonding takes place. There are several sources of strain in a tile installation, as discussed below.

Sources of strain in tile installations

There are several sources for strain generation within the tile layer. In addition to shear stresses (which, for the purposes of these discussions are always present), tensile or compressive stresses can be generated in the tile layer. The stress state can be extremely complicated for a variety of reasons, including the differences between the substrate and the tile, and because of the differences in the mechanical properties of the bonding layers. Examples of tensile (+) or compressive (-) stress sources are listed in Table I, denoted by sign, assuming a constant condition in the bonded phase. For example, contraction due to curing in a concrete substrate would generate compressive stresses in the tile layer, assuming no other stresses within the tile layer.

These strain development routes can be naturally grouped into two broad categories: tension and compression. In ceramics in general, compressive stresses are desired, but in the case of tile installations, as noted previously, excessive compressive stresses will produce buckling. However, in a directly bonded system, tensile stresses must be avoided, as they will almost always lead to cracking, either in the grout joint, the mortar bond coat, or in the tile. Even if small tensile stresses are present, cracking can occur in

Strain Source	Stress in the tile layer
Contraction due to curing of a concrete substrate	–
Flexure of a concrete substrate	
between support piers (sagging, concave tile bonded surface)	–
over support piers (a convex tile bonded surface)	+
Elastic Modulus mismatch (depends on flexure conditions)	–/+
Cracking in the substrate	+
Opening of cracks in the substrate	+
Moisture expansion of the tile	–
Cooling/Heating stresses	
Cooling from the tile side	+
Heating from the tile side	–
Thermal expansion mismatch (assumes uniform heating)	*(opposite for cooling)*
C.T.E. (tile) > C.T.E. (substrate)	–
C.T.E. (tile) < C.T.E. (substrate)	+
Pinning of the tiled surface at the walls (depends on location)	–/+
Static and dynamic loading of the tile	unclear

Table I. Sources of strain and the resulting stress in a tile layer. Tensile stresses are denoted with '+'; compressive stresses are denoted with '–'. Tensile stresses will lead to cracking of the tile layer; compressive stresses, under ideal conditions should not lead to cracking, but if sufficiently large, can cause the tile to buckle.

the bond coat, providing a location for future cracking of the tile surface — again, either within the tile itself or in the grout joints. In addition, significant shear stresses can develop between the tile and the bond coat, and/or between the bond coat and the substrate, leading to tile de-bonding.

Specifically, under tensile stress conditions within the tile, two problems can occur: 1) If the bond coat possesses a low shear strength, tensile stresses in the tile (and correspondingly compressive stresses in the bond coat) can create sufficient shear stress to cause shear failure in the tile-bond coat interface, and the tile will de-bond. 2) In conditions of high bond coat shear strength, de-bonding of the tile will not occur; the tensile strain is transferred to the tile, and tensile cracking of the tile results.

Similarly, under compressive stress conditions within the tile, compressive failure is unlikely (due to the fact that ceramics tend to be very strong in compression), so de-bonding of the tile occurs either by shear failure of the tile-bond interface, or by tensile failure of the bond through flexure of the tile. (Flexure of the tile away from the substrate will produce tensile stresses perpendicular to the tile surface.)

Allowance for stress development during the installation process has traditionally been compensated for by using the more recent analog of the sand strata method. There are two principle methods for executing this style of installation. One method is to install the tiles on a mortar screed that is still plastic. Immediately covering the freshly placed mortar with tile slows the rate of hydration in the mortar screed, thereby reducing the amount of stress exerted on the system due to shrinkage. The second method is to install the tiles using a dry-set mortar after the mortar screed has cured. Once the tiles are placed, the dry-set mortar is allowed to cure, thereby reducing the effects of shrinkage. If the tiles were installed before the mortar bed cured, additional residual stresses could develop in the tile layer, potentially leading to cracking. In addition, mortar mixes used in installations of this genre have traditionally been lean mixes to keep the internal stresses of the screed to a minimum.

Problems with cracked substrates

In cracked substrate situations, as the crack opens or closes, significant shear stresses develop which, depending on their direction, can generate tensile or compressive forces within the tile bed. Obviously, a cracked substrate represents one of the most dangerous potentials for tile installation failure.

Thermally activated stress development

Another factor is that thermal stresses generated by heating and cooling cycles are common, and thereby represent a dynamic fatigue potential. This situation is compounded by the fact that the concrete and the mortar probably do not have the same thermal expansion coefficient (CTE), that the tile CTE can vary significantly (depending on the type of tile used), and that the grout will have yet another CTE. Thermal stresses can be significant and as such, cannot be ignored.

Therefore, thermally activated strains can create significant stresses due to differences in CTE. Even a small CTE mismatch can lead to substantial strains when incurred over the distance between expansion joints. It should be noted that there can be a broad range of CTE's based on tile types (e.g. porcelain, terra cotta, etc.), thin-set mortars, joint fillers, and concrete.

As an example, a situation in which the concrete substrate and the mortar have the same CTE of $10 \times 10^{-6}/°C$, and a typical tile has a CTE of $6 \times 10^{-6}/°C$, produces a difference in CTE of $D = 4 \times 10^{-6}/°C$. If the concrete was 10°C warmer than the tile surface, this would produce a tensile strain in the tile layer of 0.04 μm/meter (40 mm/meter). Over a five meter span, this amounts to a strain of 0.2 mm (200 μm). Using the tile elastic modulus (88 GPa) shown in Figure 5, and assuming that all of the stress is concentrated in the tile layer (i.e., no stress in the concrete substrate), this would generate a tensile stress within the tile layer of 3.5 MPa. While this stress is probably not sufficient to directly cause failure, when combined with other residual stresses, it provides a significant contribution.

In the case of in-floor hydronic heating systems, systems where the heating tubes are overlaid with an approximately 2" mortar screed, there is a high potential for stress buildup within the system. For example, suppose the room to be heated is relatively cold, e.g. 10°C. It is not uncommon for the water temperature inside the heating tubes to reach 45°C to produce a desired temperature of 25°C on the surface of the tile. This results in a temperature differential of 35°C within the assembly. During the process in which the system develops its operating temperature, the lower portion of the screed is heated first and expands at a larger rate than the upper portion of the screed. Using the thermal properties detailed in the previous paragraph, a strain of 0.7 μm (700 μm) is developed over a five meter span, producing a stress within the tile of 12.3 MPa — even if only for a brief period of time.

In light of this, it becomes evident that a force-conductive bond between the tile and the screed is under considerable stress due to the strains imposed and, as such, it is reasonable to conclude that these strains are a significant contribution to tile installation failures over radiant heated floors.

Understanding stress buildup and reduction

The ceramic matrix composite analogy

Ceramic fiber reinforced ceramic matrix composites offer a "high-tech" analogy to the tile installation problem. In brittle matrix composites, if a strong bond develops between the fiber and the matrix, the composite will exhibit brittle failure. If the interface is weak, the fiber is able to deform independently of the matrix and, as such, can exhibit significant increases in toughness through the energy absorbing mechanisms of fiber pullout and crack deflection. The fiber-matrix interface must exhibit shear failure for the fiber to adequately de-bond and prevent catastrophic failure. Strong bonding leads to poor performance. In properly designed systems, it is not uncommon to observe cracking within the matrix but not in the fibers — in fact, the fibers bridge the cracks in the matrix, providing the appearance of an intact specimen.

It has also been demonstrated that fiber composites, when tested in bending (i.e., the modulus of rupture test) actually fail in a shear/compressive mode on the compressive side of the specimen, rather than in tension on the tensile side of the test specimen. The shear stresses developed during the test are significant, and, when coupled with the compressive stresses, lead to failure. This condition is analogous to the situation with rigidly bonded ceramic tile — a thin sheet of materials bonded strongly to a substrate, which can exhibit a (relatively) significant amount of bending during loading. Relieving the shear stresses would increase the strength of the sample.

In the case of small cross-section materials like fibers, the material is inherently more flexible because the strain developed in the fiber, even under substantial bending, usually does not exceed the strain limitations of the material. The same is true of tile/mortar/grout assemblages in uncoupled systems. The small cross section of the tile layer would naturally allow for greater flexibility, provided the strain limit is not exceeded. When the tile is rigidly bonded to the substrate, however, the strain is transferred to the tile through the bond coat and compounded by the combined thickness of the entire substrate-tile assembly. Once the strain limit of the tile is exceeded, fracture results. Allowing the tile layer to move independently of the substrate greatly increases the amount of flexure the substrate can accommodate without causing failure in the tile layer.

Large-scale tests on tile bonded to concrete slabs

Large-scale deflection experiments conducted at Cornell University (Ithaca, NY),[1] on tile directly bonded to reinforced concrete slabs (6.7 x 1.2 meters, 20 cm thick), demonstrated that tile would de-bond when sufficient deformation of the slab was obtained. The strain exhibited in the tile, both on the tensile and compressive side of the beam, was amplified by its rigid bonding to the concrete. In the Cornell work, substantial strains were developed, sufficient to cause buckling of the tile layer on the compression side of the flexed slabs and de-bonding and cracking on the tensile side. One inference of the test was that obtaining greater shear strength would have prevented de-bonding of the tile. Based on the analysis presented above, however, it would appear that the opposite would more likely be true. If the interface between the tile and the concrete substrate allowed the tile to flex independently of the substrate, a significant portion of the stresses would have been relieved, and the tile would have more likely withstood much greater deformations prior to de-bonding.

Flat membranes: Directly bonded "anti-fracture" and crack-isolation membranes

To date, there has been little analysis on the functioning principles of flat membranes presented to the tile installation community in general. Additionally, there is no accepted definition for "anti-fracture" within the tile industry. In principle, "anti-fracture" membranes would be applied over the entire surface to be tiled and should address most or all of the sources of strain or shape deformation encountered throughout the life of the installation.

Crack-isolation membranes, on the other hand, were designed to address existing cracks, or cracks that may develop in the future. They do not address the dynamics of the entire installation. These membranes consist of flat composite sheets or cold liquid trowel-applied materials that can be applied in two ways: 1) in narrow bands over existing cracks in the substrate, or 2) over the entire surface.

It should be noted that the tile industry refers to crack-isolation membranes and "anti-fracture" membranes as one in the same, though they are not. This is largely a marketing phenomenon.

"Crack-isolation", or flat membranes were initially developed as a means of preventing cracks from developing in the finished tile surface. However, there are several problems. Because these membranes are flat and very thin (30 - 40 mil) they are incorporated into the tile assembly in a force-conductive bond; thus the installation is left to the mercy of the strain development factors and the deformation of the substrate. What this means in practical terms, is that differential movement within a thin layer—meaning the upper and the lower portion of the membrane—is minimal at best. Additionally, the energy generated from these stresses is stored in the membrane because there is no free space incorporated into the assembly to accommodate them. One could argue, if a thicker membrane were used, that the elastic properties of the membrane could accommodate shear stresses. However, attempts in this direction have proven to be unsuccessful, due to the fact that the load bearing capacity was substantially reduced due to compressive flexure (perpendicular to the tile surface) of the membrane under static and dynamic loading conditions. In summary, it must be considered that a force-conductive bond still exists in this assembly. Therefore, it is difficult to measure or even estimate the effectiveness of current crack isolation membranes considering the multitude of possible stresses and the physical characteristics of the floor assembly. In this light, there is no reasonable way to establish meaningful guidelines for their use in today's building environment.

Creating a forgiving shear interface

The sand strata analogy

The sand strata system provided a forgiving shear plane "naturally" as an unbonded granular mass. A granular solid, or packed bed, has a limited shear cohesion. In these systems, the shear strength is directly, but weakly, related to the confining pressure. In sand strata systems, the mortar layer is relatively thin (1.0-1.5 cm), but there is a distinct interface between the mortar bed and the sand layer. Even under the worst of circumstances, the mortar will infiltrate the sand layer to a limited extent, allowing a significant amount of freedom within the sand strata. Thus, assuming the tile is installed properly, the tile is "free" to move independently of the substrate. This is how, in many ancient installations, failure within the tile layer was avoided. The sand strata method provided an effective means of uncoupling the mortar bed through the poor cohesion afforded by a packed granular mass.

The only means of reducing stress buildup between the tile and the substrate is to create a forgiving shear plane, which allows movement within the bonding system plane. It is essential that the tile, mortar bed, and grout are able to move as a coherent sheet, independent of the substrate — that is, the mortar bed must be "uncoupled" from the substrate. Bonding the tile firmly to the substrate will force stress buildup and ultimately failure. The sand strata method or, more recently, the mortar bed method, effectively uncouples the mortar bed/tile assembly through a cleavage layer of sand or a cleavage membrane.

In addition, these systems provided an effective load-distribution plane, allowing normal live load forces exerted on the tiled surface to be widely distributed throughout the assembly. Modern tile installations demand a similarly reliable shear interface. However, due to the design requirements in today's building environment, the shear interface must necessarily be lightweight, compact, and easy to install.

The uncoupling of a configured membrane

Creating a forgiving shear plane through the use of a configured polyethylene sheet-applied membrane, which is mechanically bonded to both the substrate (through a thin mortar bond coat) and the tile, has provided tile installers a solution to the problem.

The fleece, or *scrim,* on the underside of the membrane, or matting, establishes a mechanical bond to the dry-set mortar applied to the substrate. The cutback, cavity design of the upper side of the matting establishes a mechanical bond to the tile. The system allows the tile to be locked to the substrate in the vertical direction, while allowing relatively large in-plane motion. By allowing this motion, the system also allows for movement *within* cracks and behaves not unlike a shear interface created by an unbonded granular mass, as evinced with the sand strata method. Moreover, it allows the normal loading forces exerted on the tile surface to be widely distributed throughout the assembly.

The rib structure allows for free space within the bonding layer. This space is essential to provide flexibility within the bonding plane, providing greater freedom for the relief of stresses. In addition, this free space provides air channels between the membrane and the substrate, thus allowing any residual moisture in the substrate to evaporate and, thereby, permitting vapor equalization within the system. This is particularly important in today's building environment where most — if not all — tile substrates are moisture sensitive.

The most significant aspect of this solution, however, is that the objective has been achieved without the use of a force-conductive bond, thus neutralizing the vast majority of stresses in a tile installation. This does not suggest (nor is there any evidence from the field) that the tile assembly should be weakly bonded to the floor, or that the tile should be easily removed, but that the installation system allows for in-plane motion.

As pointed out previously in the analogy for thermal stress development, the system would need to allow for significant motion (under certain conditions estimated to be 700 mm over a five-meter distance) in the plane of the installation. Therefore, the use of expansion joints, with the expressed intention of allowing thermally generated stresses to be dissipated, is still a necessary part of tile installation.

Conclusions

In conclusion, ceramic tiles are hard, brittle, and unforgiving materials and, as such, are dependent upon the dimensional stability of the assembly to which they are bonded. Movement forces are present in all tile installations due to the dimensional instability of the structural components that make up the assembly. Analysis of the mechanical properties of composite systems tells us that these forces manifest themselves at the shear plane or material interfaces of the tile sandwich. In this light, failure is likely to result if the components of the tile assembly are joined together in a force-conductive bond.

The methods of installing ceramic tile have changed over the years. However, the physical dynamics of a tile assembly have not. Traditional installation methods addressed these dynamics by uncoupling the tile covering from the building structure through the use of a sand stratum or a mortar bed placed over a slip-sheet. Today, uncoupling the tile covering from the substrate can be achieved in a contemporary thin-bed application through the use of a configured, polyethylene sheet-applied membrane. This installation approach does not eliminate the need for skilled tile installers, nor does it allow poor quality workmanship. What it does is provide the opportunity for reliable tile installations on problematic substrates.

Cited Reference

1. G. Deierlein and M. G. McLaren, "Final Report of Tiled Slab Tests," (Research supported by the Tile Council of America) Cornell University, August 1994.

APPENDIX II

Sub-floor Deflection: A Word to Structural Engineers

By Bob Campbell

To determine the suitability of a floor for a tile installation, building codes specify a minimum stiffness that will support the tile without cracking it or the grout. The measure of stiffness most often used is deflection under live load as a fraction of the span length. Deflection is simply the distance the floor moves when a load is applied. There are two separate elements to consider, floor joist deflection, and sub-floor deflection.

Floor Joist Deflection

For a ceramic tile installation to be successful, the deflection of the floor joists can not exceed L/360. For example, if the joist span is 10 feet (120 inches), then the maximum allowable deflection is .333 inches. If natural stone were being installed, then the criterion is L/720. In this example, L/720 is .167 inches.

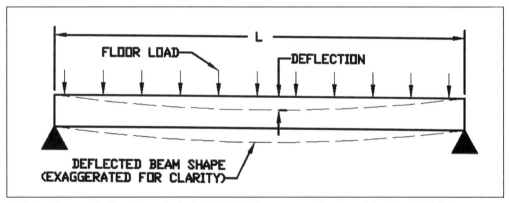

This is a diagram of a floor joist under load. The dashed lines represent the shape of the joist after deflection.

To calculate deflection, the engineer will want to know the 3 S's: joist Size, Spacing, and Span. The engineer will determine the floor loading from building codes and anticipated use of the structure. From that information, he can calculate the deflection (see below) or look it up in span tables. Span tables for common framing lumber and wood species are usually provided in building codes. Floor joists may also be an engineered wood product, such as an I-joist, or truss. These joists will require consultation with the manufacturer to determine their span-rating or deflection. Careful study of the underlying assumptions is required when using span tables.

Sub-floor deflection

The sub-floor requirements are not entirely based on deflection. The various underlayment manufacturers submit samples of their products installed on a test panel to an independent testing laboratory to perform a load/wearing test using a Robinson machine. This machine is a rotating roller assembly that can be loaded sequentially with increasing weight. The wheels are replaceable, and are soft rubber, hard rubber, and steel. The weight is increased from 100 pounds per wheel to 300 pounds per wheel. Deflection is measured, but the acceptance criteria is based on observable damage to the tile or grout. The underlayment system will receive a rating based on the highest load and hardest wheel that was successfully tested. The manufacturers will then develop installation instructions that contain the configuration limits that have proved successful.

Deflection Calculations

There are many occasions where published span tables do not address the conditions found during the remodel. Older houses may have non-standard lumber sizes. Newer homes may have minimal sized framing, but the owner wants stone. The structural engineer will have to calculate the deflection manually.

The following formula for floor deflection is from Forest Products Association publications.

$$\text{Deflection} = \frac{5 \times W \times L^3}{384 \times E \times I} + \frac{W \times L}{8 \times G \times A'}$$

W is the total load on the joist.
L is length of joist in inches.
I is the moment of inertia of the joist.
E is the modulus of elasticity for the wood.
G is the shear modulus for the wood specie.
A' is the shear area of the joist.

Bob Campbell is a mechanical engineer and moderator of the John Bridge Forums. He resides in "beautiful Eastern Tennessee." Mr. Campbell can be reached by email: bbcamp@aol.com

Appendix III

What You Ought to Know About Tile Saws

By Andy Lundberg

Choosing a tile saw can be a daunting task, especially if it is something you have not done before. But it really doesn't have to be that hard, even though there are many models and manufacturers to choose from. Normally, the choices can be pared down pretty quickly if the right criteria are considered.

Number one is the size of the tiles to be cut and whether they will require rip cutting (straight cuts) or diagonal cutting. If the cuts are to be diagonal, it is best to choose a saw that can make the cuts in one pass. To determine the length of a diagonal cut, square the length of each of the "short" sides of the triangle that will be created when you make the diagonal cut. Then add the squared numbers together and take the square root of sum. Voila, you have the length of the diagonal cut that needs to be made. For example, a 12 in. tile has a diagonal length of 16.97 in. The square of each 12 in. side is 144. Adding those together, you get 288, and the square root of that is 16.97. So if you are cutting 12 in. tiles diagonally, you should find a saw that will make cuts of at least 17 in. Most all saws will list the length of cuts they will make. If a saw manufacturer does not let you know the length of cut its product will make, take that tool off your list. (An alternate method would be to simply take a tape measure and measure the diagonal length of a 12" tile, but that would be no fun and would ensure that you never, ever use those geometry lessons, and Miss Maples would be so upset if that happened!)

There are three basic types of tile saws on the market to choose from: "box" saws, which are small plastic or metal boxes with the motor and blade located under the cutting surface, the tile being pushed through the blade; "tray" or "cart" saws where tile is set on a conveyor cart that rolls the tile under a motor and blade (in a fixed location); and rail saws, where the tile rests on a bed or platform — the motor and blade roll on rails or on an overhead bridge and pass over the tile to make the cut. Each of the three has advantages and disadvantages. Let's have a look at them.

Box Saws

Box saws are the least expensive and the most popular with DIY'ers. They are readily available, lightweight, and they run on standard electrical outlets. The blade spins under the saw table through a container of standing water which keeps the blade cool. Box saws can cut a wide variety of tiles, and they do a good job when used correctly. Many of these smaller saws can even rip-cut fairly long tiles if you don't mind trying to somehow support the tile as it hangs over the end of the "box". Typically, box saws will use blades up to 7 inches in diameter, with most using 4 inch or 5 inch blades. Because they are so small, it's easy to locate box saws near the work. They can rest on a countertop or even in a bathtub. Why a bathtub? Well, one downside is that box saws are notorious for spraying water on the user and everything near them. The bathtub can contain the water.

Other cons include a slow speed of cut, but that is understandable considering the small size of the motor (compared to motors being used on other types of tile saws). Trying to cut too fast will only bog the motor down and eventually ruin it. Small box saws are generally limited in the thickness of tiles they will cut because the blade doesn't extend far above the surface of the saw — sometimes the motor is too small to keep the blade turning. Pushing the tile over a table top will not be as smooth as using a conveyor cart to move the tile through the blade. Finally, the saws are constructed with economy in mind, and thus they tend to be less sturdy than other tile saws.

For occasional use or for use on small jobs, the box saw can be a good choice. Prices range from $70 or $80 to the high $200s.

Cart Saws

Saws using a cart to roll the material under a stationary blade fall into two categories: large and small. The smaller versions are more portable, with 1/2 to 3/4 horsepower motors. The larger, sturdier versions typically use motors of 1 hp and larger. (We'll be discussing the motor "name game" further on. I'll tell you what those horsepower ratings really mean.)

The cart saw is nice because the cart rolls the material through the cut while the operator holds it against a backstop. Straight cuts are a snap. A guide is included to help make rip cuts (straight cuts), and there are other guides to help make 45 degree cuts, miter cuts and variable angle cuts. These attachments are sometimes included with the saw, or they are available at additional cost. The saws I'm talking about are generally favored by professional contractors and some "power" DIY'ers. The largest of these saws will cut 24 in. tiles on the diagonal. (Yes, for those of you utilizing your geometry, that is a 33.94 in. rip cut.) That's a big tile and a big saw, so big that it pushes the envelope of "portable" saws. Cart saws employ a pump, located in a pan underneath the cart, to direct water onto a diamond blade.

The smaller versions of the rolling cart saw sell for $250 to $350. They will usually rip-cut a 12 to14 inch tile and diagonally cut a 10 to 12 inch tile. Small saws with small size motors will not cut hard tile and stone as fast as the models with larger motors. Usually these smaller versions are direct drive from the motor to the blade, and almost all use plastic water pans. They are very portable, however, and easy to set up close to the job. Either universal motors or induction motors may be used. Universal motors, resembling those used on right angle grinders, run at a higher rpm, have a bit more horsepower and are shorter lived than induction motors. They are often very loud as well, since they must employ a right angle gearbox to transmit the correct revolutions per minute (rpm) from the motor to the blade. Induction motors are much quieter, sometimes as much as 70%, and they run at slower rpm. I'll be talking about the effect of rpm on blades later. These small saws are a nice choice for cutting 12 inch tiles easily and accurately.

It is sometimes possible to diagonally cut larger tiles with smaller saws by cutting halfway through the tile in one direction and then turning it around to complete the cut from the other side. This method, while not ideal, is a serviceable way to get though the occasional larger cut. Contractors often keep small cart saws for repair jobs, and they are very popular with DIYers, too. With the proper blade for the material being cut, the small cart saw will cut just about any tile on the market, no matter how hard.

The larger versions of the cart saw are the workhorses for most tile contractors. In general, they will rip cut 18 inch tiles and diagonally cut 12 inch tiles. They use 1 hp or larger capacitor-start motors and are equipped with a belt to turn the blade shaft — this as opposed to the less expensive direct drive models.

Things to look for are good quality bearings on the cart and on the blade shaft, sturdy overall construction of the saw and the ability to adjust or tweak the alignment of the blade in order to ensure straight cuts. A high quality, continuous duty motor is also desirable. The water pan on a good cart saw will be of plastic or metal. It is simply a matter of personal preference. The plastic pan is lighter to carry, but some users judge metal to be more durable.

Equipped with relatively high horsepower motors, cart saws will cut most any material available. The proper blade for the material being cut is still important, but because of higher horsepower and torque, the larger cart saws will cut a wider hardness range of materials with the same blade.

As larger tiles become more common, the popularity of big cart saws increases. A common delineation for these models would be saws that rip 18 inch tiles, those that will rip 24 inch tiles and, finally, saws that will rip 36 inch tiles. If large, hard or thick tiles are going to be cut often, and optimum efficiency is the goal, a large version of the cart saw is the way to go.

Rail Saws

The third main type of saw is the rail saw. On this saw the material remains stationary, and the motor and blade travel on a rail system through the tile as it is cut. Saws using this method to cut larger tiles are often more compact than their counterparts with stationary cutting heads, even though both cut the same size tiles. The entire section of the tile being cut is supported on the cutting bed. This helps to make for smoother cuts and reduces chances of tiles being broken. (On cart saws, large tiles are often unsupported, and thus they incur a slightly greater chance of being chipped or broken.) With larger tiles, especially those which are 24 inches and larger on the diagonal, it is easier to make accurate cuts if the tile doesn't move and the blade can be directed through the cut.

One important characteristic of rail saws is that because of the way they are designed, a permanent split capacitor direct drive motor is often used. These motors usually have smaller profiles (needed for this design) and less torque than comparably rated capacitor start motors. There is less room for windings in the smaller frame.

Rail saws tend to be lengthy. They must be longer than the maximum length of cut the tile saw is rated for. With the rail design, the tile to be cut cannot extend beyond either end of the saw, as it can with other types of tile saws.

A nice feature of rail saws is that the rails will tilt and allow the cutting head to do miter cuts. This method is far superior to what is attainable on a cart type saw where you have to hold the tile at an angle to the cart and move it through the blade.

The best of the rail saws will make very accurate, long cuts, and this is what rail saws are best suited for. Because these saws are also used in the stone industry, there are models that will cut material measuring 3 meters and longer, but the price and size of these units is well beyond the scope of a typical tile job.

Motors

Once a saw style has been chosen, it is important to know a little about the motor that will turn the blade that will ultimately cut the tile. My intent here is to provide enough information about electric motors to enable anyone contemplating a purchase to make an informed decision. Motor types that might typically be found in tile saws are permanent magnet (DC), universal (AC/DC) and AC (single phase).

I'm going to focus primarily on larger saws with motors of 1.5 hp and up, but everything I'm about to present will apply to the smaller, less powerful motors used on portable tile saws as well.

We should consider a few things when looking at a motor. Horsepower is the most cited factor, but it is only one of several things that should be considered. In the case of a tile saw, a motor's service factor, code and duty will play important roles in how that horsepower is applied to the material being cut.

The first thing to remember is that horsepower ratings can be very deceiving. All 1 hp or 1.5hp motors are not equal and will not cut tile with the same efficiency or speed. Just thinking about the different physical sizes of motors on the market that are rated at the same horsepower will tell you how this can be true. To begin to understand what the horsepower rating means, you have to understand how that number is assigned and what factors are considered in assigning it.

Horsepower is calculated by multiplying torque times speed, and dividing by 5250. Torque is measured in foot pounds (lb. ft.), and speed is measured in revolutions per minute (rpm). An important thing to note here is that the rated horsepower of the motor is calculated at the specific motor speed and torque designated by the manufacturer of the motor. This information is listed on the serial number plate. If torque or speed changes due to operating conditions, so does the actual horsepower. When the motor is actually working (cutting through a tile), its rpm (speed) will likely vary each time the blade is in the cut. This means the actual horsepower delivered to the cut will be different each time. The manufacturer of the motor can manipulate listed horsepower by choosing to rate the motor using a different amperage on the serial number plate. Doing this will change the rpm and torque rating, and therefore the horsepower that can be used. We'll discuss this aspect of motor classification in more detail later in this section. The motor "name game" is often used to confuse the user about the kind of motor that is supplied with the saw.

So while horsepower rating is probably the factor most cited by users of tile saws, other characteristics of motors must also be considered. On the serial number plate of the motor, besides horsepower, there are several listed items that affect motor performance significantly. We will first discuss the duty rating, called "rating" on the serial number plate. On tile saw motors you may see ratings listed as "Saw Duty, Intermittent" or "Int" and then a number, such as "Int 30." You might also see "continuous" or "cont."

In order for a saw to be rated "continuous duty," it must be able to pull the rated horsepower all day, every day, without overheating or shutting down. Motors able to achieve this rating are the more expensive motors on the market. They are built to be used in the most extreme workloads. Although you will not cut tile all day everyday, you could do that, and you wouldn't be putting your saw through anything it couldn't handle.

To be rated "intermittent duty," a motor must be able to supply the rated horsepower for 5 minutes, 15 minutes, 30 minutes or 60 minutes straight without overheating or shutting down. The minutes will be noted after the intermittent rating, such as

"Intermittent 30." This intermittent rating is generally acceptable because tile cutting usually puts only an intermittent workload on the saw motor.

The "saw duty" rating means almost nothing. To be saw duty rated at a certain horsepower, a motor needs to hit that horsepower rating for just a very short time. An example would be a common table saw used to cut through a 2 by 4 stud. It does not have to be able to maintain that horsepower without overheating or shutting down at all; it just has to hit it for the second or two it takes to make the cut. With a rating like that, it is very hard to tell what you are getting. The motors are usually lower in cost, lighter in duty, and they may or may not perform well in tile applications. There really isn't a good way to know except by trial and error.

One way a manufacturer can play games with horsepower ratings is to rate a motor as saw duty or intermittent duty with a higher horsepower rating than could be used if it were to be rated as a continuous duty motor. How a motor is rated is up to the motor manufacturer or the original equipment manufacturer (OEM), which in this case is the manufacturer of the saw itself. A motor rated at 3/4 hp continuous duty could also be rated 1 hp intermittent, or 1.25, or 1.5 hp saw duty. This is legal, and in many cases it is left up to the OEM. A manufacturer may choose to rate a motor with a higher horse-power and lower duty rating in order to advertise the higher horsepower.

Another way to rate a motor at higher horsepower is to list an amperage draw that is not readily available when using the saw. When a motor is rated, the horsepower is given on the serial number plate, and the amps the motor uses to achieve that horsepower are given also. There are small saws on the market which are saw duty rated at 2.5 hp, listing the amps at 30. They will pull 2.5 hp, but they do it by drawing 30 amps on a 110 volt circuit. Of course, it is almost impossible to find a 30 amp circuit breaker on a 110 volt service (household current), so when the saw is put under load, trying to draw 30 amps to provide 2.5 hp, it blows breakers. Now, technically speaking, the manufacturer told the truth. If the user could find a way to provide the 30 amps, the motor would provide 2.5 hp. Once again, though, finding the 30 amp circuit to use in normal everyday tile cutting locations is not going to happen, and using anything under 30 amps to turn the motor will mean the motor will not perform at its rated horsepower but at levels well below. The same "2.5 hp" motor used on a 15-amp breaker might have a rating of only 3/4 hp. And even if a 30 amp circuit could be found, all wiring, including any extension cords, would have to be sized for 30 amps — 10 gauge or larger.

Try to look for a motor with amperage listed under 15 so that it will run on common household circuits. At most, listed amperage draw should be under 20. In everyday applications, anything higher than this will trip breakers.

When cutting tile, torque is also important. Some granites and porcelains can be pretty tough to cut, and the higher the torque a motor is able to produce, the faster the cut can be made. Motors sold in the U.S. have a rating listed under "Code" on the serial number plate that helps to determine the amount of start-up torque a motor has. An alphabetic letter is used to designate torque. The later a letter appears in the alphabet, the higher the torque of the motor. On larger 1.5 hp saws, a rating of "J" or better works well. It is possible to have a tile saw with a higher horsepower motor, but lower start-up torque code, which will not cut tile as effectively as the lower horsepower saw with better start-up torque. The possibility exists because under load, the motor with the lower start-up torque will not be able to maintain rpm well and will lose cutting power.

Another rating to check is the "service factor." The service factor is listed as a number that designates how well a motor can handle being overloaded on a continuous basis. A motor that has a service factor of 1.15 should perform when it is overloaded by 15% without overheating or sustaining damage. When no service factor is listed, it is assumed to be 1.0. However a 1.5 hp with a 1.15 service factor is actually a 1.725 hp motor (1.5 x 1.15). It is good to have that reserve capability in an application like tile sawing.

These are not all the design factors involved or listed on a motor, but they are the most important in tile saw applications. Much of this information is understandably overlooked when making a decision to buy a saw because it is not readily available to the user. Better information will allow a better buying decision.

Blades

Perhaps the best way to address diamond blades (used for cutting tile) is to answer the most frequently asked questions about them.

1. Just what is a diamond blade and how does it work?

A diamond blade consists of a core, generally made of steel, and a rim or outer edge that does the grinding. Rather than actually cutting material as a wood blade does, a diamond blade is considered a grinding wheel. Whether the blade has a continuous rim or segments attached to the core, the principle is the same. Diamonds are imbedded in a mixture of metal powders throughout the rim or segment. Those diamonds that are exposed on the edge grind away at the material being cut. As the diamonds fracture and wear out, the metal powder around them also wears away and lets them fall out. When the diamonds on the outer edge fall out they expose new sharp diamonds from underneath. This dulling and sharpening process continues throughout the life of the blade until the rim is worn out.

2. How do I pick the right blade, and aren't they all the same?

All blades are not the same. A blade consists of a core, metal powders and diamonds. The size of the diamond, the concentration (amount) of diamond, the quality of the diamond and the type and mixture of the bonding agent or powders used all affect the way a blade will cut. The less expensive blades use lower quality diamond chips which fracture more quickly than their higher quality cousins. Since the diamond deposit is fracturing more quickly, the powders that hold the diamond in place have to wear more quickly, too, so the used diamonds will fall out and new diamonds will be exposed. That is why these blades tend to wear more quickly. For tile applications, porcelain and granite are some of the harder materials that have to be cut. There are blades on the market that are designed especially for the purpose. These specialized blades may use larger, better quality diamonds to grind more effectively. They will use a specific mix of powders and diamonds designed to cut the hard material with more efficiency. When cutting soft body tile, it is possible to use smaller, lower quality diamonds. This explains the lower cost of "general purpose" blades.

3. Can I sharpen a blade/what if my blade won't cut as fast anymore?

If there is rim left and the blade is running true, it can be sharpened. Sharpening exposes new, sharp diamonds by wearing away a layer of dull diamonds from the surface of the rim. The nice thing about diamond blades is that once sharpened they work as well as new. Sharpen by cutting cinder block, day old mortar, conditioning sticks sold for that purpose, or even soft bricks. Remember that you are wearing a layer of dull diamonds off the rim and that may require several cuts to accomplish. If a layer could be worn off in only a few cuts, then the blade would not last very long in everyday use, and users would be very unhappy with it.

4. Can I use different size blades on tile saws, and what difference does it make if I do?

On many saws you can choose to use a 7", 8", or 10" blade, especially on the better quality professional type saws. If the depth of cut needed is covered by the size blade you choose, there is no problem using a smaller blade, which will save on blade price. The general rule is that when using a smaller blade, the surface speed of the rim is slower. This makes the blade act softer and wear a bit faster. The difference is probably not noticeable in everyday use. Other saws, especially those with fixed heads, as well as tabletop style saws, require a specific size blade in order to function. It pays to know as much as possible about the saw you want to buy before making a final decision.

5. What is the difference between a blade that is segmented, one that has a turbo style rim, or one with a continuous rim?

Because of the separations in the rim, segmented blades tend to chip the tiles being cut. Turbo style blades cause less chipping, but chipping is still apparent. Continuous rim blades give the smoothest cut of all, which is why they are used 95% of the time.

6. Do I have to cut wet? How much water do I need to use?

Blades are designated to be used wet, or wet/dry, and this will be stated somewhere on the blade or packaging. Dry blades can be used with water, which will cut down on dust, and this is a good idea indoors. Even using a spray bottle helps. Blades designated as wet should be used with water. Saws that use water pumps to provide the water usually provide more water than is needed. There are ways of cutting back the water flow to the blade to keep the mess at a minimum and still cool the blade. A wet blade used dry may warp and cause chipping in the material being cut. It may get so dull that it will not cut at all.

7. Why does my tile chip when I get near the end?

This can be caused by a couple of things. Pushing the blade too hard or fast through the material can cause chipping because the blade will tend to bow or flex in the cut. Then, as the end of the cut is reached, the blade will try to "straighten" itself back up. As there is very little material left at the end of the cut, the last section of tile chips off. This happens when a blade is dull, too. When the user has a difficult time pushing the material through the cut because the blade is dull, problems will occur. Also, a blade that is not running true, or one that is wobbling in the cut, may do the same thing. A wobbling blade can also cause excessive chipping throughout the cut.

8. My cut isn't straight. What do I do?

The same thing that causes chipping (above) can make a blade run slightly off course. As the blade bows or bends in the cut, it tends to head off to the side.

Additionally, the saw can be out of alignment. To remedy an alignment problem, contact the manufacturer or check the owners manual for instructions. To determine if the saw is truly at fault, a carpenter's square can be used in place of a piece of tile. If the blade runs along the edge of the carpenters square for the entire length of the cut without developing a gap or pushing against the square, the saw is aligned properly and another solution must be found.

Manual Tile Cutters

Tile cutters are so prevalent they could almost require their own chapter. A pretty good rule of thumb is, you get what you pay for. Cutters range in cost for a 12" model from $17 to $150. Cutters are available to cut tiles in lengths up to 36", and just about every size in between. Cutters work by scoring the tile and then breaking the tile at the score mark. Most tiles will snap pretty well along a score line. What delineates a quality cutter is its ability to make nice straight score lines and break the tiles with little or no chipping.

The less expensive cutters slide on poor quality rails and have a lot of "play" in the handle. Over time they are difficult to slide, and because of the play, it is difficult to score straight lines. Low quality cutters really aren't made to last a long time. You will see a lot of plastic, and replacement parts can be non-existent.

High quality cutters use bearings or other special sliding mechanisms to move the scoring wheel across the cut. They are tightly fit with very little play. They use more sophisticated methods to "break" the tile. The difference between these cutters and the low-end machines is usually very noticeable — in quality of construction and performance. The higher end models are made to be used daily and should last the average user years, or even a lifetime, depending on use. Replacement parts are available to ensure long useful life.

The rubber meets the road on cutters when it comes to the scoring wheel. A good score across the tile makes all the difference. Wheels do wear out and must be replaced periodically, and there are even different qualities and sizes of wheels. They are listed by diameter in millimeters (mm) and occasionally (just to complicate things more) by application or quality, such as "standard" or "premium." Better quality wheels can be expected to last longer and to work better on harder materials. Most cutters will do the job on most tiles, but hard, brittle tiles sometimes require a special wheel. In general, smaller diameter wheels work better than larger diameter wheels on hard tile.

If only straight cuts are going to be made, especially on standard tiles, cutters can do the job well and affordably.

Summary

To make a good decision when buying a tile saw, know the size and type of tile that will make up the majority of tiles to be cut, and make sure the saw will accommodate that size tile. Choose the type of saw that will best meet your needs, i.e., box, cart or rail. Be aware of the type and quality of the motor used on the saw, and make sure it will run on standard outlets. Following these steps will ensure success in cutting materials for any tile project.

Addendum

Or use the Joann Miller time tested method: "Pick the pretty one!"

Andy Lundberg is products manager for Target/Felker Saws, Olathe, Kansas. Joann Miller is one of Target/Felker's valued employees. Andy can be reached via email at: customerservice@felkersaws.com

APPENDIX IV

INSTALLATION OF SWAN CORPORATION SHOWER RECEPTORS

The Swan Corporation makes a range of products from several materials including its own Swanstone™ and Veritek™. Find them on the Internet at http://www.swan-stone.com

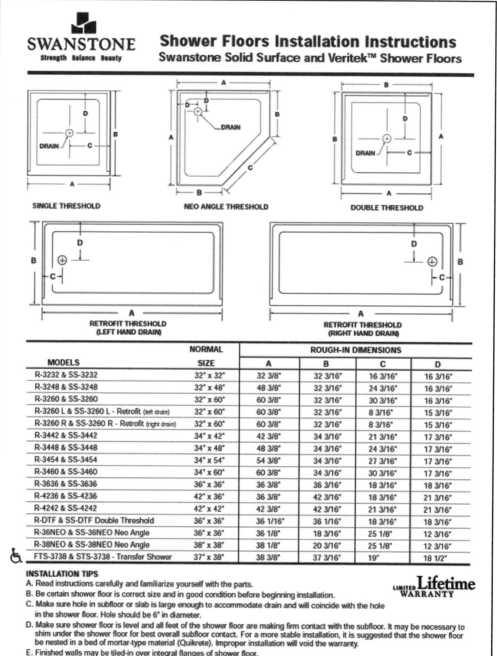

Shower Floors Installation Instructions
Swanstone Solid Surface and Veritek™ Shower Floors

SINGLE THRESHOLD   NEO ANGLE THRESHOLD   DOUBLE THRESHOLD

RETROFIT THRESHOLD (LEFT HAND DRAIN)   RETROFIT THRESHOLD (RIGHT HAND DRAIN)

MODELS	NORMAL SIZE	ROUGH-IN DIMENSIONS			
		A	B	C	D
R-3232 & SS-3232	32" x 32"	32 3/8"	32 3/16"	16 3/16"	16 3/16"
R-3248 & SS-3248	32" x 48"	48 3/8"	32 3/16"	24 3/16"	16 3/16"
R-3260 & SS-3260	32" x 60"	60 3/8"	32 3/16"	30 3/16"	16 3/16"
R-3260 L & SS-3260 L - Retrofit (left drain)	32" x 60"	60 3/8"	32 3/16"	8 3/16"	15 3/16"
R-3260 R & SS-3260 R - Retrofit (right drain)	32" x 60"	60 3/8"	32 3/16"	8 3/16"	15 3/16"
R-3442 & SS-3442	34" x 42"	42 3/8"	34 3/16"	21 3/16"	17 3/16"
R-3448 & SS-3448	34" x 48"	48 3/8"	34 3/16"	24 3/16"	17 3/16"
R-3454 & SS-3454	34" x 54"	54 3/8"	34 3/16"	27 3/16"	17 3/16"
R-3460 & SS-3460	34" x 60"	60 3/8"	34 3/16"	30 3/16"	17 3/16"
R-3636 & SS-3636	36" x 36"	36 3/8"	36 3/16"	18 3/16"	18 3/16"
R-4236 & SS-4236	42" x 36"	36 3/8"	42 3/16"	18 3/16"	21 3/16"
R-4242 & SS-4242	42" x 42"	42 3/8"	42 3/16"	21 3/16"	21 3/16"
R-DTF & SS-DTF Double Threshold	36" x 36"	36 1/16"	36 1/16"	18 3/16"	18 3/16"
R-36NEO & SS-36NEO Neo Angle	36" x 36"	36 1/8"	18 3/16"	25 1/8"	12 3/16"
R-38NEO & SS-38NEO Neo Angle	38" x 38"	38 1/8"	20 3/16"	25 1/8"	12 3/16"
FTS-3738 & STS-3738 - Transfer Shower	37" x 38"	38 3/8"	37 3/16"	19"	18 1/2"

INSTALLATION TIPS
A. Read instructions carefully and familiarize yourself with the parts.
B. Be certain shower floor is correct size and in good condition before beginning installation.
C. Make sure hole in subfloor or slab is large enough to accommodate drain and will coincide with the hole in the shower floor. Hole should be 6" in diameter.
D. Make sure shower floor is level and all feet of the shower floor are making firm contact with the subfloor. It may be necessary to shim under the shower floor for best overall subfloor contact. For a more stable installation, it is suggested that the shower floor be nested in a bed of mortar-type material (Quikrete). Improper installation will void the warranty.
E. Finished walls may be tiled-in over integral flanges of shower floor.

LIMITED **Lifetime** WARRANTY

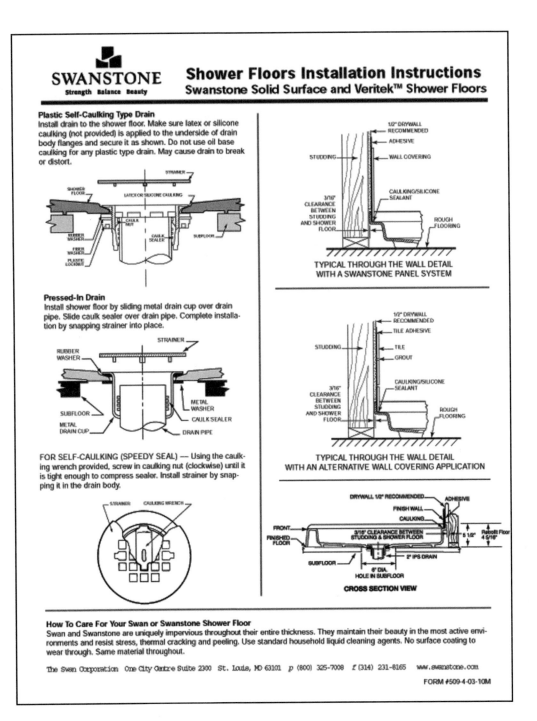

SWANSTONE
Strength Balance Beauty

Shower Floors Installation Instructions
Swanstone Solid Surface and Veritek™ Shower Floors

Plastic Self-Caulking Type Drain
Install drain to the shower floor. Make sure latex or silicone caulking (not provided) is applied to the underside of drain body flanges and secure it as shown. Do not use oil base caulking for any plastic type drain. May cause drain to break or distort.

Pressed-In Drain
Install shower floor by sliding metal drain cup over drain pipe. Slide caulk sealer over drain pipe. Complete installation by snapping strainer into place.

FOR SELF-CAULKING (SPEEDY SEAL) — Using the caulking wrench provided, screw in caulking nut (clockwise) until it is tight enough to compress sealer. Install strainer by snapping it in the drain body.

TYPICAL THROUGH THE WALL DETAIL WITH A SWANSTONE PANEL SYSTEM

TYPICAL THROUGH THE WALL DETAIL WITH AN ALTERNATIVE WALL COVERING APPLICATION

CROSS SECTION VIEW

How To Care For Your Swan or Swanstone Shower Floor
Swan and Swanstone are uniquely impervious throughout their entire thickness. They maintain their beauty in the most active environments and resist stress, thermal cracking and peeling. Use standard household liquid cleaning agents. No surface coating to wear through. Same material throughout.

The Swan Corporation One City Centre Suite 2300 St. Louis, MO 63101 p (800) 325-7008 f (314) 231-8165 www.swanstone.com

FORM #509-4-03-10M

APPENDIX V

CHOOSING BETWEEN ORIENTED STRANDBOARD AND PLYWOOD

Manufacturers of oriented strandboard and plywood claim both products work well. But using panels made of wood chips makes some builders nervous. Like it or not, osb will define the future of the structural sheathing market.

By Paul Fisette – © 1997

The issue for most builders who choose between plywood and osb is durability. Osb looks like, and is, a bunch of wood chips glued together. Detractors of osb are quick to say: "osb falls apart". This opinion has a familiar tone. Plywood suffered the same criticism not too long ago. Delamination of early plywood sheathings gave plywood a bad name. Many "old-timers" swore by solid board sheathing until the day they hung up their aprons. Not many builders share that view today.

Background

Portland Manufacturing Company made the first structural plywood from western woods in 1905. This plywood, like all structural plywood made until the mid 1930's, was bonded with non-waterproof blood and soybean glue. Delaminations were routine until waterproof synthetic resins were developed during world war II. The technical fix for delamination was inspired by the 1950's housing boom. In the late 1960's advances in adhesive technology brought southern pine plywood to residential builders. Today, southern pine plywood accounts for about half of all structural plywood sold.

MacMillan Bloedel opened the first viable waferboard facility at Hudson Bay, Saskatchewan in 1963. Aspenite, the first generation waferboard (called chipboard by many builders), was manufactured from the abundant supply of aspen found in the region. Technology involving the random alignment of wood-fiber in waferboard soon gave way to the development of structurally superior oriented strandboard. Elmendorf Manufacturing Company made the first osb in Clairmont, NH just 14 years ago.

Technical Merits

All 3 model building codes use the phrase "wood structural panel" to describe the use of plywood and osb. Codes recognize these two materials as the same. Likewise, APA the Engineered Wood Association, the agency responsible for approving more than 75% of the structural panels used in residential construction, treat osb and plywood as equals in their published performance guidelines. And wood scientists agree that the structural performance of osb and plywood are equivalent.

Osb and plywood share the same exposure durability classifications: Interior,

Exposure 1 (95% of all structural panels), Exposure 2 and Exterior. They share the same set of performance standards and span ratings. Both materials are installed on roofs, walls and floors using one set of recommendations. Installation requirements prescribing the use of H-clips on roofs, blocking on floors and allowance of single-layer floor systems are identical. The weights of osb and plywood are similar: 7/16-inch osb and 1/2-inch plywood weigh in at 46 and 48 pounds. However, 3/4-inch Sturd-I-Floor plywood weighs 70 pounds, 10 pounds less than its osb counterpart. Even the storage recommendations are the same: keep panels off of the ground and protected from weather.

Professor Poo Chow, a researcher at the University of Illinois, studied the withdrawal and head pull-through performance of nails and staples in plywood, waferboard and osb. Chow found that in both dry and 6-cycle aged tests: osb and waferboard performed equal to or better than CD-grade plywood. The results of another independent study conducted by Raymond LaTona at the Weyerhauser Technology Center in Tacoma also showed that withdrawal strengths in osb and plywood are the same. But, while the two products may perform the same structurally, they are undeniably different materials.

To begin with, the composition of each material is different. Plywood is made from thin sheets of veneer that are cross-laminated and glued together with a hot-press. Imagine the raw log as a pencil being sharpened in a big pencil sharpener. The wood veneer is literally peeled from the log as it is spun. Resulting veneers have pure tangential grain orientation, since the slicing follows the growth rings of the log. Throughout the thickness of the panel, the grain of each layer is positioned in a perpendicular direction to the adjacent layer. There is always an odd number of layers in plywood panels so that the panel is balanced around its central axis. This strategy makes plywood stable and less likely to shrink, swell, cup or warp.

Logs are ground into thin wood strands to produce oriented strandboard. Dried strands are mixed with wax and adhesive, formed into thick mats, and then hot-pressed into panels. Don't mistake osb for chipboard or waferboard. Osb is different. The strands in osb are aligned. "Strand plies" are positioned as alternating layers that run perpendicular to each other. This structure mimics plywood. Waferboard, a weaker and less-stiff cousin of osb, is a homogeneous, random composition. Osb is engineered to have strength and stiffness equivalent to plywood.

Performance is similar in many ways, but there are differences in the service provided by osb and plywood. All wood products expand when they get wet. When osb is exposed to wet conditions, it expands faster around the perimeter of the panel than it does in the middle. Swollen edges of osb panels can telegraph through thin coverings like asphalt roof shingles.

The term ghost lines or roof ridging was coined to describe the effect of osb edge swelling under thin roof shingles. The Structural Board Association (SBA), a trade association that represents osb manufacturers in North America, has issued a technical bulletin outlining a plan to prevent this phenomenon. SBA correctly indicates that dry storage, proper installation, adequate roof ventilation and application of a warm-side vapor barrier will help prevent roof ridging.

Irreversible edge swelling has been the biggest knock on osb. Manufacturers have done a good job of addressing this issue at the manufacturing facility and during transportation by coating panel edges. But the reality is that builders don't limit osb use to full-sized sheets. The edges of cut sheets are seldom if ever treated in the field. Houses under construction get rained on. And if you use osb in an area of very high humidity, like over an improperly vented attic or over a poorly constructed crawlspace, you are asking for trouble.

Osb responds more slowly to changes in relative humidity and exposure to liquid water. It takes longer for water to soak osb and conversely, once water gets into osb it is very slow to leave. The longer that water remains within osb the more likely it is to rot. Wood species has a significant impact. If osb is made from aspen or poplar, it gets a big fat zero with regard to natural decay resistance. Many of the western woods used to manufacture plywood at least have moderate decay resistance.

Recently we've heard that walls in many Southeastern homes covered with the Exterior Finish and Insulation System (EIFS) were rotting. Rigid foam insulation was applied over osb and coated with a stucco-like covering. When the exterior foam boards were removed, wet, rotted, crumbling osb was exposed. Osb was slammed in the press. The problem really isn't osb's fault. All cases I'm familiar with were caused by improper installation of flashing or protective coverings.

Louisiana-Pacific's osb inner-seal siding also made the news recently. LP just settled a class action suit to the tune of $350 million. The claims were that osb siding was rotting on the walls of many homes in the South and Pacific Northwest. Both are very moist climates. LP said the problems were caused by improper installation. But builders and consultants involved in this case think the material doesn't work in permanently exposed applications. To my knowledge, there has not been a problem of similar scale associated with plywood siding. Osb, in its current state of development, is more sensitive to moist conditions. Plywood, although not immune, is somewhat forgiving. Plywood actually gets saturated much faster than osb, but it is not prone to edge swelling and it dries out much more quickly.

On the plus side, osb is a more consistent product. It is truly an engineered material. You never have a soft spot in the panel because 2 knot holes overlap. You don't have to worry about knot holes at the edge of a panel where you are nailing. Delaminations are virtually nonexistent.

Osb is perhaps 50 strands thick, so its characteristics are averaged out over many more "layers" than plywood. Osb is consistently stiff. Plywood has a broader range of variability. During the manufacturing process, plywood veneers are randomly selected and stacked up into panels. You may get 4 veneers of earlywood stacked above 1 veneer of latewood. Who knows? Most plywood panels are overbuilt to cover the statistical range that guarantees each sheet of plywood meets the minimum standard. Osb, on average, is 7% less stiff because it stays closer to its target spec. However, osb feels stiffer when you walk across a floor covered with it because there are no occasional weak panels like plywood. Smaller trees can be used to make osb. Wood fiber is used more efficiently in osb.

Osb is stronger than plywood in shear. Shear values, through its thickness, are about 2 times greater than plywood. This is one of the reasons osb is used for webs of wooden I-joists. However, nail-holding ability controls performance in shear wall applications. So both products perform equally well as shear-wall components.

Approved Use

It is human nature to be afraid of a new product. A builder's reputation often hangs on the ability of new technology to deliver on its promise. Homeowners expect builders to select materials and systems that perform well. Builders need assurance from manufacturers that new products will work. Manufacturers are not always right. But right or wrong, a manufacturer's support is often where the rubber meets the road.

Subfloors and underlayments serve as structural platforms and as a base for flooring products. Osb and plywood are equals structurally, but flooring manufacturers make different recommendations regarding their use as a substrate.

The National Oak Flooring Association (NOFA) in Memphis recommends either 5/8-inch and thicker plywood, 3/4-inch osb or 1-x6-inch dense, group1 softwood boards installed at a diagonal under hardwood flooring. The NOFA recommendation is based on research conducted by Joe Loferski at Virginia Tech, Blacksburg, VA. In his study, Loferski simulated what happens on a real construction site. He built several full-sized floors out of boards, plywood and osb and weathered them for 5 weeks before installing hardwood flooring. Finished floor systems were cycled in an environmental chamber to simulate the changes that occur in summer and winter months.

The study showed that solid boards installed at a diagonal were far and away the best system. Statistically, 5/8-inch plywood and 3/4-inch osb worked the same. But two significant observations were made during the study: Some of the plywood delaminated during the weathering experiment and new patches had to be spliced into the subfloor system. Also, researchers learned that the best floor of all was the control specimen, which had been protected from any weathering. This speaks volumes for the importance of protecting materials during transport, storage and early stages of construction.

If you are planning to use osb as a subfloor OR underlayment for your next tile floor, you may want to think again. Joe Tarver, Executive Director of the National Tile Contractors Association, Jackson, MS says, " Osb is not an acceptable substrate to receive ceramic tile, period!" NTCA lists osb, along with pressboard and luan plywood, as "not acceptable" in its reference manual. It has to do with thickness swell. They feel that if osb gets wet, it transfers stress and causes the tile to fail.

The Resilient Floor Covering Institute, a trade association that represents manufacturers of vinyl sheet-flooring and tiles, also puts the nix on osb. RFCI installation specifications recommend plywood as an underlayment material. Osb is acceptable as a subfloor material. Manufacturers have not seen a deluge of failures due to the use of osb under resilient flooring. However, they have received complaints of edge swelling that has telegraphed through their flooring products. Manufactures feel more comfortable guaranteeing their products when they are installed over plywood.

Wall sheathing: No news is good news. All manufacturers of siding products I contacted agree that osb and plywood are equals. Kevin Chung, Engineer with Western Wood Products Association in Seattle assures us, "There have been no problems reported from the field. Nail-holding and racking resistance are the same." Chung has noticed some concern about the use of osb among builders, but is quick to add, "There is no reason for any concern. Both products serve equally well as a nailbase."

Roof sheathing is a mixed bag. The National Roofing Contractors Association (NRCA) in Rosemont, IL and the Asphalt Roofing Manufacturers Association (ARMA) in Rockville, MD both recommend the use of APA performance rated osb and plywood panels. However, ARMA, NRCA and representatives from at least 2 roofing manufacturers, Cellotex and TAMKO, prefer plywood roof decks. Warranties on shingles are extended to both substrates, but manufactures feel more comfortable with plywood. Mark Graham, NRCA's associate director of technical services says, "We hear a lot of complaints related to dimensional stability. And a disproportionate number are related to osb. So we are a little bit cautious." Grahm also acknowledges that APA, an organization he clearly respects, is standing firmly behind the osb product.

Florida's Dade county is the only building code district in the country that prohibits the use of osb as a roof deck. Damage to roofs during hurricane Andrew were originally blamed on osb's poor nail-holding power. Dade's banning of osb spawned several research initiatives to explore the suitability of osb as a structural sheathing.

Research conducted by APA, Chow, LaTona and others have conclusively proven osb seaworthy. Many experts think the ban makes no sense. Dade's position is perceived by many industry insiders to be a political maneuver to satisfy public concern.

Market Rap

Osb has earned its reputation as a low-cost substitute for plywood. In fact, recent price quotes from Denver, Boston and Atlanta put 7/16-inch osb $3.00 to as much as $5.00 per sheet lower than 1/2-inch cdx plywood. This price spread means that a builder can save $700.00 on a 2,500 square foot house if osb is substituted for plywood sheathing on floors, walls, and roofs. A substantial savings to be sure. The trend among builders is to switch to osb. APA's market data indicates that more than half the structural panels used in residential construction in 1995 were osb. But price is not the whole story.

A bumper crop of news stories highlighting contractor ripoffs has left consumers reeling. Reports indicate that some homeowners worry about builders "cheaping out" when they use osb. Customers become suspicious that builders are trying to put something over on them: charging for an expensive product like plywood and substituting it with something cheap, like osb. When it comes to structural integrity, cost is less of an issue among consumers than structural performance.

"It looks like a bunch of junk pounded together.", is how one homeowner described osb to me. Another homeowner asked, " What the hell is going on? Aren't there any more trees?" Public perception is that we are getting stuck with scraps. The uninitiated don't appreciate the high-level of science and technology used to produce engineered wood products. They think that "glued-together" is not as good as "nailed-together". And oddly, plywood is perceived as solid wood to a lay person.

Customers don't want technical explanations about many things. For example: Most do not want to know how blown-in fiberglass insulation performs differently than batt insulation. They typically don't want to know what weight roof shingle you are using; or even what depth floor joist you have speced. However, customers are nervous about engineered wood because all they see are little pieces of wood stuck together. Osb is so visually striking that customers need a technical explanation about this material from their builders.

Future Watch

Osb is unceremoniously pushing plywood aside as the structural panel of choice. Twenty-one osb plants are scheduled to open between 1995 and 1997. Nobody is building plywood plants. In fact they are closing down. Production of structural plywood is forecast to drop by 7% in 1996, while osb production is projected to increase 25%. Good news for builders: The increase in osb production is expected to depress the price of all structural panels. Also, strong supplies reduce price volatility. Prices remain stable when the distribution chain expects adequate supplies.

Market data show that conversion from plywood to osb among builders is irregular. Northeastern and Southwestern housing markets are still plywood markets. North central and Southeastern regions have largely converted to osb. In some areas of the Pacific Northwest where plywood was born, you are hard-pressed to find a plywood-skinned house.

One thing is certain: osb is in our future. Osb products will improve. Production will reflect market needs. Perhaps thickness-swell will be included in future performance standards. It should. Osb manufacturers can formulate their process to provide virtually any property they want. They can build panels to resist high relative humidity, deliver more strength, or provide a harder surface. It becomes a question of cost vs performance and we will dictate the final product.

Contact Information:
Paul R. Fisette, Director
Building Materials and Wood Technology
126 Holdsworth Natural Resources Center
University of Massachusetts, Amherst, MA 01003
Tel: +1 (413) 545-1771 Email: pfisette@forwild.umass.edu

APPENDIX VI

TILE BACKER BOARD INSTALLATION TIPS

PROPER PREPARATION IS THE KEY TO CERAMIC TILE PERFORMANCE

By Jim Reicherts

Ceramic and stone tile remain two of the most desirable finishes for residential and commercial applications. On walls and floors, tile provides a lasting impression while adding dimension, color and durability to any room.

But while a top-notch tile job may be remembered for how it looks, a truly superior application withstands the rigors of everyday life and maintains its beauty year after year. The key to achieving that standard begins long before the first tile is set in place.

For centuries, ceramic and stone tile was installed into a bed of mortar, stucco or other compatible cementitious or stone-based material. As a result, the tile was adequately supported and moisture was absorbed by the substrate materials, which allowed the entire assembly to cure evenly and remain that way for years.

But with the relatively recent advent of wood (and now light-gauge steel) frame construction, disparate frame, prep and finish materials are often thrust together in the same wall or floor assembly. These include wood, gypsum, metal and tile. As a result, moisture, created either during construction or after completion and absorbed by the above materials, can react adversely within the entire assembly, causing problems such as delamination, leaks, cracks and other failures that affect the appearance and structural integrity of the finished job.

The invention of cementitious backer units or "CBUs" has met the demand among contractors and homeowners for a construction material that is economical, easy to use and reliable in its performance. For stone and ceramic tile jobs, CBUs give wood or metal frame construction the ability to provide a compatible and stable surface for long-lasting tile installation.

Simply, CBUs are factory-produced mortar beds. They are lightweight, workable and available in standard panel sizes for fast and easy installation. Made from a combination of portland cement, aggregates and fiberglass reinforcement, CBUs become an ideal substrate for ceramic and stone tile on both walls and floors, especially in "wet" areas such as kitchens, baths and entries. The leading CBU is DUROCK® Brand Cement Board, which happens to be manufactured by United States Gypsum Company.

CBUs distribute loads and absorb force. Whether this force is applied to a wall by a

213

person falling against it, or whether it results from a concentrated load (a chair leg or a refrigerator wheel), high-quality CBUs help prevent damage to the ceramic tile finish.

That said, CBUs must be installed properly to deliver reliable and durable support. U.S. Gypsum offers a step-by-step guide to help contractors and homeowners prepare for, and thus ensure, a superior and long-lasting ceramic or stone tile installation.

Step One: Standards and Compliance

Not all CBUs are created equally. Contractors and homeowners can ensure they are installing quality CBUs by selecting materials that meet standards set by the American National Standards Institute (ANSI) and promoted and proliferated by the Tile Council of America through its "2003 Handbook for Ceramic Tile Installation."

The ANSI standards, specifically A118.9 and A108.11, reflect several key aspects of a CBU's makeup, performance and installation. These include bond strength, flexural strength, fire resistance/flame spread, fungus/bacteria resistance, fastener holding strength and floor service performance levels.

Along with meeting the minimum CBU product standards, contractors and home-owners also need to comply with building codes regarding wall and floor construction, as well as fire resistance ratings. Despite their low density (half that of concrete), DUROCK Cement Board and other CBUs meet most code requirements as a substrate for ceramic tile for both wall and floor construction over properly designed framing.

Local codes may also dictate moisture-control methods, such as a vapor retarder or water barrier installed behind the tile backer board as an extra layer of protection to block and shed moisture from either side of the wall or floor assembly.

Step Two: Hanging the Panels

CBUs can be easily cut with a utility knife or a power saw – the latter equipped with a dust-collection devise and the worker fitted with a mask or respirator and eye protection.

The panels can be applied to the wall either vertically or horizontally, provided their vertical ends or edges are adequately supported by the framing members (wall studs). Specifically, the panel ends or edges must extend at least 5/8 inch onto a stud or other structural nailing surface – where two panels abut vertically along the same stud length.

CBUs must be installed flat to ensure a quality tile job. Where the board meets the raised rim of a tub or shower base, for instance, avoid placing the board over the rim. Instead, leave a small (1/16 inch) gap between the board and rim in order to maintain the even plane of the panel surface. This will also permit the installation of a thin flashing or water-resistant membrane that will extend over the rim and ensure drainage of any moisture that might accumulate in that area.

CBUs can be fastened to the structural frame without pre-drilling, allowing for fast installation. Specifically, nails or screws are driven so the bottom of the fastener head is flush to the board surface with care taken not to "overdrive" the head of the fasteners below the surface of the board, which may fracture the panel and reduce the holding strength of the fasteners.

For horizontal wall panel joints, maintain a small (1/16 to 1/8 inch) gap between adjacent boards. This gap will be filled by the tile-setting mortar, which will bond the panels together and keep the joint (and surface of the finished tile job) from cracking under everyday use.

Step Three: Prepping the Surface

With the CBU panels properly hung and fastened to the wall frame or floor assembly, it's time to prep the surface of the backer board for the installation of stone or ceramic tile. Often, the cement boards will abut gypsum panels outside of the tiled area. Because panels are available in the same thicknesses as gypsum panels, the transition can be seamless.

Specifically, the process for bridging a CBU-to-gypsum panel joint is similar to the tape-and-joint treatment procedure commonly used for non-tiled walls. In areas that will be getting wet, such as in showers, thin set mortar is used over the alkaline-resistant mesh tape. Outside the shower enclosure, drywall compound may be used.

At the Corners

The outside corners of a tiled wall can pose some interesting challenges. The key is to create outside corners that allow the ceramic or stone tiles to wrap around the wall while maintaining a flush, flat appearance. For that reason, the use of metal corner bead – common for non-tiled corners – is to be avoided because it tends to protrude to far past the flat plane of the wall. Instead, install reinforcing tape and joint treatment materials for finishing outside corner joints, which produce a square and flat corner for an easier (and more attractive) tile installation.

Installing Backer Board on the Floor

For the installation of floor tile, CBU panels are typically applied directly onto a wood subfloor (plywood or OSB) with both adhesive and fasteners. This combination helps eliminate voids and movement between the sheathing and the protective layer of the cement board and also results in a stiffer (and thus more durable) floor.

First, tile-setting mortar is trowel-applied to the subfloor, providing leveling and an adhesive layer for the cement board. Full or cut panels are then fastened with screws (at 8 inches on center) to subfloor panels and ideally to the floor joists. In addition, the joints of the CBUs should be offset from the sub-floor panel joints. Finish up by taping over all the joints with backer board tape and thin set mortar.

Jim Reicherts is business manager for Durock brand cement board at United States Gypsum Company. Visit USG at: http://www.usg.com/

Appenidix VII

Cementitious Backer Unit Installation on Floors

By John Kipper

The American National Standards Institute (ANSI) defines a cementitious backer unit (CBU) as "a nailable/screwable backerboard or underlayment panel which is composed of stable portland cement, aggregates, and reinforcements that have a significant ability to remain unaffected by prolonged exposure to moisture." CBUs are lifeblood for thousands of tile contractors, who rely on them to ensure a tile job that will last indefinitely.

The structural integrity of a CBU is not compromised by the introduction of moisture. CBUs remain dimensionally stable as tile substrates and have high compressive strengths. The highest compressive strength for a 1/4" thick CBU is 7000 psi, achieved by James Hardie Building Products' HardiBacker® EZ Grid.™ This is according to American Society for Testing and Materials (ASTM) test method D2394. For tile installations on interior floors with a wood subfloor, CBUs offer a convenience, reliability, and long-term cost savings that cannot be overstated.

All CBUs conform to ANSI A118.9, which provides definitions, general requirements, and testing procedures. The size of the aggregates in the CBU depends on the CBU production method. Generally, glass mesh CBUs contain large, abrasive aggregates while fiber cement CBUs have finely ground aggregates that are non-abrasive and easy to work with. CBUs are constantly evolving as manufacturers go to great lengths to provide contractors and do-it-yourselfers lighter, stronger, and easier-to-use panels. For example, James Hardie, a leader in fiber cement technology, created HardiBacker EZ Grid with an embossed one-inch grid pattern for easy measuring and a recessed fastener pattern for easy nailing.

Unless the installer desires the increased height of a 1/2 in. backer board, 1/4 in. thick CBUs are generally used for floor installations. 1/2 in. thick CBUs are used primarily for wall installations.

The following is a set of guidelines for installing CBUs on floors as a tile substrate. While these guidelines are presented in accordance with ANSI A108.11, they should not replace detailed installation instructions provided by the CBU manufacturer.

Before any job is started, be sure the ambient room temperature is between 50°F and 100°F and that there is plenty of ventilation. Ensure that the subfloor is suitable for tile installation. The subfloor should not be damaged; loose, warped or rotted sections of floor should be replaced. Make certain the subfloor is clean and has a flat surface. The subfloor should consist of a minimum 5/8 in. exterior grade plywood or 23/32" exterior grade OSB, complying with local building codes and ANSI A108.11.

Floor joist spacing typically should not exceed 16 in. on center. The goal in building a subfloor system is to limit deflection so that it does not exceed L/360 of the span, including live and dead design loads. If the floor deflection is greater than L/360, it is possible that the tile will crack after installation. If the subfloor design consists of tongue-and-groove plywood, do not use glue between grooves. Room for expansion and contraction of plywood must be profided. The CBU may be installed over Vinyl Composition Tile (VCT) and other resilient flooring, but all other existing floor coverings, including cushioned vinyl, should be removed first.

Required materials to complete the job are the CBU, latex or acrylic modified thin-set mortar (complying with ANSI A118.4), dry-set mortar (use between subfloor and backerboard only) (complying with ANSI A118.1), 2" wide high strength alkali-resistant glass fiber CBU reinforcing tape, and fasteners. The fasteners should be long enough to ensure 3/4" penetration into the subfloor. Typically, the fasteners are minimum 1-1/4" long corrosion-resistant roofing nails or minimum 1-1/4" long No. 8 x 0.375" HD self-drilling, corrosion-resistant, ribbed waferhead screws. Do not use dry wall nails or dry-wall screws to install CBU's as these fasteners will corrode.

When installation is about to begin, determine the layout of sheets so that your entire subfloor will be covered. The most common size of CBU is 3 feet by 5 feet, so, allowing for scraps and awkward cuts, a 40 square foot bathroom, would probably require four sheets of CBU. Using a straightedge as a guide, cut the CBU sheets down to size, if necessary. This is done by scoring the face of the sheet with a carbide tipped scoring knife and then snapping it upward along the line. A circular saw with a carbide or diamond tooth blade may be used for large cutouts. If using HardiBacker EZ Grid, a circular saw with a carbide or diamond tooth blade or a fiber cement shear may be used. For small holes, a carbide tipped masonry bit may be used, or you can score around the perimeter and break the hole out from the face side with a hammer. Smooth the rough edges with a rasp or coarse sandpaper. Glass mesh CBUs or CBUs with large aggregates will not provide clean holes as will fiber cement boards. When cutting the CBU, always wear safety glasses and appropriate respiratory protection.

After cuts have been made, it is recommended that you lay the board temporarily in its intended location to ensure that the cuts were correct and the layout looks good. When laying CBU sheets, stagger all sheet joints and don't align the CBU joints with subfloor joints. Also, never allow the corners of four adjacent CBU sheets to meet at one point, as this would create a spot of weakness in the installation.

Keep the outer edge of CBU sheets 1/8 in. back from walls and cabinet bases. Some manufacturers also recommend setting a 1/8 in. gap between the edges of every sheet, so manufacturer installation instructions should be always consulted. Similarly, movement joints (or expansion joints) should be provided in accordance with ANSI A108, Section AN-3.7. Common areas where movement joints are provided occur when the CBU sheets are being applied over existing structural joints, where the floor changes in direction (such as in "L" shaped rooms), where the tiled area is large, and where changes occur in backing materials.

Once the layout is confirmed and the cuts have been made, apply a leveling bed of dry-set mortar or modified thinset to the subfloor with a 1/4 in. square-notched trowel. Embed the CBU sheets firmly and evenly in the wet mortar, and fasten them to the subfloor with the above specified nails or screws spaced every 8 in. over the entire surface. When using a product such as HardiBacker EZ Grid, use the recessed fastener pattern as a guide. Keep the fasteners between 3/8 in. and 3/4 in. from sheet edges and 2 inches in from sheet corners. Fastener heads should be flush with the surface without overdriving. Fill all joints of CBU sheets with tile setting material and tape the joints according to the CBU manufacturer's requirements. When taping the CBU joints, do not use paper tape and drywall joint compound. Do not proceed with a ceramic tile installation where the aforementioned has been done.

At this point, the installation of the CBUs is complete. Tiles should be adhered to the floor using a latex or acrylic modified thinset that complies with ANSI A118.1 and a trowel suitable for the size and type of tiles being used.

It should be noted here that CBUs cannot be considered structural load-bearing members unless so approved by the manufacturer and recognized for such use by local building codes. Lastly, CBUs should not be used on floors that are sloped to a drain, such as shower floors.

John Kipper is Marketing Manager – Interior Products for the James Hardie Building Products company. Email: John.Kipper@jameshardie.com You can access the James Hardie web site at: http://www.jameshardie.com

Appendix VIII

Joist Curvature verses Sheathing Curvature and the Probable Role of Each on Ceramic Tile Performance

Keith T. Bretzfield and Frank E. Woeste

Introduction

The cracking of ceramic tile and grout is a common problem in residential floor applications. Prior to 2001, the design criteria set forth by the Tile Council of America (TCA) in the Handbook for Ceramic Tile Installation stated "design floor areas over which tile is to be applied to have a deflection not greater than L/360 of the span" (TCA, 2000). A common misconception among joist designers was that this L/360 deflection requirement in TCA was the same L/360 building code deflection limit for residential floor joists under a uniform design live load of 40 psf. In 2001, the language of the provision was changed to "design floor areas over which tile is to be applied to have a deflection not greater than L/360 of the span when measured under 300 lbs. concentrated load (see ASTM C627)" (TCA, 2001). Thus, in 2001, it became clear to us that there were two L/360's involved and no known relationship between the two L/360's could be established by engineering analyses.

One widely accepted cause for tile cracking is the deflection of the floor system beneath the tile. The primary objective of this paper is to demonstrate that curvature, rather than deflection, may be the primary geometric factor that causes cracking of the tile and grout. A secondary objective is to differentiate between the curvature of the sheathing and the curvature of the joists in a floor assembly.

ASTM C627

The ASTM C627 test is the standard test method for evaluating ceramic tile installation systems. The C627 testing procedure utilizes the Robinson-Type Floor Tester to evaluate "complete ceramic floor tile installation systems for failure under loads" (ASTM, 1993). Per the 2001 TCA specifications, all plywood floor assemblies must be rated using this test. The Robinson-Type Floor Tester consists of a 4 ft square plywood assembly. The plywood is placed on four 1-5/8" square wooden members, simulating joist supports, four feet in length. These "floor joists" are fully supported along their length by a concrete base, eliminating any joist deflection from the test. The plywood is installed with the face grain perpendicular to the floor joists to ensure maximum stiffness.

The load is applied to the assembly utilizing three caster wheels with differing applied loads dependent on the load cycle. These dynamic, concentrated loads pass over the tile system in a continuous circular motion, causing the plywood to deflect throughout the testing procedure. Figure 1 depicts one concentrated load of the Robinson-Type Floor Tester and the cross-section of the subfloor and underlayment that rests on 2 x 2's (fully supported by a 4' x 4' concrete slab not shown).

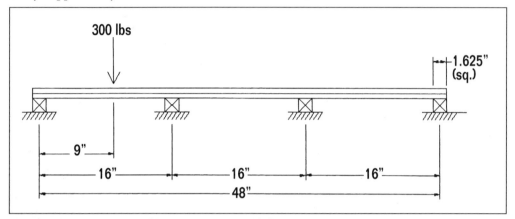

Figure 1   Cross-sectional view of the test specimen assembly for the Robinson-Type Floor Tester with applied load creating maximum moment on the floor sheathing layers.

Figure 1 depicts the 16" joist spacing case with the 15" load radius as specified by ASTM C627. The maximum moment will be created 9" from the outside support. This maximum moment was the basis of determining the curvature of the plywood assembly.

Curvature of Floor Sheathing

The curvature of a beam, C, is defined as the reciprocal of the radius of curvature, •. The radius of curvature is the radius of the elastic curve of the deflected beam. The curvature of a beam can be calculated using Equation 1.

$$C = \frac{1}{\rho} = \frac{M}{EI}$$ [1]

where:
  • = radius pf curvature,
  M = bending moment,
  E = modulus of elasticity, and
  I = moment of inertia.

As the formula dictates, curvature is directly proportional to the applied moment at the section of the beam in question. Therefore, the point on the beam with the highest moment will have the highest curvature, C, or minimum radius of curvature, •. This point on the beam shown in Figure 1 will have the greatest deformation caused by the bending moment, and it is believed to be the critical point on the beam (sheathing span) that may contribute to tile cracking and grout failure.

Figure 2 represents a model of a tile and sheathing interface showing an exaggerated gap that would occur beneath one tile assuming no adhesive contact between the tile and sheathing. The width of the tile is represented as Tw. The relationship between the gap distance, •, the radius of curvature, and the tile width can be seen in Equation 2.

$$\delta = \rho - \frac{1}{2}\sqrt{4\rho^2 - T_w^2} \qquad\qquad [2]$$

Assuming a constant moment over the width of the tile, as the width of the tile is increased, the gap distance, •, will increase. As the radius of curvature is increased, the net effect will be to decrease the gap distance.

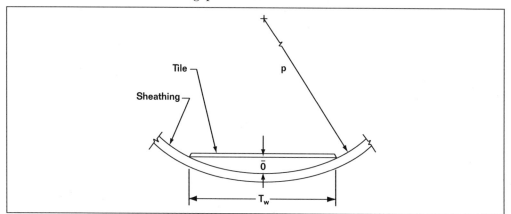

Figure 2   The tile and sheathing interface model showing an exaggerated gap between the single tile and the floor sheathing.

TCA Residential Plywood Assemblies

The 2002 Edition of the Handbook for Ceramic Tile Installation offers four recommended plywood subfloor assemblies that can be used for residential ceramic tile installation. Table 1 shows the minimum radius of curvature for the 16" and 24" joist spacing assemblies.

Table 1. Minimum radius of curvature for TCA-2002 subfloor layer and overlay layer specifications

TCA Assembly	Subfloor Layer	Overlay Layer	$EI_{Subfloor}$ (lb-in2)	$EI_{Overlay}$ (lb-in2)	M_{max} (lb-in)	$\bullet_{min}$ (in)
F142-02	19/32" 20 oc Rated Sturdi-I-Floor or Rated Sheathing	19/32" 20 oc Rated Sturdi-I-Floor or Rated Sheathing	221,400	221,400	927	526
F147-02	23/32" 24 oc Rated Sturdi-I-Floor or Rated Sheathing	3/8" 24 oc Rated Sheathing	347,400	70,200	1301	353
F149-02	23/32" 24 oc Rated Sturdi-I-Floor or Rated Sheathing	23/32" 24 oc Rated Sturdi-I-Floor or Rated Sheating	347,400	347,400	1301	588

When determining the curvature of the sheathing systems, no composite action between layers and no effects due to any uncoupling system were factored into the calculations. The radius of curvature ranges from a minimum of 353 inches for the F147-02 assembly to a maximum of 588 inches for the F149-02 assembly. The only difference between these two assemblies is the thickness of the overlay layer. A 92% increase in overlay layer thickness led to a 67% increase in minimum radius of curvature for these specific systems. Therefore, the thicknesses of the sheathing layers have a large impact on the predicted curvature of the overall floor system.

Curvature of Joists

The deflection of joists has often been pointed to as the primary cause of tile cracking and grout failure. Yet, at this time, there is no ceramic tile test that addresses the impact of joist deflection on expected tile floor performance. For this reason, the minimum radius of curvature of joists that would be applicable to the TCA recommended assemblies were calculated for comparison with the sheathing system values. No. 2 2 x 10 Southern Pine members were assumed as the floor joist members. The maximum span length was calculated using a deflection limit of L/360 under live load only. Table 2 shows the minimum radius of curvature at the center span of the floor joists.

Table 2. Minimum radius of curvature at center span of floor joist when the joist span is limited by a live load deflection of L/360

Live Load (psf)	Dead Load (psf)	Joist Spacing (in)	W_{LL} (lb/in)	E (psi)	I (in⁴)	L_{max} (ft)	W_{TL} (lb/in)	M_{max} (in-lb)	p_{min} (in)
40	10	16	4.44	1,600,000	98.93	16.4	5.56	26,839	5,898
40	10	19.2	5.33	1,600,000	98.93	15.4	6.67	28,521	5,550
40	10	24	6.67	1,600,000	98.93	14.3	8.33	30,723	5,152

The radius of curvature values are approximately 10 times greater than the radius of curvature values for the plywood systems, and thus the predicted curvature of the joists is only 10% of the predicted sheathing curvature. These values were calculated assuming independent curvatures between the joists and the plywood assembly.

Conclusions

The current method of designing ceramic tile floor assemblies based on deflections may not be the best or most reliable approach. Ceramic tile is a brittle material that cannot withstand significant bending stresses. A design procedure based on curvature, rather than deflection, could provide a more accurate and representative response to actual applied loads.

The predicted curvature of the joists used in these assemblies is approximately 10% of the predicted curvature of the sheathing systems. This fact suggests the possibility that limiting the curvature of the plywood assembly by design may help prevent tile cracking and grout problems in residential applications.

In cooperation with Schluter Systems, we are planning tests to validate our curvature theory as it relates to tile floor performance predicted by the ASTM C627 test. We will be utilizing the new Universal Tester developed by TTMAC cooperators and designed by Tool Development, Inc., Newmarket, Ontario. Among several unique features, the design allows for the inclusion of full size joists and their deflection behavior as part of the ASTM C627 test. Two tests will be conducted with identical tile installations, except in one case the joists will be designed to the L/360 live load deflection limit, and in the second case, the joists will be design to the L/720 deflection limit.

Based on our proposed theory, we do not expect differences in test results based on ASTM C627 test criteria. This experiment is expected to indicate that the sheathing and installation system should be the primary focus area for improving tile performance at the field level.

Figure 3   Floor system is tested using a Robinson type floor testing machine.

References

American Society for Testing and Materials (ASTM). 2001. C627-93 (1999) Standard test method for evaluating ceramic floor tile installation systems using the Robinson-Type Floor Tester. Annual Book of Standards, Volume 15.2, ASTM, 100 Barr Harbor Drive, West Conshohocken, PA.

Tile Council of America, Inc. (TCA). 2000. Handbook for Ceramic Tile Installation. TCA, 100 Clemson Research Blvd., Anderson, SC.

Tile Council of America, Inc. (TCA). 2001. Handbook for Ceramic Tile Installation. TCA, 100 Clemson Research Blvd., Anderson, SC.

TTMAC. 2002. Specification Guide 09300 Tile Installation Manual. TTMAC, 30 Capstan Gate, Unit 5, Concord, Ontario, Canada.

Keith T. Bretzfield is a former graduate Research Assistant and Frank E. Woeste is Prefessor Emeritus, Biological Systems Engineering Department, Virginia Tech University, Blacksburg, Virginia 24061. This article was previously published by the Terrazzo Tile and Marble Association of Canada (L'Association Canadienne de Terrazzo, Tuile et Marbre).

TTMAC
30 Capstan Gate, Unit 5, Concord, Ontario L4K 3E8
Tel: (905) 660-9640 • (800) 201-8599
Fax: (905) 660-5706

Index

picture frame returns; 105
pipe, galvanized; 81-82
plastic sheeting (poly); 14-15, 26, 82, 84, 88, 91, 130
plumbing; xvi, 3, 71, 74, 75, 76, 77-78, 80, 81-82, 89, 90, 121, 126-127, 132-133, 135, 153, 176
plywood; 14, 16, 19, 20, 22, 23, 35, 36, 94, 109, 110, 131, 152, 153, 160, 163, 164, 165, 181-182, 184, 207, 208, 209, 210, 211, 216, 217-218
porcelain; 3, 4, 5, 6, 38, 59, 115-116, 125, 157-158, 167, 169, 187, 199, 200
porch; 59, 60, 61, 63
portland cement; 4, 22, 23, 24, 30, 32, 34, 50, 83, 96, 110, 168, 177, 213, 217
poultry netting (chicken wire); xi, 15, 26, 84, 164
pre-slope; 82-83, 84, 85, 127, 130, 175

quarter-round; 91, 117, 118

range tops; 161
re-bars; 28
reference lines; 40, 41, 42, 46, 56, 58
reinforcing; 15, 26, 28, 30, 38, 70, 84, 91, 92, 93, 134, 153, 216, 218
risers (drain pipes); 63, 75, 78, 133, 134
risers (drain risers);63, 75, 78, 133, 134
risers (step risers); 63, 75, 78, 133, 134

Saltillo Pavers; 4
saws; 8, 9, 38-39, 54, 70, 76, 195, 196, 197, 198, 199, 201, 202
Schluter Systems; xvii, 29, 34, 35, 109, 123, 131, 132-133, 159, 160, 181
screeds, mud; 23, 26, 83, 85, 136
sealers; 67, 167, 169, 171
self-leveling cement (SLC); 32, 34
shovel; 24, 25, 95, 96, 97, 98, 110, 114
shower bases, plastic; 82, 90
shower floor; 71, 76, 83, 84, 86, 90, 91, 94, 112, 114, 115, 126, 127, 128, 130, 131, 135, 136-137, 138, 139, 146, 175, 176, 219
shower pans (shower liners); 82, 85-86, 87
    dam corners; 87, 88, 89, 90

shower valves; 78, 82, 121
showers; xiv, 7, 30, 69, 70, 73, 74, 75, 87, 88, 89, 90, 92, 100, 103, 106, 109, 113, 114, 118, 119, 127, 129, 131, 135, 139-140, 143, 169, 171, 172, 175, 176, 177, 215
sink cabinets; 152
sinks; 152, 153, 160, 163
sistering (partnering); 17, 72
slabs; 8, 13, 14, 27, 28, 38, 119, 181-182, 184, 188
slate; 17, 59, 61, 63, 118, 154, 157, 159, 163, 168, 169
slip resistance; 5
soapstone; 159
sole plate; 72, 85
spacers; 108, 118, 120, 124, 148
sponges; 65
stain (grout stain); 169, 171
standard wall tiles; 3, 116, 125, 158, 161, 162, 173
standing around; 54, 68, 103, 129
steam showers; 131
stone; xiv, xviii, 1, 2, 5, 6, 11, 14, 15, 17, 18, 19, 20, 22, 23, 27, 28, 29, 38-39, 41, 65-66, 67, 68, 106, 109, 113, 116, 118, 119, 120, 121, 129, 151, 153, 156, 158, 159, 167, 168, 169, 170, 171, 172, 177, 179, 193, 194, 196, 197, 213, 214, 215, 216
straightedges; 85, 94, 95, 104, 105, 106, 114, 136
stress cracks; 28, 29
structural cracks; 28
studs; 72, 73, 74, 87, 92, 107, 129, 130, 132, 177, 214
Sturd-I-Floor®; 14, 18-19, 35, 208
subfloors; 24, 34, 35, 84, 209-210

termites; 72, 73
terracotta tiles; 4
thin set; 7, 15, 20, 21, 22, 31, 32, 34, 35, 36, 38, 50, 51, 52, 53, 59, 69, 84, 107-108, 115, 116, 118, 119, 123, 124, 125, 128, 130, 131, 132, 134, 138, 139, 140, 141-142, 143, 148, 153, 154, 159, 160, 165, 173, 174, 215, 216
three-four-five method; 41, 42, 43, 56
Tile Council of America; xi, xvii, 10, 11,